Caught Between the Dog and the Fireplug,
–or–
How to Survive Public Service

Caught Between the Dog
and the Fireplug,
−or−

How to Survive Public Service

Kenneth Ashworth

GEORGETOWN UNIVERSITY PRESS / WASHINGTON, D.C.

Georgetown University Press, Washington, D.C. 20007
© 2001 by Georgetown University Press. All rights reserved.

Printed in the United States of America

10 9 8 7

This volume is printed on acid-free, offset book paper.

Library of Congress Cataloging-in-Publication Data
Ashworth, Kenneth H.
    Caught between the dog and the fireplug, or How to survive public service /
Kenneth Ashworth.
        p.   cm.
    Includes index.
    ISBN 0-87840-847-9 (pbk. : alk. paper)
    1. Civil service.   2. Public administration.   3. Bureaucracy.
4. Career development.   I. Title: How to survive public service.   II. Title.

JF1601 A75 2001
650.1'3—dc21   00-047678

To my mother, Mae Ashworth

"Little fragments of my fleece that I have left on the hedges of life."

— Justice Oliver Wendell Holmes,
Preface to *Collected Legal Papers*, 1920

Contents

Foreword

It has long been obvious that the most useful writings about administration, politics, and leadership are those written by reflective practitioners, doers with a taste for thinking hard about what they were doing and how they were doing it.

During my life as a "public executive" in a dozen different kinds of organizations, I learned that much of each task was actually teaching—that is, helping colleagues understand the purpose and nature of whatever-it-was we were trying to do together. I consequently found much inspiration in the writings of those who had "been there, done that"—practical thinkers such as Confucius and Caesar, Machiavelli and Clausewitz and Madison, Woodrow Wilson and Winston Churchill and Jean Monnet, Barnard and Brownlow and Appleby.

When I had my fling at teaching public administration, I initially didn't think of my own experience as "teaching material." But the more teaching I did, the more I found that I was drawing on my own lives and works—both to illustrate in a practical way the concepts and theories I was expounding, and to enliven the learning process itself.

Ken Ashworth, who seems to have drawn the same conclusion from a wholly different experience, has been the very model of a public executive. Educated in public administration, economics, and educational philosophy, he has worked in the federal and municipal governments, in academic administration, and latterly as a high official of the nation's second largest state. For twenty-one years, from 1976 to 1997, he was Commissioner of Higher Education for the State of Texas, outlasting five governors and 10 chairmen of the Texas Higher Education Coordinating Board, which oversees all the universities, colleges, and community colleges in the state.

In our customary parlance he has never held "political office"; he was always a "civil servant," a servant expected to be civil to politicians. But he has been acutely aware that he was always in "policy politics," which meant that he couldn't be "neutral" on any policy question that touched higher education in that enormous state. His survival for two decades in so visible and vulnerable a position through several swings in Texas politics epitomizes the famous British definition: a civil servant "is not neutral, but is loyal to one government at a time."

In these letters to "Kim," the author's androgynous nephew/niece, Ken Ashworth unwraps the experience and exposes the ambiguities of life in large public-interest organizations.

It soon becomes clear that he thinks of the public servant's role as an *entrepreneur* — a word that in too many vocabularies connotes a profit-seeking business. He guesses that "Kim" will always be constrained by administrative mandates and political expectations. But his own experience has shown him that the larger an organization and the wider its reach, the looser it has to be to work at all. That means there is lots of room for "entrepreneurship," for pioneering, for imagination, for personal get-up-and-go — lots more room than is usually visible from the outside, or even from the inside to those who think it's always someone else's turn to act first.

The bigger the problems to be tackled, the more real power is in practice diffused, and the larger the number of people who can exercise it — if they are willing to work at it. Even in organizations whose "leaders" still depict them with boxes piled up in pyramids, there are leaders at every "level." The complexity of organizations is distributing ever more widely the opportunity to lead — and thus multiplying the requirement for leaders.

The "advisory opinions" in this book are valuable not only for the practical wisdom they contain, but also for their tone and voice — informal, humorous, written in plain English. Ken Ashworth illustrates through style as well as substance why he has been successful as a public executive, and why he has therefore emerged with a vocation to teach.

"Bureaucrat" has long been a pejorative description of drones working lazily to get routine things done. This book is a wonderful antidote to that image. It reveals a seasoned executive with long and successful experience in bringing people together to serve the public interest — without losing either his élan vital or his sense of humor.

Harlan Cleveland
Political scientist and public executive,
president emeritus of the World Academy of Art and Science,
former president of the American Society for
Public Administration, and
author or co-author of numerous books on
executive leadership and international affairs

Preface

The idea of putting together a series of short essays about my personal experience in government came out of my teaching in the Lyndon B. Johnson School of Public Affairs at the University of Texas and at Texas A&M University in the George Bush School of Government and Public Service and in the College of Education. In returning to teaching after a lifelong public service career, ending with twenty-one years as the Texas Commissioner of Higher Education, my initial approach was to avoid telling "war stories" to my students or dwelling on my work experience. I suppose I was trying to deny my arrival at the age of anecdotage, as Louis Brownlow has called it. But all too frequently some concept or theory or "construct" we were discussing in class could be elucidated and enlivened by an example of an actual experience or event, usually from my own past. My students quickly began to tell me that it was especially useful to them for me to draw on practical experiences from my government career to illustrate the academic theories or models about policy making that we were studying in the course.

The format of using "letters" to a young bureaucrat for this book provided me several advantages. Each letter could serve as a brief essay on a subject that is important for public servants to examine. Second, my writing could be very informal and more easily accessible to younger readers than a textbook or a memoir. And, third, through the use of actual experiences and side comments I could try to pique readers' continuing interest as well as to enlighten them. And finally, in addressing my letters to "Kim," I make clear that my advice is as much addressed to young women as to young men (not as Lent Upson began his "letters" on public administration, a book of fifty years ago: "To my attentive young Gentlemen").

Students told me repeatedly that they want to know what it is really like "in the trenches." They want to know what kind of situations they are probably going to encounter, how nasty can it really get? Is this a place of fulfillment? How do real people respond to the kinds of things that most beginning employees never expect to encounter in a government career?

Students are sometimes a little perplexed by the theories or models they encounter in their classes because they have not yet had extensive work experience and are not familiar with how they will apply these general frameworks on the job. In these "letters" I have tried to address both of these student needs. I have drawn on specific events in order to generalize from them about the kinds of things that actually happen in living out a long public service career. At other times I have gone in the other direction; I start with a general idea and move to the specific with an on-the-job illustration.

I know from my own career experience and from my mentoring of rising public servants that no young man or woman is going to shape public policy and improve government services to the people by studying only theories and models and conceptual frameworks described by scholars and researchers of public affairs. And this is true irrespective of how insightful and accurate those academic analyses may be. Young people will have to be in the thick of things, learn how to write a good briefing memo, know how to "play the game," be willing to take risks and know the consequences when they do, experience the exhilaration as well as the possible penalties of having the courage to be venturesome. And we can't just provide them with impressive entry-level credentials and turn them loose to go out and learn these things on the job. And certainly no good school of public affairs or public administration is doing only that.

Nonetheless, from what my students have been saying to me I thought I might expand on the practical end of their training through these "letters." First, I could impress upon them how important are the general models and theories they are studying, for in the beginning these will provide practically the only refuge for perspective and understanding amidst seeming chaos, uncertainty, and confusion. Second, I could provide some additional mortar that might fill the niches between the academic subjects and the courses in skill training they are studying.

These "letters" can probably be of greatest use in courses in public administration and public affairs and policymaking as a supplement to other readings. Because most of my years were spent in higher education administration, the letters will also be useful in preparing educational administrators. And the book should be of more than passing interest to practitioners in government and higher education.

Because the book is unique to the literature of public administration, I have been told that I may need to explain how it can be used in teaching. However, I will not presume to do that. If its use is not evident to faculty members, then no possible explanation from me, with far less teaching experience, will serve much purpose.

Another suggestion was that I need to "name names" and spell out who each of the protagonists is in the vignettes and anecdotes I provide. I simply must disagree. My intent is to reach the students and readers as directly as I can. I am not writing a history of my career or a memoir. I suspect most readers of these letters could care less about who these old geezers are, many of whom are dead and most of whom are retired. In my view, if I have been successful, all of us in these letters are stage props to create the drama of real life in the public service for the delectation of aspiring bureaucrats.

Others have suggested that it would be useful to the reader to know what positions I held as I experienced and learned from the events I describe in these letters. Let me say first why I did not elaborate on this in the context of the letters themselves. I wanted to give my letters written to a niece or nephew as much verisimilitude as possible. As an uncle I would not repeatedly introduce myself and explain my career to my own relative. Moreover, I could not do so without destroying the setting and context of my letters and without stalling their flow and informality, and my occasional free association. I did not want students immersed in a program of studying for the public service to turn to this book each week during a course as one more dreadful "reading assignment." I wanted them to pick it up with interest and maybe even enthusiasm and say, "I wonder what this old codger has to say that might help me in my job when I graduate next year." For this reason there are also no footnotes, only a few notes at the end for the curious about references and quotations.

In addition, for purposes of benefiting from the book, I'm not sure readers really need to know exactly what positions I held. If they find this book of interest it should be because they get a realistic feel for what public service jobs are like, what dilemmas and choices they will face, and what a difference they can make as individuals. To them it should not matter what position I held or whether some event I describe took place in California or Texas, Washington or Austin, on a university campus or in a federal agency. My wish would be that each student reader would think of me as a garrulous and relatively obscure uncle, working somewhere in government and near the end of his career, who has taken enough interest in his niece or nephew to put down some gratuitous advice and counsel, and one who is immensely proud of his young relative's decision to enter the public service.

But for those whose curiosity has sustained them to the end of this preface and have further interest about my career there follows a brief description of the positions I have held in the public service.

- Management Analyst, Office of the Secretary, U.S. Department of the Treasury, Washington, D.C., 1959–60 (after receiving a master's degree in public administration from Syracuse University, 1959, and a B.A. in economics from the University of Texas at Austin, 1958)

- Project Analyst, Urban Renewal Administration, Washington, D.C., 1960–61
- Assistant Director for Redevelopment, National Association of Housing and Redevelopment Officials, Washington, D.C., 1961–63
- Assistant Director, San Francisco Redevelopment Agency, San Francisco, California, 1963–65
- Director, Division of Facilities Grants, Office of Education, Department of Health, Education, and Welfare, Washington, D.C., 1965–66
- Director of Federal Programs, Texas Higher Education Coordinating Board, Austin, Texas, 1966–69
- Assistant to the Vice Chancellor for Academic Affairs, University of Texas System Administration, Austin, Texas, 1969–70 (after receiving a Ph.D. in the history and philosophy of education from the University of Texas at Austin, 1969)
- Vice Chancellor for Academic Affairs, University of Texas System Administration, Austin, Texas, 1970–73
- Executive Vice President, University of Texas at San Antonio, 1973–76
- Commissioner of Higher Education, Texas Higher Education Coordinating Board, Austin, Texas, 1976–97
- Visiting Professor, Texas A&M University and the University of Texas at Austin since 1997

Kenneth H. Ashworth

re: *Working with politicians*

Dear Kim

Well, I suppose you know by now how thoroughly you have disappointed your mother and father. They cannot imagine what got into you to turn down those admissions offers you had in hand from the Harvard School of Business and the Wharton School of Finance to attend what they consider some podunk university to study public administration, of all things! They have complained to me that they didn't even know such a degree existed.

They hope, I believe, that as your uncle I might talk you out of your decision. After all, they had come to cherish fond visions of you becoming the microchip baron or maybe cornering the market on soap. They've been reading about MBAs fresh out of college starting with salaries over $100,000. And now instead, you have chosen a highly questionable and unpredictable future in the public service. They have left it to me to inform you that they have not yet been able to bring themselves to tell the neighbors, who they know never expected you to amount to much anyway. If your parents continue to give you grief over your choice, you should bite your tongue, but you might take consolation in something Arthur Miller said about why he became a playwright and did not follow his father and uncles into business. He said, "Oh, I didn't have the discipline. To be a businessman you have to have the discipline to put everything interesting out of your mind to make money."

Knowing the lack of support you are receiving in this decision, I feel I may need to find moments now and then to drop you a note to explain some of the finer points of the career you are now embarked upon. If I can maintain the discipline, I do—at least for the moment—intend to send you some of my passing thoughts from my experience of almost four decades in this field. I'll try not to preach, just observe, generalize, talk big and tell a few stories. A lot of what I will tell you will come from my work experience at various levels of government: local, state, and federal. Although a lot of what I draw on will come from my experience in working with a governing board and with governors and legislators, whatever you end up doing, you should find what I share with you to be transferable to your work. Whatever you do in the public service, there will always be somebody to whom you are accountable and who is giving you directions and applying advice and criticism, even if you are in a so-called independent agency.

So over the months ahead in your studies, I will try to make the point that there is at least one in the family who supports your totally unexpected decision about your future career in the service of the people.

Perhaps there is nowhere better to start for your first lesson from this old government functionary than with some advice on dealing with politicians. A large portion of your time as a public servant will be spent with elected politicians, trying to convince them of policy initiatives or changes you have found to be needed. And part of your experience will include being kicked around or being on the receiving end of abuse from elected officials, most of it mild but some probably quite severe. Consequently, this topic can probably bear a little elaboration to prepare you for your future dealings with politicians.

About a year ago I had to go to the capitol on some business, and after I parked my car and I was crossing the mall I noticed my stomach was tying itself into knots and I had this unexplained depression and sense of dread. I knew suddenly that Pavlov was right. The legislature was not even in session and there I was with a conditioned reflex to the treatment I so often receive before committee hearings and in dealing with individual legislators. It was complete, even to Pavlov's ringing of bells, in this case the bells calling the legislature into session.

This reaction is just part of my usual biennial manic-depressive mood swings that go with having the legislature in town. I can be manic at noon when a "bad ol' bill" looks like it's dead in a committee and then depressive by mid-afternoon when I learn that the committee has met on an emergency posting and voted the bill out and sent it to the Calendars Committee to schedule a floor vote. Or I might feel great when I hear that an important bill looks like it will probably pass this session because a conference committee between the two houses has been appointed and will work out the minor differences in the two versions of the bill. And then I learn that the senator chairing the committee is refusing to convene the conferees for a vote until a dog of a bill of his is voted out of the House. And when you have several bills you are concerned about, you can find yourself manic and depressed at the same time.

Sometimes a bad ol' bill will be passed by one house as a favor to one of its members or to help a group of legislators who need to go back home and be able to brag about what they got accomplished. The members of one house will do this in full expectation that the bill will die in the other house. Such was the case one year with a bill to create by statute nearly 250 new degree programs in universities in south Texas, including doctoral degrees and new colleges of engineering and law and pharmacy and veterinary medicine and other professional fields. This bill would have created these programs without the review and analysis of my agency, the higher education coordinating board, which had been established by the legislature decades earlier to oversee and prevent just such unnecessary and costly duplication of degree programs. The bill was passed in the House to help the legislator sponsoring the bill and House colleagues to "bring home the bacon." The House passed it with the clear belief that such a bill would never pass the Senate or get by the governor. But after it passed the House, the House sponsors, and others in the Senate who wanted credit for this bacon as well, suddenly realized that the governor could never afford to veto such a bill if it reached her desk. She desperately needed votes from their region in the next election. Consequently, there was a "full-court" press put on to pass the bill out of the Senate as well, and it remained a cliffhanger for the entire session.

With so many bad ol' bills being introduced every session in legislatures nationwide and in the U.S. Congress, you come to appreciate the foresight of the founding fathers in knowing this would occur. They wisely made it exceptionally difficult to pass any bill. They protected us all by requiring that for anybody's idea to become imposed upon the people as a new law it must garner enough support to pass both houses and then be signed into law by the governor or the president. And if the governor or president refuses to sign it and vetoes the proposal, the two houses will then have to gather exceptional support and re-pass the proposal in both houses by a two-thirds majority. Thankfully this provides many places to kill or modify a bill or to tie it up until it dies.

You will quickly learn there are far more bills introduced in every legislative session that need to die than need to pass. I suppose every state has the same saying, "No person's life, liberty, or property is safe so long as the legislature is in session." Yet some critics of government claim that these kinds of requirements lead to gridlock and they feel it should be much easier to pass bills quickly that seem popular with the voters. But after you have

watched a legislature very long, you will agree with the founding fathers:
It is better to have a little gridlock than for a bunch of bad ol' bills to pass
every session, laws that the voters would then have to live with until they
could get them repealed. There's an old saying, "There are three things you
should never watch being made: sausage, cottage cheese, and legislation."

There are many ways a bill can be killed. And you will need to learn
these points to apply choke holds. A committee chair in either house may
decide to lock it up in a subcommittee. Or if two even slightly different versions of a bill pass the two houses, it might get waylaid in the conference
committee, or it might get modified so that it is not so bad a bill as it started
out being. Or the Speaker of the House or the lieutenant governor may
arrange for the bill to never reach the floor for a vote. Or the governor can
help a bill to die by saying in advance she will veto it. Even if it's a bill the
governor may have to sign for political reasons, she may work quietly with
legislators in one or both houses to be certain it never arrives at her desk to
embarrass her into having to sign it. Or if she's vetoed it, she can work to be
certain that at least one of the two houses can't get the two-thirds votes
necessary to override her refusal to sign it into law.

But those who are promoting an idea or proposal never count on just
the most visible and direct way to have their way, that is, to pass the substantive bill itself. They are always looking for a fallback option to salvage
at least part of what they seek to achieve by attaching it to some other bill,
ideally a related bill they know has to pass that session. Their challenge is
to find a bill to which their attachment will be germane. If it is not germane
to the purpose of the bill they are loading onto, their attachment faces the
risk of being removed on a point of order. But what others with less-
deserving proposals attempt to do can provide you a lesson on how to have
your way on more worthy issues you will pursue in the future.

Because bills can be killed so easily, politicians have to be willing to
amend their proposals to attract enough votes even to get it through their
own chamber. That means thoroughly bad bills with no redeeming social
values can rarely get passed. The only exception is where a bad ol' bill intended to benefit one area or one city or one military base or one university
begins to get broadened to include benefits to additional legislators' districts
in order to garner more votes for passage. A bad ol' bill loaded up with
enough "bad ol' amendments" to gather enough votes to pass is called a don-
key barbecue. Everybody gets a free piece of ass. This is where the governor
or the president can spoil the party, however, if he has the courage to veto it.

Playing with "free votes" in one house while counting on the other
house to kill a bill can be risky, however. In Washington for years the House

of Representatives used to pass a bill to impose constraints and regulations on the use of animals for research purposes in medical schools across the country. The American Medical Association (AMA), working on behalf of the medical schools, could be relied upon to always oppose the bill and to ensure its demise every session in a Senate committee. With assured death in the other chamber the bill for animal rights each session became a popular "free vote" for every member of the House. They could vote for the bill in the House and then go home and tell their constituents they were looking after the protection of everybody's pets, and if they felt like it they could even cozy up a bit to the anti-vivisectionists.

One year the bill once again passed the House and came before the same Senate committee where it was expected to be summarily dealt with in the usual manner. The chair, Senator Warren Magnuson, a lifelong bachelor who had just recently married, commented musingly, "I know we kill this bill every session, but my young bride told me at breakfast this morning she sure wished we could pass it. She's worried about our two little dogs getting out of the house someday and getting picked up by those people who collect stray dogs and sell them for medical research."

The Republican minority leader from Colorado on the committee was notorious for opposing any kind of federal control and regulations and was predictably anti-government intervention on everything. The senator from Colorado said, "Mr. Chairman, let me tell you a little story. Our dog disappeared in Denver last year and my wife and I walked the streets, we knocked on doors, we posted signs about him, we talked to neighbors, and we simply couldn't find him. We were devastated at losing him. Then my wife suggested we go to the medical school as a last resort just to see if he might be there. That's where we found him, waiting to be cut on by those doctors." Everyone sitting there picked his chin up off the floor when he then added, "Senator Magnuson, I will join you in reporting this bill out to the floor with a recommendation that it do pass." With two such powerful Senate leaders supporting the bill it passed despite all that the AMA and the lobbyists for the medical schools could do to defeat it.

So, back to where I was: What do politicians do to you in committee hearings? One thing you learn early is that legislators are very current-issue oriented. What's been in the papers and on television and might have gotten the attention of the voters? Those are the issues that often get dragged into a hearing on totally unrelated topics and get aired at length. This permits members to make their positions clear on what's in the morning news, what's on the minds of their voters. You can see your silk purse of a hearing quickly become a pig's ear if there is press coverage at your hearing and the questions and statements on your testimony devolve into a diatribe on something from the "City and State" page of a local newspaper.

Some legislators become notorious for their grandstanding and posturing for the voters. Once I was berated and abused for over two hours by two committee members about how I had for years denied their constituents their constitutional, legal, and rightfully deserved benefits from the state. When the committee broke for lunch the television crews heard what had been going on and showed up in force. When the committee reconvened with cameras all over the room, the morning performance was repeated, almost word for word. I was hardly permitted to respond or defend myself in either the original performance or in the replay. I was to stand there and take it, a necessary prop or "straight man." I was not to play an active role other than to serve as a convenient foil and target of abuse. It is a humiliating thing to have to put up with, but often there is very little you can do.

That is one thing you learn early. As a paid public servant you are never equal to legislative committee members, and you should never expect to be. Moreover, committee members will rarely discipline each other when one of them is boring in on a civil servant. Why should they make an enemy or alienate a vote they need on something else just to help you out? After all, this is part of what you get paid for, and you are merely incidental to what each of them is trying to get done that day anyway. They are courting each other for votes, they have cut deals, and they have committed their votes. You are expected to tolerate the abuse you receive and you must put up with it. Occasionally a member may intervene to throw you a soft-pitch question or to elicit a response he knows you have been wanting to make. Be thankful for such small help. It is very infrequent.

Once I did get some serious help and it came in such a subtle form that the senator in the chair never caught on. The committee vice chair was presiding and he could not resist his rare opportunity to perform for a large group of hometown constituents present at the hearing. He proceeded to abuse me as he had so often before. His accusations became so outrageous that I refused to remain silent or acquiescent any longer. As he continued making outrageous and unsupportable charges, I warmed to my task and began to make strong and pointed responses, denials, and corrections of facts. The vice chair was increasingly losing control, and since he was in the chair it did not appear anyone else on the committee could correct the drift of the altercation. Finally another senator called out, "Mr. Chairman, point of order." The intensity was partly broken simply by his interrupting our exchange. The vice chair asked what the point of order was. The committee member winked at me as he said, "The witness should be instructed to confine his remarks to the topic of this hearing." The vice chair was so absorbed in his performance for his claque of supporters that he missed the scattered laughter around the room, but he banged his gavel and said severely to me, "Yes, the witness is admonished to restrict himself to the topic under consideration." Nothing could have pleased me more and we all went back to the business before the committee.

It is very risky to respond in kind to legislators in most cases. In this case I was in dangerous waters. You may quickly find that rather than only one or two committee members being on the attack, you have all of them down on your neck. The ranks close quickly if you do not stay in your allotted subordinate role with legislators.

Specifically, they get after witnesses in a number of ways. They may start by keeping you waiting to testify by running in ahead of you other unscheduled witnesses or those scheduled to appear later. Sometimes this is unavoidable for a committee, but a chair who wants to send a message of displeasure to a witness can keep him waiting all day or several days by this technique. And the costs of keeping state executives and their staffs idly waiting are not a consideration even to the most efficiency minded of legislators. It is more important to make clear who is in charge and who is subservient.

You sometimes will find yourself fielding questions that can become increasingly accusatory and abusive, often presented as in cross-examination, pointed and rapid fire, in an effort to confuse you, make you appear stupid, or lead you to a predetermined end. And it is the nature of the proceedings that you never know where a question is coming from next or what kind of off-the-wall grilling you may get. I will not advise you to relax and bear with it, because it is impossible to relax. It is some of the most intense intellectual effort you will ever encounter.

If members are determined to intimidate you or to try to embarrass you, they may show little regard for facts or circumstances. For four years we were criticized for having more space per employee in our agency quarters than the new state standard recommended. The fact that our ten-year lease had been executed several years before the legislature set the new space standard was irrelevant. We clearly were not following state guidelines and were accused of being wasteful and uncooperative.

They may ask why the staff travels so much or why your people are not out in the field more to see conditions first hand. Or why you printed a report in-house rather than contracting it out. Or why you contracted out a printing job you could have done more cheaply in-house. Or why did you extend a contract for services or why did you not extend an existing contract rather than incur the costs of getting new bids?

You also learn soon that there is abundant wisdom in the saying, "No good deed goes unpunished." In our administration of the federally insured student loan program, we had managed to accumulate surplus funds beyond what were needed to cover debt service, above what was needed to keep the costs of student loans low, and more than sufficient to cover losses of unpaid loans. The state was leasing a privately owned building for our agency at considerable expense to the taxpayers. We did some calculations about how much we could save the state on our next ten-year lease if we were permitted to use the surplus funds we had accumulated in the loan program to build a new facility to be owned thereafter by the state. So we presented our proposal to the legislature.

It was at that hearing that I learned not to expect beatification but to take solace in martyrdom. The only thing the committee members heard was that we had somehow accumulated $9 million that they could get their hands on to spend on something else—which they promptly proceeded to do, continuing to appropriate funds for us to lease space. That was over ten years and untold millions of tax dollars ago.

Another case arose with our recognition of the desperate need to place more African American and Hispanic faculty members in our university classrooms. We devised a program to lend money to minority graduate students to complete their doctorates. The program would permit these students to have a fifth of their total indebtedness paid off by the state for each year they worked at a university in our state after completing their doctorates. The legislature thought it was a wonderful program and passed authorizing legislation. But since it required new funds they directed us to seek support for it from private sources and foundations.

We spent two years trying to raise such funds, only to be told repeatedly by possible donors, "This is a fine program, but it needs to be funded by the state, not by us because it will be an ongoing program spread over many years." When we returned to the legislature two years later and explained our situation, the House Appropriations Committee looked around for a source of funds for this fine program and found it. They took it from our agency's *operating* budget. The gratitude for our proposing this program was summed up in one legislator's angry question to me when I objected that this would injure our agency and was not an appropriate way to fund the new program. He said, "You mean to say, doctor, that your operating budget is more important to you than helping minorities get doctoral degrees? It appears you have lost sight of the purpose of your agency." And, indeed, our budget was cut to pay for the program. Fortunately we got part of that funding restored in the Senate.

As you sit there before a committee giving your testimony, a multitude of thoughts go through your mind. Stay calm and in control of yourself, show respect, never appear arrogant, avoid any sense of self-importance, try to be responsive and helpful, and keep your answers as short and cogent as possible. And never blow up or show your impatience.

With experience over the years you would think that testifying before legislative committees would become easier. But it doesn't. You learn to be more aware of what is going on behind what is superficially obvious. As the questions come at you from all sides you must consider what is the best and most appropriate response. For example, a legislator may throw you a soft pitch, but you need to consider that if you hit the pitch as hard as he wants you to and as you are tempted to do, it is likely to draw a reaction from other legislators who hold a different view. In fact, is the easy question a kindness to you from a sympathetic member or is he trying to use you and the answer he thinks you will give him in order to irritate or embarrass another member of the committee? Is this a leading question? Where are this line of questioning and my answers taking me? Will it be better to respond succinctly and risk being misunderstood or to explain this complex issue more fully and perhaps lose the attention of the committee members? Do I answer this as best I can from the data I have at my command here or do I give a short reply and promise to provide more information later? And as you are processing these thoughts and making your responses, you notice that half the committee is in conversations with each other or not paying attention.

One day as I was being cross-examined and tossed from pillar to post among the committee members an aberrant thought crossed my mind. I recalled a scene from the movie *Dr. Strangelove*. There was a character named Jack D. Ripper who was lamenting his war experience to another officer named Mandrake. Ripper was reproaching himself for how he had broken under torture by the Japanese during World War II and had given his interrogators more than his name, rank, and serial number. Then he asked Mandrake how he had behaved under similar torture. Mandrake replied, "Oh, I don't know that they cared all that much about what I *said*. I rather think they were having a bit of fun."

Then there is the question: "We know, of course, where your board and your agency stand on this problem, but tell us how you feel about this personally." Beware. You have no privilege to represent an agency position and hold a different personal opinion in public. To state a differing personal position is to immediately undercut your agency, your board, and your job in that agency. It seems so self-evident after you have once fallen for that simple invitation to separate yourself from the agency position you must justify and defend. In fact, with this question, there will be occasions when you do, indeed, have a strong personal view different from the one you must defend in public. You just don't have the prerogative to state it publicly. It can even be a risk to state it privately.

A senator devised on his own on his computer a new formula for how the legislature should fund higher education. And as chair of the Senate Finance Committee he was in a position to push to substitute his version for the formula that the universities and our agency had developed and been fine-tuning and updating every two years for several decades. The senator invited me for a private discussion to ask me to endorse his innovation, his new formulas. I explained that to accede to this request I would first have to abandon a financing method I had agreed to with the universities, one I had pledged to the presidents I would defend before the legislature. Second, I would have to disassociate myself from my own board's formal adoption of recommendations to the legislature to use that method of financing. I explained the situation I was in and why I could not now choose to endorse his plan personally when the one I was officially wedded to was on the table before the legislature.

I did offer the services of our agency to assist him with his new model for financing and to do trial runs of data and his formulas for him. He pointed out that the universities were abandoning the old method and were going to endorse his approach since he was promising them more money if they would accept his new formula. I told him they had that prerogative, but I did not. They were pledged only to each other; I was pledged to all of them as a group. In the end, he saw me as less than cooperative and felt I was being inflexible and hardheaded. I did not feel I had a choice in the matter. I had to do what my job and my pledges required of me.

We all may wonder what motivates legislators in their own particular ways of dealing with public servants. Most of all they want their way in what they pursue. The political process is distinctly different from the practices followed in most of our working hours as civil servants. We focus principally upon developing solutions to problems and implementing and carrying out programs. In contrast, the politicians' problem is to reach agreement with other politicians and policymakers so that some version of what they want to achieve and what others are pursuing can move forward. That means they become masters of trade-offs, at swapping, at making deals, and at compromise.

Those of us in administrative posts carrying out public programs don't have the politician's latitude to wheel and deal and be unpredictable or to always be flexible and willing to modify a position we have taken earlier. We don't have favors to trade or chits to call in. Consequently, we sometimes become part of the problem in legislators' eyes because we can't capitulate easily, put deals on the table quickly, or compromise away standards or procedures. The politician's position was best encapsulated by Illinois Senator Everett Dirksen, when he said, "I am a man of fixed and unbending principles—the first of which is to be flexible at all times."

We administrators tend to be more concerned than legislators about what is required to give greater predictability and stability to our activities and our rulings that affect people every day. Our jobs require us to pursue consistency. Politicians are more often looking for change and new accommodations. We prefer to tinker with programs or procedures on the margin and fine-tune what exists. They often prefer to sweep out the old and introduce something entirely new. No wonder our two camps often look upon each other with considerable distrust and skepticism.

Moreover, politicians have needs we bureaucrats don't have. They need to impress their voters and the pleaders for special treatment and satisfy supplicants for exceptions and favors. We bureaucrats can be obstacles to those needs because favors, exceptions, and special pleaders are the bane of our existence. To us these kinds of people are asking us to be unfair and to treat themselves and other citizens unequally. To the politician such requests represent a chance to do a favor, to make someone indebted to them, to create the potential for some future trade they may need in order to move something on their agenda.

In addition, legislators are performing for other politicians, particularly the leadership in both houses. They all want better committee assignments and aspire to hold committee chairs—or to chair a more important committee. So they are grandstanding to look good in the legislature as well as with their voters. And some are courting supporters and voters they may need in order to pursue the next higher office they aspire to.

And finally, of course, most of them serve because they want to make a difference. They see conditions they want to correct or improve, circumstances they want to get placed on the public agenda, solutions they want to try out, changes they want to make in how governments do things. And it may sound cynical, but when one of them does something for you, a mere bureaucrat, it may very well be to get you indebted to him so he can ask you for something in exchange later. Even when they are your personal friends, politicians don't see a request to balance the ledger as unusual or out of line. Why would it be inconsistent to ask a friend for a favor, especially if he has already done one for you? What are friends for? All of this is in the nature of being a politician. It's just that elected politicians move the public agenda differently than we career public servants do. And for the good of the nation, we can be thankful for that. Both approaches contribute to the way our system of government works. Efficiency and consistency are worthy goals, but so are change and accommodation.

In terms of individual personal relations with legislators, you will find most of them are pleasant or certainly tolerable. Many politicians are downright charming. After all, they have not gotten to where they are by always being nasty or threatening to other people. And in being charming they feel this entitles them to press to the very edge of what is socially acceptable to obtain what is politically desirable.

Yet one underrated pleasure of life is to watch obnoxious politicians get their comeuppance. Those who are overbearing and generally abusive of their positions are often taken care of by their own colleagues. There was one east Texas legislator who was renowned for his outrageous and arrogant demands upon state agencies and his colleagues. Fred was one of those politicians who truly felt, "If it turns out reincarnation is the way the universe works, I want to come back as me." Many of his fellow House members had a chance to observe him in all his glory on one occasion as they walked from a parking lot to a university reception for the legislature. He was leaning out of his car window and screaming at three policemen to move a goddamned barricade to permit him to park in front of the building where the reception was being held. The other legislators might walk from the parking lot a block away but not Fred. When the police officers did not move fast enough for his satisfaction, he blew his horn at them and began pushing them and the barricade with his car.

Fred's brother-in-law was serving as a dormitory proctor at one of the universities, a special privilege Fred insisted on by virtue of his august position in the legislature. The young brother-in-law was generating substantial personal income by requiring that all laundry in the dormitory be handled through a laundry service that provided him with a commission. He had also moved a pool table from the lobby into one of the rooms of his suite and was charging students to use it. He had also moved his girlfriend into his apartment. Then the university discovered he was not even enrolled at the university. Fred wanted to know what the university's problem was with his relative; after all, he was going to marry the girl. I tell you these tidbits to help you see Fred in all his resplendent dignity.

During one slow day in the House there was a large delegation of school teachers from across the state in the gallery watching the House debate bills on education and do its business. Fred received a note purported to be from one of the teachers upstairs, saying how she was from his district and how much she admired his work and how she had been ecstatically watching him for hours. This epistle was followed a little later with another note from the young lady, saying that it would make her so proud to see him at work and would he please go to one of the microphones and say something on one of the bills for her. He did this, of course, and the word soon spread among his colleagues in the chamber what was going on. Legislators caucused in a corner to compete in creativity about the next note to send to him. This continued for some time as the notes became more and more personal. Finally a note arrived in which the teacher said she had called back to her school superintendent and had arranged to take the next day off and she would be able to stay overnight. If he could possibly be able to meet her after the day's work, he should give her a signal. Perhaps he could stand up and comb his hair. She pointed out, incidentally, that she was the teacher in the lavender dress (chosen from among those in the gallery by Fred's colleagues for her pulchritude). Good old Fred nearly stripped himself bald, looking up toward the young lady as he stood and vigorously preened away.

There was another politician whose practice was to vote against programs and appropriations and then return home to take credit for projects funded under them. On one occasion he told the people holding a dedication ceremony that he could only be present briefly before he would have to dash out to catch a plane. He demanded to be put first on the program. His peremptory request so angered the dignitaries gathering for the ceremony that they directed everyone to turn the clocks in the courthouse and their watches back fifteen minutes. When the senator arrived he saw the clocks and proceeded to use this windfall in time to move around the room and greet the voters. Finally his staff caught on to what had been done just in time to get him out the door and to the airport to catch his plane. Unfortunately he had not had time to stay for the dedication ceremony.

Dislike among colleagues can be intense. When one member of the Texas legislature had a heart attack, two colleagues got into an argument over which of them was entitled to take credit for causing it.

You learn in this business as you go. When I was first in this line of work I was crossing the Senate floor during a hearing and a senator jumped up from a table and came across the chamber yelling at me. When he reached me he accused me of "messing around" with one of his bills. If I didn't back off he'd take care of me in my agency's financing bill. He was right about what I had been doing, and as chair of the Senate Finance Committee he could deliver on his threat. I was going about it all the wrong way. I had some unrealistic idea that I could work quietly and unknown behind the scenes.

There are few if any secrets in the legislative process. In fact, a political secret is an oxymoron. There really is no alternative to confronting the sponsor of legislation you disagree with. If you voice your first opposition at a hearing on the bill you will get roasted in public. You might as well get barbecued in private by seeing the bill sponsor and explaining your position. Besides, to oppose a bill when it is being heard before a committee is nearly always too late to do any good anyway. The deals have been made, the favors swapped, the votes pledged and counted, and you'll be going public as an opponent for no practical purpose. Also you might remember this: If you do have ideas on how a bill can be improved, telling the committee and sponsor for the first time at the hearing is far too late. You have an amendment? Talk to the bill sponsor. He doesn't like it? Find a sponsor for your amendment on the committee.

One senator I met with to talk about a bad ol' bill he was carrying listened from behind his desk with a scowl on his face as he glared at me over his half-moon glasses. When I finished, he said, "I'm gonna get you *fired* this session. I'm tired of you messin' with my schools." He had not heard a word I had said. But he could not accuse me of working behind his back.

Often you go to see a governor or legislator or other elected official to ask for help, not to discuss matters you disagree on. Since appointments with busy politicians are so difficult to get, many people make the mistake of bringing their whole load of hay of every idea they have saved up for months and then proceed to unload all of it. That is a mistake. Identify the two or three things you need help on most and ask only for those and make your case on them. Even better, keep the requests to not more than two if possible. If you raise too many topics they will all seem of equal value to a politician still thinking about her last appointment and what she still has to follow up on and about the meeting coming up when she can finally get you out of her office. And when you are gone she is likely to forget *all* of your multiple requests.

Another word of advice on lobbying legislators. Don't feel that you have to talk to the legislator himself or herself on all the issues you need help and support on. It is often more effective to talk with the legislator's aide or the committee clerk handling most of his business. These people generally are not as pressed for time and can give you more attention and listen at greater length. If you can get them to buy into your cause and you provide them with the information and arguments they will need to sell your position, they can become an in-house lobbyist for you. When their boss asks about it, they are ready and informed. In briefing them, you help them to look good with their bosses. They can also pick the right moment to present your position, when the legislator is receptive or dealing with an ancillary matter.

A legislator who was particularly obstreperous was threatening a lobbyist one day and I overheard the lobbyist say, "You know, Carl, you really do try to scare people, don't you? You bluff, you bully, you push against them with your belly, you yell in their faces. If I didn't know you were a lawyer and that you know better than to hit anybody, I would swear at times you were about to slug somebody. Why do you do it?"

Carl laughed as though he had been caught out and replied, "Because it works on so many people."

Once a legislator asked me to do something for the son of his major political donor, to make a particular exception for the boy, and I had to tell him I had no legal authority to do it. I explained that I had turned down dozens of similar requests and I couldn't legally or in good conscience do what he asked of me. The word would quickly get out that I wasn't holding fast to the position I had to enforce under the law. He listened to what I said and then he said quietly in his most pleasant manner, "You don't understand. I'm asking you to do this for me as a personal favor." As they say in West Virginia, "Everything here is politics, except politics. That's personal."

When I again said I could not do what he asked, he said in a less pleasant voice that he would remember this at the next budget hearing. Sure enough, he remembered the following year. He had arranged with the chair that in the final markup of the appropriations bill he be given the personal privilege of making the motion to cut our request.

In another case I had to say "no" to the overweening aspirations of a legislator to convert his local branch campus into a separate university and I testified on behalf of my governing board against his bill. On the floor of the House in debate on the appropriations bill, he reduced the line item for my salary. He worked with the Senate conferees to see that it was not restored. In the many years I knew him after he left the legislature he sent several messages through mutual acquaintances about how much he regretted later having done such a small-minded thing. But at the time it had not seemed small to him. I still remember watching from the gallery as he looked up at me from the House floor and smiled as his amendment passed to cut my salary.

I had another legislator ask me to overlook and write off an unpaid student loan of one of her constituents. I refused to do it and as a result she would call me to her office on other business and leave me waiting each time for an hour before she could manage to work me in. But her later political problems dwarfed this into insignificance.

When I first took my job many legislators wanted to send me a message about their unhappiness with me and our board. The message came as they would introduce a bill to abolish our agency. The requests for such a bill were so frequent that the Office of Legislative Counsel kept a folder at hand with multiple copies of a standard bill to abolish us. The form provided two blank spaces, a place for the sponsor to enter his or her name and a space for the bill number. Over the years that practice has declined as we spend more time "on the hill" talking to legislators and making ourselves available for more direct reprimands and complaints.

However, a few years ago one senator took great umbrage at our board denying his university's request to purchase an empty "white elephant" of a building some fifteen miles from the campus. One of our board members referring to the facility as "an old sausage factory" did not soften his feelings about our board members and their action to support the staff recommendation for disapproval of the proposed purchase. So later the senator introduced a bill to abolish our board and transfer any functions that might indeed be found necessary to other agencies. Since he was chair of the Senate Finance Committee by that time, he had substantial leverage on his colleagues and he treated the bill as important to him.

The night of the hearing on his bill I was called to testify. I started off listing the essential functions assigned to us by the legislature and which we had been carrying out for several decades. But I said I knew change is inevitable and certainly we all knew where the final authority rested as to any changes that might be made concerning our agency. I said I was reminded of Lord Tennyson's *Death of King Arthur*. I said, "As you will recall at the end King Arthur is dying and is on his funeral bier on the river. The King calls his grieving knights to him. And Tennyson describes the King's response to their lament:

> And slowly answered Arthur from the barge,
> "The old order changeth, yielding place to new,
> And God fulfills Himself in many ways,
> Lest one good custom should corrupt the world."

I then went on to say that we thought in following their statutes our work had been good, but if in their eyes we had corrupted the world, then they certainly held the power to cause us to yield our place to something new. I said perhaps no university or college would defend our continuation. If not, that possibly could be to our credit. If we had failed the legislature or had offended them individually in some way we would, of course, accept their decision.

The committee turned to other matters and nothing further was said about the bill. The members were either so confounded by my quoting poetry to them they did not know what to do or they felt the message of dissatisfaction by their chair had been received and understood.

However, I was criticized later by one of my own staff members. He said I had been disingenuous when I said to this group of legislators, "As you will recall . . . ," and then referred to Tennyson. Perhaps I was temporarily insane. I know I did not feel as cocky as that testimony sounds to me as I reread it today. I do know by hindsight I would handle the situation differently today, even though the bill did get dropped.

The worst abuse of legislative power I ever witnessed was by a House member who wanted a new university in his district. His "window of opportunity" opened when he became chairman of the House Calendars Committee, the body that schedules bills to go to the floor for final voting. He informed all House members that if they had any bills they wanted to reach the floor for passage that session they would have to support his bill for a new university. Coincidentally, this was the session when my higher education agency was up for sunset review. This meant that if the bill reauthorizing our agency's existence did not pass out of the session, our agency would be forced to go out of business during the following three months. The legislator wanting the new university informed us that any opposition to his bill by us would doom our reauthorizing bill to die in his Calendars Committee.

Not surprisingly, the Calendars Committee chair's bill passed the House, and it was quickly defeated in the Senate. At that point, he became what some legislators referred to as "the thirty-second senator" of the thirty-one–member Senate. He crossed the rotunda and explained to six senators who had voted against his bill that their bills now in the House would all die in his committee unless they reconsidered their votes.

His bill then passed the Senate, but only after he had to agree to a provision added by the Senate and insisted on by Governor William Clements. The amendment required prior approval for establishing the new university by our agency *after* the legislative session was ended.

Our own "sunset" or reauthorization bill reached the floor of the House and passed just before midnight during the very last hour of the legislative session. After the session ended, our agency, as a result of his bill as amended, was then placed in the unusual position of being able to veto an act passed by both houses and signed into law by the governor. This provision arose because neither house of the legislature nor the governor was willing or able to kill the new university and they passed that nasty job on to our agency.

To this date no new university has been approved by our board or authorized by the legislature for that district. Unpopular as our agency may be with politicians, we have proved useful to them on occasion.

For all the associated unpleasantness, though, you must always be willing to meet with your opposition and your enemies. There are lots of advantages. First, you might bring them around to your point of view. Or, remote as the possibility might seem at the time, they might bring you around to their point of view. Or, more likely, you might work out an accommodation between you, even if it's just temporary. Your opponents will have to respect your openness and might even admire your courage in entering the lion's den to meet with them. And if nothing else, you will get a better idea of their arguments and the forces you will have to overcome to prevail in your position. There is no downside that I have ever found in meeting with my opposition—except, perhaps, the occasional concern about assassination.

Incidentally, don't ever fall for the commonly heard criticism that compromise is dishonorable or reprehensible. That's bull. It is not selling out or capitulation. Look it up. The dictionary says compromise is consent reached through *mutual* concessions. It is the alternative to gridlock and inaction. It is the lubricant to governing.

Back to meeting with your opponents. There is a byproduct I came to recognize. You tend to come to know your enemies better than even your friends because you have to spend more time with them and talk more persuasively with them. They might become useful allies on other issues in the future, which will tell you that they are never really enemies as much as they are merely temporary opponents. You are at the moment political adversaries, but that may be the case only on this particular issue. If you show you aren't self-righteous and "holier than thou" they might be willing to help you with a favor. Like all politicians, they sometimes like being asked for help. You can show them you are not above obligating yourself to them just a bit. Your asking for help gives them face and respect and shows that you see them and yourself as equals, even as you disagree over some substantive issue in another area. As more than one politician has said, "I never had a friend who couldn't become an enemy or an enemy who couldn't become a friend."

In the end you need to understand that it is inevitable in dealing with politicians that you are going to have at least some of them mad at you from

time to time. One or two may be mad at you all the time. You will find that if you are going to carry out the responsibilities of your job this is absolutely unavoidable. And unpleasant as it is to have people of power and prestige angry at you and to have to live with their emotional explosions and attacks, you will discover that there is usually a much larger number of other politicians who are looking on and who recognize that you are doing what you are expected to do. It is the nature of political relationships, however, that these other politicians don't often speak up to defend or explain what you are doing. Why should they? As a result you can feel alone and unappreciated. One of my board chairmen, Harry Provence, summed it up best. Once when I was whining and complaining about my unpopularity and being caught so often between two opposing groups, he said, "You don't understand. Your job description is to stand between the dog and the fireplug."

Harry's characterization of my job resulted in the enclosed cartoon, drawn by one of our college presidents, Carl "Cheesie" Nelson. You will see he actually made me into the *fireplug*. But he clearly captured the idea; I had a wet leg much of the time—and so will you when you get in this line of work.

It is more than merely rationalizing to say that you need to have some politicians mad at you some of the time. A public agency is given certain duties and responsibilities by the legislature and perhaps by the governor, and if you do the job given to you, it is inevitable that you will create hostility from a few of those legislators and their constituencies. It is inescapable that you are going to offend some of them and some of their constituents. If you do not accrue such hostility, it may very well mean you are not carrying out well the job the legislators as a body have assigned to you. In striving to be popular or inoffensive you may be letting somebody down. If you fail to do your job, then it puts that job back on those who delegated it to you in the first place. And they probably gave you that job to do because they, as a group, do not want to deal with it or find that they cannot deal with it effectively. Some of them have come to know that in the political process legislative votes alone should not control every decision. Sometimes the political leaders need someone else to provide the obstacles they do not want to set up or to state the rationale for denying some colleague's unreasonable demands. You help them to hold the line without their having to say "no" directly.

Even if the only thing ever erected in your name is a pissing post, consider it an honor if it's done for the right reasons.

When a legislator is looking a colleague in the eye who is pressing him for his vote on a bill and he doesn't know enough about the bill to give the reasons why he can't vote for it, that legislator may find it very helpful to use you as a foil. He will be off the hook in committing himself too quickly if he can say, "I know you probably have a really good bill here, but you know we gave Agency X or Commissioner Whatzit responsibility to report to us on these kinds of things before we take action. It's all very complicated. I hate to put you off, but I'd like to find out what they think about the bill before I commit myself on it."

In other words, it is important for you to have the right people mad at you. Lyndon Johnson used to say, "Ever'body needs a sumbitch sometime." Consequently, if you work too assiduously to avoid controversy and try to keep everybody happy, you may just be inviting a much more significant group of politicians to see you as ineffectual. Some people need you to be their sumbitch sometimes. If you never make an enemy you will probably soon be considered to be inconsequential. Good politicians know very well that the quality of a person is often known best by the enemies he makes. If you let them down by avoiding the unpleasant accoutrements of your job, in time a growing group of them will come to be unhappy with you. So get on with doing your job and at least have the *right* politicians angry with you.

But expect no reward or recognition for your unpopularity. To expect this in an active political arena is about as realistic as to think that a bull in his field will not charge you because you are a vegetarian.

Like it or not, this is all part of the workings of our democratic system of government, or as Justice Oliver Wendell Holmes might have labeled it, "sparks in an active workshop." If you want to play a meaningful role you have to get into the fray. James Q. Wilson said making policy in the United States is like a barroom brawl. "Anybody can join in, the combatants fight all comers and sometimes change sides, no referee is in charge, and the fight lasts . . . indefinitely."

You have to remember, it is not *you* and it's not *them*. It's what you and the elected politicians *together* constitute: a way of finding a public course of action in your area of responsibility that is in keeping with the sentiments of the people, those you serve, those who speak for those you serve, those who pay for what you do, and sometimes those who have no one but you to speak for them. If you come to understand what is going on and what to expect as you live in the midst of the political process you can be a more effective player. You will come to accept the attendant discomforts as a condition to continuing progress.

I can't resist one more word of advice. Don't pander to politicians, or for that matter, those above you in the organization. Ask yourself, "Am I doing this or taking this position on this issue because I know it will make so-and-so happy?" If you are, odds are you are probably cutting corners on your analysis and neglecting the duties of your office and your obligations to others. It is so tempting to want to do something to be liked, to want to placate a powerful adversary, to anticipate what you think are the desires or preferences of a governing body, all to make your job a little less unpleasant. Like so many temptations, this is a dangerous one.

If you are reluctant to face confrontation and stress you might wonder after this dose of cynicism and war stories why I have stayed with it. If it is so bad why didn't I get out? How can I continue to work with an agency or an administration or with politicians when I disagree with their positions strongly and where disagreement brings mistreatment? Harry Truman used to say, "If you can't stand the heat don't come in the kitchen." I would extend his metaphor to say that working in the kitchen is sometimes the best way to change the menu. Or as George C. Marshall, one of the men President Truman most admired, said, "You don't take a post of this sort and then resign when the man who has the constitutional responsibility to make decisions makes one you don't like." Part of your staying or going depends on the issue. You can't fall on your sword every time you disagree with your board or the courts or the governor or the attorney general or, in Marshall's case, with the president.

Harry McPherson, longtime aide to Lyndon Johnson, asked himself this as well: "Why am I here? Why did I choose this 'experience,' instead of beginning a law practice and finding a responsible place in a small community?" His answer is probably what lies in part behind your own decision to become a public servant, "Partly because I want to find out what goes on in the councils of power. . . . Partly because I want to 'do good,' and a decade after Roosevelt it still seems as if Washington is the grand arena for doing good. Partly—perhaps chiefly—because I want to cast a shadow, to feel, however vicariously, that I have affected significant events and therefore exist."

My public information director is getting restless. She wants to brief me on what not to say at our next meeting. I am hosting lunch for the press to provide them with background information on issues of interest to us this session. One skeptic says that's my first mistake, to think I can educate the press.

Your admiring

Uncle Ken

P.S.: Incidentally, from my collection of quotes, I found a few that fit the topic of this letter. Here they are.

Watching a legislature in session is like attending an Italian opera. One person gets up to sing and four others stab him in the back.
— *A legislative witticism*

I don't want to start any kind of precedent here, but I would like to read your bill a couple of minutes before I take a position on it.
— *Texas Senator Kent Caperton*

All my constituents like trees. The problem is 50 percent like them vertically and the other 50 percent like them horizontally.
— *California Representative Douglas H. Bosco*

Yes, you may speak briefly on this topic, but I doubt you can.
— *Texas Lieutenant Governor Bill Hobby*

re: *Working with the press*

The price of freedom of religion or of speech or of the press is that we must put up with, and even pay for, a good deal of rubbish.

— *Justice Robert Jackson*

The weight of the first amendment is on the reporter's side, because the assumption underlying the first amendment is that secrecy and the control of news are all too inviting, all too easily achieved, and, in general, all too undesirable.

— *Alexander Bickel*

If a reporter is not a "disturber of the peace," he should go into cost accounting.

— *Harrison Salisbury*

NOVEMBER

Dear Kim

I decided as I finished my last letter with those quotations from politicians that I am going to open each of my letters to you with a quotation or two that's been meaningful to me and might interest you. Incidentally you should start collecting quotations and vignettes from your reading and experience that you think you might find useful in your future speech making and writing. I guarantee you that they'll come in handy later.

You'll remember when I signed off last time I closed with some disparaging remark about educating the press. Yet I truly wonder what bureaucrats and government officials would become if they didn't have the press watching and reporting to the people on everything we do.

There must forever be a permanent tension between the desire of the press to know everything government does and the desire of government officials to keep secret or confidential as much of what they do as possible. This is one of the separations of power not addressed in our Constitution except as implied in the First Amendment. If ever the press knew everything as it was being worked up, drafted, studied, considered, negotiated, and executed, governments would be crippled in getting some of their most important and sensitive work done. If the press could report before a meeting what an ambassador was going to demand and also what position he was prepared to retreat to and settle for, how effective would his negotiations be? If candid differences of opinion among executives and their advisers were openly aired in the media how could decision makers obtain candid views or consider differing opinions or develop the best options for public action? If personnel evaluations relating to important appointments were openly published in the press, when would there ever again be an honest evaluation made and how could merit ever again play a role in promotions?

But if ever a government can decide for itself everything that it wishes to keep secret, the ability of the people to control that government will end. Some of the first things to be hidden from the press and the people would be waste, mistakes, fraud, corruption, and favoritism and nepotism. So as a bureaucrat you will find yourself living within this ongoing, permanent tension between the press always trying to find out more than may make you comfortable and your need to protect certain information from premature release.

You will have to put up with that unresolved and continuing tension even when it seems unfair at times. And at times it will indeed be unfair, namely when someone in the press or television exercises his or her power to shock, to astonish, to feed the public's insatiable appetite and curiosity, to pursue events with a seemingly prurient perversity, more in the interest of entertaining than in informing the public.

Yet my advice to you on dealing with the press is to work closely with them. You may in time come to an entirely cynical view of the media, based on your own experience, but I would advise you not to start out cynical—perhaps only skeptical. My own view is, except for the few who have ceased to be reporters and have become high-paid, egotistical performers, the press is the most underpaid branch of government. And, in my opinion, the First Amendment indirectly makes the press an integral part of our representative system of government.

Early in my career I worked with people who deliberately never returned a phone call from the media before a publication or filming deadline.

And they had a studied knowledge of when those deadlines were. They had the misguided belief that in this way they were punishing the press and media. Yet they went on to wonder why they had such bad relations with reporters.

When I go through my phone messages at the office I always put the press calls as near the top as I can. "Unavailable for comment" always sounds evasive to the public, like you have something to hide. But if the reporter can't talk with you what else can she say? I advise you to learn the deadline times for the press and television stations you deal with and then try hard to get back to reporters on their schedules. Your relations with them will be much better when they realize you are trying to help them do their jobs. If they ask you something and you don't know, say you don't know. If you know but can't say, say you can't say.

Once I was asked by a reporter whether I knew what the governor was going to do on a particular issue. When I said I thought I did, she asked what he was going to do. I said I couldn't tell. She asked, "Why not?" I said if I did I would never again know anything the governor or any other public official was going to do. "Oh!"

But don't be reluctant to "go on background" and "off the record" with a reporter. Often that is the way to brief a reporter on the history and context of the situation and the major players involved. Another reason you will need to explain the background for a story is because reporters turn over and you are often dealing with a new personality. Explaining the background and context off the record also gives you the opportunity to present something that is your view or an interpretation you would like the reporter to consider and think about but which you don't want attributed to you, something you are willing to tell her, but not something you want to be quoted on. If you can help the reporter to see the story in the full context, her report will be better for her and for you both. Then offer to go back on the record at anytime so the reporter can get some direct quotes for her story. And don't be reluctant to advise a reporter about who holds another view on the subject. This will show your confidence in your position and help her to get an opposing view for her story.

This is where you need to become "quote conscious." Give some thought to how to state your position succinctly and cogently. Long, rambling statements with numerous qualifications and "on the other hands" will quickly get you labeled as "Dullsville" and "booorring." On something like a request for a statement about some person's death or someone's move to a higher position don't be reluctant to say you want a few minutes to think on the matter and you will call right back. But it is better if you foresee you may be called about some issue or person and have something ready to say. Anticipate what you are likely to be called on during the next week or so and keep a folder of notes ready at hand when the calls do come. It helps to have notes on the points you want to get across. In your comments try to en- capsulate your position. Like it or not, we live in an age of sound bites. Learn to think about your story from the point of view of the reporter and try to meet her needs.

Does this work? I can refer only to my own good treatment by the press and give you one testimonial. On one occasion I was explaining to a group of agency heads how I try to work with the press and again I had no idea a reporter was in the audience. She identified herself and then said, "Do you receive flowers and cards from the press? You should."

A little humility helps. A reporter, Michael Kinsley, once wrote a story about Charles Wick, a wealthy California investor and lawyer and former bandleader and a principal strategist in President Reagan's election, and Kinsley had written in part, "By all accounts, Wick is a jackass." Several years later Wick invited him to lunch. At one point during the meal the reporter finally commented about how nice it was for Wick to invite him to lunch since he had once written that he was a jackass. Wick replied, "I don't mind criticism from the press, as long as it is accurate."

Of course there is always danger in trying to explain complex issues in very short statements. But there is also danger in talking too much. Try to overcome your wish to educate the world on all the reasoning behind your every position. At a press briefing before a legislative session I had pointed out how short funds would be for higher education that year, and at the end of the meeting a reporter from El Paso asked, "What does this mean for the prospects of the doctoral programs being developed by our university?"

I should have said, "The University has some areas of special strengths and we look forward to working with them on their strongest proposals." Instead I explained that in the context of very tight money, the state would have to be very selective about where to spend its limited funds on expand- ing new programs. I said El Paso, hundreds of miles to the west of most of the state's population, was not a place likely to receive approval of numer- ous new doctoral programs. Then to add insult to injury, I said that although the university in El Paso was a strong regional institution, it should never aspire to become equal to the two major flagship campuses in the state. All very true statements.

The El Paso senator, an Anglo woman running for reelection in a pre- dominately Hispanic district, needed nothing so much for her reelection as a dumb, old, bald-headed, white man as a target, and I had conveniently stuck my head up. The president of the university needed nothing so much as a statement she could use to show how her school had been unforgivably slighted and unjustly relegated to an unfair subordinate role in the state. They both seized their opportunities with enthusiasm and gusto. The senator called for my resignation, then asked the governor and my board to fire me, and finally, when all else failed, called for my early retirement. I had managed to turn a press briefing into a session-long headache for myself. The university president proceeded to develop new doctoral programs as fast as possible and sent them in to make the point about how unfair we would be if we did not approve them all. As Henry Rosovsky put it in a somewhat similar situation, "There is a price of specificity in an age of the pet peeve." Vagueness has its virtues.

Immediately after the article came out the reporter who had written it called to assure me he had written a balanced article containing all my reasoning and explanations, but that the editors 600 miles away had trimmed it to fit the space available—and put it on the front page. He felt terrible about what had happened. It wasn't his fault and I told him I knew that. I told him I suffered frequently from a malady common to cattle country, foot in mouth disease.

Misquotes? If you talk to reporters, you will be misquoted. It is very rarely intentional. And calling the reporter's boss or the publisher about a misquote is a good way to make an enemy of a reporter, or at least a less sympathetic listener. Besides, what is the best you can expect from such a call? A correction or retraction on an obscure inside page of a later edition? Better to call the reporter, point out the problem and make clear that it stops between you, no complaints higher up. She will owe you one. And usually she will be more careful in future stories. I have had reporters I have treated this way call to check the accuracy of future stories.

Still worried about going off the record? Every reporter knows there will be future stories where he will need your help. Reporters will very rarely violate your request not to be quoted, certainly not intentionally. But you might remember that very often you are being recorded as the reporter makes notes. So don't plan to backtrack on what you actually said. When you have been speaking off the record and you go back on the record, don't forget that what you now say is quotable and attributable. Once I thought an interview was over, because the reporter and I had begun to chat about other topics of mutual interest. Then at the end he casually asked, "Oh, incidentally, how does your board feel about taking on this new assignment from the governor?" Forgetting that I was speaking for the record, I gave a casual response. What I said was on the front page of the *Dallas Morning*

News the next day, "About like a mule looking at a new gate." It was obviously a slow news day.

It helps immensely to know if the media are present when you are making a speech or giving a lecture. When in doubt, assume they're there. I was addressing a class of administrative interns at a university once and someone asked what it looked like for tax revenues in the upcoming session of the legislature. Since I had just had lunch with the governor's and the legislature's budget directors and had been told in detail what was projected, I saw no harm in sharing liberally what they had told me. After all, I was in a classroom of third- or fourth-level administrators who couldn't possibly make any use of the information. They wouldn't even be back on their campuses for a couple of weeks. Unfortunately there was a reporter in the back of the room. It was a slow news day in the college town. The next day the story filed by the *Eagle* reporter was front-page news across the state. Deservedly, I received irate calls from the governor, the lieutenant governor, and the state comptroller, all wanting to know just when I had assumed responsibility for making revenue projections for the state. Incidentally, such conversations with angry politicians go far better if you happen to be able to call back later than to have to take the call while the person telephoning is still primed at the peak of his or her anger. But if you're there, you'd better take the call.

In working with the media you need to be conscious of how to get your point across. Don't ever assume a reporter knows much of anything about what your agency does or what you do, especially television reporters. And they could care less about the points *you* want to convey to the public. Half the time they've already got their slant on their story and they're performing. You are a prop or mere fixture. And you might remember they practice "wash basin" reporting. They put in the plug, fill the basin with water, stir it around with their fingertips, and pull the plug when they're through with that topic. Then with somebody else they put the plug in again and fill the sink with a new basin of water, an entirely new subject, and stir it around again. That basin has been filled so often by the time they get back to you again for another story, they don't remember much of what was in that sink the last time you washed together. So it's a risk to leave yourself at their mercies — and to their script. Let me illustrate.

In my early career I prepared carefully for several television interviews and I had organized everything I wanted to say. I was ready to roll when the key questions would be put to me. I had my lecture all ready. A few minutes into the interviews the television reporter said, "Thank you very much. That gives us what we need for the story." She and her cameraman began to pack up. And she had never asked a single key question I was waiting for. I had never touched on what was important to get across to the public. So in future interviews I began to rephrase questions to get my stuff in. Or, on occasion, I would ignore the question altogether and "dance with the girl who brung me," as the saying goes. Often it made no difference, because the reporter wasn't listening to my answer anyway while getting ready for her next question.

What I'm saying is this. Don't let the people interviewing you control the interview. Decide on the one or, at most, two points you want to get across and then bore in on these. Keep the discussion focused on what you want to say even if you have to talk around the questions being put to you. And hone a couple of sound bites beforehand. Those are probably the only thing that won't be on the floor of the editing booth at the station for your fifteen seconds of glory anyway.

As much as the public seems to prefer television reporting over reading newspapers, it is the print press that you need to pay the most attention to if you want to reach politicians and other policymakers. In the first place most of them don't spend much time watching television anyway; they get their reports on TV items from their staffs. Nearly all of them get some kind of clipping service, and they do go through these. They read the clips because they can glance over them in between meetings or during hearings and while traveling. And since they are engrossed in truly trying to solve public problems and address public needs, they need more information and in greater depth than television gives to anything except occasionally in a special report. *USA Today* has tried to emulate television in fragmentary coverage but television, even CNN, has not tried to do what only the print press can do.

Now I am going to tell you two stories about the press. The first is a story of how helpful the press can be when all else fails. Reporters will sometimes call to ask you if anything is going on they might look into. When that happens to me I often give them a trail to brighten their day—even if it probably blights somebody else's week.

A few years ago I got such a call. And truly there was one situation that was getting increasingly out of hand that I simply could not figure out how to address or expose. The call was from a very thoughtful and accurate reporter with the *Houston Chronicle*, Nancy Stancill. I referred her to an interesting advertisement that had been placed recently in the Austin paper by a community junior college located in Killeen. The ad said the college was seeking a number of men fluent in Spanish who were familiar with the use of small arms and automatic weapons to participate in a special class offered at the school. From this modest referral grew months of articles about the college.

This state-supported community college had started with ambitious plans and hopes in the 1960s but due to its location it simply could not grow to its planned size and fulfill its local aspirations. The quite large college-age population in the area was unusual. It consisted largely of young people assigned to Fort Hood for military training, and it turned out they were too busy or not interested in swelling the rolls of the new college just outside the main gate.

The new college president was a very enterprising individual and he undertook several plans to expand his school. He created a private university to offer junior and senior level classes to fit on top of his freshman and sophomore classes at the public community college. He became president of both schools and received two salaries along with his two titles. In a further step toward efficiency and economy, his board at the community college also served as the trustees for the private university as well. He then also became chancellor over his new "American Educational Complex." His new private university leased space from the community college, and business arrangements were further facilitated by having the two coterminous presidents and coextensive boards agree upon contractual relations between the two schools. Arm's length meant close enough for an embrace.

This led to an innovative approach whereby a new building was constructed on the campus by a private foundation established by the college, and the debt on the building was rapidly amortized by income from the private university paid to the foundation. Then, in turn, the foundation used $300,000 of these newly found resources to build a home and make a gift of it to the chancellor personally, not to the public college or to his private university.

All this was revealed to me by a local anonymous whistle-blower. When I turned the documents I had received over to the state auditor, who substantiated the reports, he, in turn, passed the matter to the attorney general, who then passed it on to the local district attorney for investigation and prosecution. The locally elected district attorney reported to the attorney general that he had examined the allegations against these fine, outstanding, and upright local institutions of higher education and could find no basis to pursue the matter further. Case closed.

I think it was John Dewey who observed that if you think democracy works best at the local level, you have obviously not lived in an American small town.

Contemporaneously with these events I was receiving complaints from institutions around the country about why we could not control the aggressive activities of this community college to expand its operations overseas. I was told the college was using unethical and questionable methods to extend its educational offerings on military bases around the world and to ships at sea. Complaints about this college ranged over questionable underbidding on costs, deficient academic requirements, poor quality controls, hiring of unqualified military personnel for faculty positions as a means for obtaining preference over other college competitors, and in general, strong-arm methods of displacing other schools.

It was reported to me that the president/chancellor of this college had used his board chairman's contacts with President Lyndon Johnson in order to use the White House to help promote the presence of their college on military bases. The technique I was informed of was this: Arrangements were made for the chancellor to use a telephone and a secretary to place his calls. The secretary, at the chancellor's direction, would call an overseas base commander and announce, "Please hold, the White House is calling." The chancellor would then say, as we might imagine, to the general standing at attention beside his bed in his skivvies, "I have just been talking with the President and he tells me you need more educational programs on your base. I will be on your base next Wednesday to talk with you about what we can offer you from our college." The complainants also alleged that the board (or boards) of the educational complex was actually paying a commission to its executive for each of the contracts he closed in addition to his regular salary.

After Nancy Stancill took on the story, she maintained a continuing drumroll of stories exposing what she turned up, such as the college running up $1.7 million in travel expenses from the college through an agency owned by the daughter of the school's business officer; the chancellor claiming $3,500 in cab fares for 218 taxi trips in one week while in Washington, D.C., the teaching of secret and classified courses for selected Army officers; and the state of Texas and the Defense Department both paying over a million dollars for the same courses in "drivers education" required of military personnel stationed at Fort Hood and being trained to drive tanks and other military vehicles.

People in Killeen who had for years wanted to reveal wrongdoings at the college began to call to give Nancy leads and to send materials. Her problem was that they often wanted to meet to talk with her alone in obscure and secluded locations, usually under the cover of darkness, causing her concern for her safety. They told her they were worried about *their* safety.

To add to her worries she had been told by one contact that an opposition candidate who had run against an incumbent on the college board had been killed in an unexplained one-car accident on a remote road in the area. The interviews she was granted at the college were filmed by the college and conducted in the most intimidating settings the administrators could arrange. Every inquiry she made for information required a formal open-records request under state law.

After months of reporting, tongue clucking, and no response from any government agency, local or state, and after continuing dilatory, uncooperative, and thoroughly obstructing responses from the school, Nancy seemed to have run out of steam and it appeared the story would die. She came to me again. I suggested that she use her open-records authority to obtain two separate sets of records and compare them. Having seen how no possible opportunity for financial gain had remained unexploited by the college, I suspected that still another opportunity had been discovered by the college and was all too tempting for them not to have used it.

From the college Nancy obtained the list of every employee of the college teaching at the home campus and on all military bases and ships at sea worldwide and their social security numbers. From the state Teacher Retirement System she obtained her second request, a list of all employees of the college, along with their social security numbers, whose retirement withholdings were being matched by funds provided by the state legislature. She sat alone in a room at the Teacher Retirement System and matched up the lists. She discovered dozens of names of people who had never taught on the home campus of the college or ever been in the state of Texas and whose retirement accounts were being enriched at the expense of Texas taxpayers.

At last she had a story that brought the state auditor's office back into the act. He found that the college owed the state over $700,000. This story finally brought down the chancellor. His business officer succeeded him to the chancellor's job and he also was forced to resign over additional scandals that Nancy continued to expose.

Need I say more about the importance of the press as an effective branch of government?

But before I make the press look too holy, let me say that not every reporter is always fair or ethical. When former Congressman Joe Kilgore was on the board of regents of the University of Texas he got taken advantage of by such a reporter. Frank Erwin, the irascible and no-holds-barred chairman of the board, gave an off-the-record interview to a reporter about how the board had voted unanimously in closed executive session to fire the university's president. Erwin insisted he could not be quoted, so the reporter called

Kilgore and discussed other university business at length, but she never mentioned or touched on Erwin's statement to her about firing the president.

In her article the next day she reported on her interview with Kilgore and then threw in, without attribution, the story Erwin had given her. Her story implied, as was intended, that Kilgore was the source for her information about firing the president.

At the next board meeting Kilgore made certain the reporter was present and then brought up the article and said, "Now, Mr. Chairman, every member of this board knows we have never voted on the question of firing the president, either in public or in secret meeting. The report of a unanimous vote by this board in executive session to fire him is totally erroneous. I raise this matter so that any member present who disagrees with my statement may speak up now." No member, including Frank Erwin, the chairman, said anything, for there had never been such a vote.

But the next day the reporter wrote that Regent Kilgore had moved to rescind the previous vote to fire the president and his motion failed for lack of a second.

My plane is landing so I have to shut down my laptop. I'm coming up here to answer to a legislator and the local chamber of commerce about why their university should not be allowed to open a law school and a college of pharmacy.

Your penurious

Uncle Ken

re: *Learning from your boss*

If you want to hit a bird on the wing, you must have all your will in focus, you must not be thinking about yourself, and equally, you must not be thinking about your neighbor; you must be living in your eye on that bird. Every achievement is a bird on the wing.
— *Justice Oliver Wendell Holmes*

He suffered from the disadvantage of remoteness from people who could stand up to him.
— *Sir Edgar Williams in referring to General Bernard Montgomery*

Had he never been placed in authority, nobody would ever have doubted his capacity for it.
— *Tacitus*

DECEMBER

Dear Kim

You have probably noted that I am trying to send you one of these epistles every month and, compared to the high tuition and fees you are paying, to give you some free advice. During your career you'll receive a lot of that. But remember what Huck Finn said that night after he attended a revival meeting. When he came back to the raft he reported to Jim that the preacher's advice and counsel had been abundant and generous and it was all free—and it was worth it too. So for what it's worth, this month's sage advice will be on learning from your boss—or bosses.

But first I want to make a few comments on the nature of the career you are embarked upon. Since you have been in class now for a couple of months, you have your roster of courses for your first semester and you've probably looked ahead to the curriculum lying ahead of you. You will note how heavily they focus on preparation needed for your first job. This is because the school wants to be able to place you when you graduate, "job-wise," as you young people say. So they are very concerned about your job-entry skills. They also know that if they are very careful over the next two years and don't do anything to mess you up, you'll go out and be successful. This will help to enhance the reputation of their school and make the faculty look good.

In the letters I send in the months ahead you will find very little of help to you in getting your first job. My assumption is that you have chosen this career not to remain a policy analyst all your life or to get stuck in your entry position, but to become a policy*maker*. So I have this loose construct in my mind to try to write in these letters to you about things that will help you in your fourth or fifth job some years down the line. In those earlier jobs you will just have to make out as best you can on your own and with what help you can find from courses in statistics, quantitative economics, cost-benefit analysis, organization and management, public finance, political science numerology, PPBS, PERT charting, management by objectives, zero-based budgeting, and reinventing government. Those are the proverbs; I intend to work by parables.

So, charging right ahead, a few words on your mental health. I am sure you have heard the observation questioning whether anyone is psychologically fit for elected office who is willing to submit himself and his family to what running for public office entails—years of confrontation, stress, and exposure as well as loss of privacy and private time for a job that pays little compared to other fields in which a person with the same talents could succeed magnificently. And whether you ever seek elected office, you are headed for much that same kind of life if you aspire to rise to the top in the career public service. Consequently, I regret to have to observe that your desire to be a leader and to play a significant role in society reveals in you a form of egregious neurosis. Psychologists have long known that anyone who wants to feel special, such as someone who aspires to leadership, who feels driven to play a hero role in society, exhibits one of the most common and potent forms of denying his or her own mortality. To want to be a leader is a death-denying and death-defying obsession.

Therefore, you may as well acknowledge that you start with this neurosis. And then, encumbered with that malady, you will proceed into a career in public policymaking, where the demands of the job are that you constantly resolve polarized positions and make decisions and act among

competing and conflicting options. And as you are forced to make those unhappy choices, you will be forever judged on your performance between the
extremes of bifurcated public expectations. One view will be that you do too
little, the other that you do too much. That you regulate when you should
be promoting. That you are an adversary when you should be an advocate.
One group will say that you show insufficient vision and another that you
propose more than you can deliver. One group will say that you compromise
away your position, the opposite that you are unyielding and inflexible.

As a senator once said to me, "When I agree with you, you are operating within powers we have delegated to you; when I disagree with you,
you are exceeding your authority." Your public life will be spent between extremes on almost every important policy decision you make. As F. Scott
Fitzgerald put it, you must have "the ability to hold two opposed ideas in
the mind at the same time, and still retain the ability to function." Can you
recognize the classical symptoms I am describing here? Some would call this
a job in which only a schizophrenic could survive—and you will spend full
time at it.

And rather than receiving canonization and sainthood, which you will
come to feel you deserve for your dedicated service as a public hero, you instead will take an abundance of abuse and criticism. The public is a fickle
mistress. Therefore, I urge you to revel in whatever fulfillment you can find
in oblation.

But there is one rationalization that I can offer to help you feel a little
better in your own mental illnesses. Never forget that you will cause at least
half of the people you rule against or whose wishes you have frustrated or
denied to suffer periodic fits of paranoia. They will know you are part of a
conspiracy out to get them, that life is unfair to them, that they are unjustly
persecuted. They will feel this way because they will not be able to conceive
how anyone using reason and logic could possibly come to a position opposite from their own reasoning and logic. One of the few pleasures in life
allowed to public officials is the ability to bring out the paranoia of others.

Now for a harder look at the world you are about to enter. It is in the
nature of human societies that the predominant groups of people will try to
control the use of governments for their own benefits or to promote their
own points of view. It is in the nature of a *democratic* society that, given time,
those who do manage to gain control of governments screw things up.
Those who gain control neglect or ignore the needs of other groups, or they
so blatantly favor themselves that they force other groups to come together
to establish a new balance in the uses of the powers of government. As a

public servant you will live out your career in the vortex of this permanent and ongoing tension among competing groups and live with the periodic "changing of the guard" wherever you work in government. As a consequence, you may not survive in every position you occupy. As a thinking person you will choose to favor in your mind and perhaps in your actions some groups over others. Such choices will put you at risk. But it will be your preferences about whom you seek to assist that will distinguish you from the chaff and the flotsam that make up far too much of every bureaucracy in this country, public and private.

Unfortunately, today there is much disaffection for public servants and extensive distrust of government. Although the problems and circumstances you will deal with during your career, compared with those I have dealt with in mine, will be similar in many ways, they will be very different in others. And part of the big difference is that during my time "on watch" there has been a more generally accepted feeling that government can make a difference in how the world works. We have believed that problems *can* be dealt with effectively by government and that it is desirable for humans to try to bring order into rapidly changing social and economic conditions through the uses of government. I'm not sure many of us from the older generations of public servants are really "social engineers," as we are often pejoratively labeled, but at least we believe government should do major tinkering around the edges. We believe fervently that it is a task of government to try to protect those unfairly taken advantage of and to help those who get left out or who can't find ways to take care of their basic needs when things are changing too fast or in ways they can't comprehend. Furthermore, we do think government should assist those intentionally denied a role or place due to prejudice or neglect.

That earlier faith in the capacity of government to address our social and economic ills has diminished greatly from when I began my career. In that sense our job has been easier than yours will be. Old problems have become more intractable. New diversity in culture, behavior, and values challenges older, more conforming expectations. Even increased equality challenges roles that formerly were accepted and which have been narrowly defined and enforced in subtle and not so subtle ways. Moreover, problems we used to cope with inside a state or within our own nation are beyond control by our governments as they extend across national borders. International problems that used to have a clean definition and which we knew how to respond to when they existed between two superpowers have evolved into nasty situations where a single U.S. answer can no longer serve.

And without the age-old Machiavellian threat of external attack or invasion to draw us together, we now have the luxury of tearing at each other without putting the nation at risk against a major enemy.

The failure of government to be able to cope effectively with these more insoluble problems has been made worse by an assortment of other changes. You'll recognize them: the dehydration of "debate" of public issues, the devolution of news reporting into entertainment and the exploitation of ignorance by radio and television, runaway costs of campaigning for public office along with the resulting compromising of elected officials, and the tendency of elected officials to track public opinion to guide their policy decisions, to mention but the more obvious. You have your own list but to these I have to add reductions in services to the public due to funding cuts, fudging at the truth by officials on public issues, new constraints on government due to the runaway national debt—all of these contribute to a loss of trust in government and public officials.

So, as you well know, I was not being entirely facetious when I said that your parents and neighbors and school chums can't understand how you could decide to enter the public service with all the other career choices available to you. But you will learn something they will never understand: You are headed for being part of the elite of the American society by this choice of profession you have made. Think about this: In the next couple of decades hundreds of thousands of civil servants from the baby boomer generation will be retiring each year. All the universities of this country together are graduating each year under 30,000 majors in public administration, public affairs, and policy development. Only a third of those are at the graduate level. You are almost certain to become a player in the policymaking process of this nation. In this role you will become part of the elite because of the small ranks you will join and the resulting disproportionate weight you will carry as you and the agencies you work among affect and carry out public policies.

As you enter this field, where you will serve mostly unrecognized and often vilified, at a time when those who hate and demean government have achieved greater volubility and visibility, you need to reflect on your predecessors. You should remember with pride what has been accomplished for the people of this country by individuals in your kind of work, people who believed in the application of conscious human intention to the scrambled conditions of our times. Again, you can make your own list, but here are a few that come to mind quickly: the national highway system, flood control, radio and television broadcast systems, space exploration, public lands and parks and forests, disaster assistance, safety of foods and drugs, assistance to small businesses and farmers, extension of civil rights, care for the elderly, oversight of monopolies, promotion of trade, support for the underprivileged and handicapped, low-income housing, regulation of sales of securities, and "to care for him who shall have borne the battle and for his widow, and his orphan."

I want to say again how pleased I am that you are now irrevocably committed to this field of rampant psychopathology, for you are joining the ranks of a few good men and women who strive to make the conditions of mankind more tolerable. It is not science and technology alone that improve humanity's lot on this planet or enable this meager globe to support over six billion people, a growth of over four and a half billion since the previous crossing of a century mark in 1900. Government organizations and their acts and services all play a significant role along with technology. The public service will tax your every talent, test who you really are and what you believe in, try your courage to the sticking point, and scare the hell out of you a lot of the time. Just remember Edith Hamilton's translation of an ancient Greek definition of happiness: "the exercise of vital powers along lines of excellence in a life affording them scope." Be content; you have found your way to such a place, on a vessel struggling to sail between Scylla and Charybdis—that is, between a rock and a hard place. An old Chinese curse says, "May you live in interesting times." Welcome to the melee.

Now to the topic I set out to give advice on. Don't think for a minute that when you finally graduate you will have left all your teachers and instructors behind. Right away in your very first job you should set your boss up as your new teacher—or I should say bosses, both the ones nearby and the head of your agency or organization or even those in higher positions. They will immediately serve you as both good and bad examples of leadership and supervision.

They don't need to know you have made them into your new teachers. Just plan to watch them closely. In your own mind you can learn from their actions and statements and style and behavior. Harold Stoke, Queens College president, summed it up well when he said that the president is the principal teacher on a campus because everybody, faculty and staff, are studying him constantly as to what he says and does and what he reveals as being important to him. Most bosses don't know this about themselves but it is true of all of them. They are watched from inside their organizations much more than they know.

Because you aspire to reach the top someday, you should become an understudy to your bosses. You have the opportunity to make their every performance a rehearsal for yourself. Before your boss copes with a problem, devise in your mind your own response. Before every public statement she must make, think how you would say it and what you would say. With every crisis that comes, large and small, ask what you would do.

You must be like the first chair violinist, the concertmaster to a small symphony orchestra. Ever wonder why he always looks so worried—besides having to bring a perfect 440 A to the orchestra to tune to? It's because he may have to stand in for the conductor some night. As Harlan Cleveland used to say, "You can always recognize a successful executive by the worried look on his deputy's face."

Consider the opportunity. One night Leonard Bernstein, a young pianist, made the most of his. I have always gotten goose bumps reading what the *New York Times* wrote in an editorial two days later:

> There are many variations of one of the six best stories in the world: the young corporal takes over the platoon when all the officers are down; the captain, with the dead admiral at his side, signals the fleet to go ahead; the young actress, fresh from Corinth or Ashtabula, steps into the star's role; the junior clerk, alone in the office, makes the instantaneous decision that saves the firm from ruin. The adventure of Leonard Bernstein, 25-year-old assistant conductor of the Philharmonic, who blithely mounted the podium at Carnegie Sunday afternoon when Conductor Bruno Walter became ill, belongs in the list. The corporals and captains must be brave, the young actress beautiful and talented, the clerk quick on his feet. Likewise, Mr. Bernstein had to have something approaching genius to make full use of his opportunity. It's a good American success story.

Whether your boss is making a speech or testifying before a committee or making a presentation to your board, you should be on the edge of your seat, ready in your mind to take over instantly when she falls over in an epileptic fit. That means you will need to learn as much about every issue as your boss does. And why shouldn't you expect to do that? If for no other reason, it will quickly make you more useful to her and the organization. But it also means you need to read what she writes about her work and to find ways to be where she speaks about her job and the issues of your agency. Is she articulate? Is she persuasive? What's her style of communicating? Is she dull and boring, serious and convincing, witty and humorous? There is so much you can learn from watching how she handles hostile questions and how she gets her key points across in the short time she is usually allotted. Could you improve on how she communicates the mission and work of your agency? Does she let her personal feelings show? Does that help her or hurt her?

But the ultimate learning experience for you is to compare how your boss does her job against how you would do it. In the beginning, of course, you are going to find that due to her experience and command of your field of endeavor your ideas rarely can equal hers. Nonetheless, you will be learning by trying. You will be putting your ideas up for measurement against an expert—or so let us hope.

Let me describe for you the marks of failure you can watch for among aides to leaders. First, they constitute an "amen corner" or claque. They nod their heads and by body language show their complete agreement with their boss—or their contempt and disdain for his opponents. The second mark is that they think they are present to be entertained and to watch the show. Third, they don't bother to take notes on what is happening, follow-ups to be made, promises their boss has just made in the heat of his presentation, or individual interests revealed by panelists or constituents. Fourth, they may even strut; they are so immensely happy to be there and be seen and bask in the glory and prestige of their boss.

Indeed, you will encounter now and then an agency head who brings with him such an entourage of lackeys and admirers. But such a person is rarely leading anyone to anywhere important so it is immaterial how many such followers he has accompany him along the way.

I recall once as a lowly subordinate when I was accompanying my agency's chairman to a Senate appropriations hearing. As the hearing ended I commented to several others on the staff about a serious misstatement of fact our chairman had just made in his testimony. Although they had caught his misstatement as well, they were all intimidated by his stature and persona and remarked to me that it wasn't all that important. But as we crossed the rotunda to repeat the performance in the other house, I was bold enough to call the error to our chairman's attention. His comment was, "Oh, for God's sake, thanks for correcting that. They would've caught that in the House committee for sure. Why don't people speak up and tell me this kind of thing?"

So, as you watch your boss's style and behavior, what should you look for that you might want to emulate later? I would put near the top this: Does he reward candor and tolerate disagreement and differences of opinion inside his staff? Most subordinates are highly "cue conscious." It does not take most employees long to sense what the boss wants and what he will reward.

Writing about his relations with President Nixon while serving as his general counsel, John Dean said, "I wanted very much to be what I thought he wanted to find." Subordinates like this try to be just a half-step ahead of their boss, thus permitting them time to place their foot anywhere the boss might imply or hint he wants it to fall. This is rather like the most formal version of the Japanese language, which developed and was refined out of palace life and courtier behavior. The verbs are at the *end* of sentences — in order to permit the speaker the opportunity to alter what he is saying as he says it. He has time to read the expression and reactions of the person he is addressing. In those days a person's life, liberty, and property could depend on a verb form.

Vice President John Nance Garner remarked fondly as one of his young staff men dashed out the door, "I really like that boy. You give him an order and he runs like a scalded dog."

Incidentally, once you get to a top position, you will need to be aware that people are in fact often looking for cues as to what you want them to do. Those anxious to please can misinterpret the wishes of their bosses, especially when the boss holds a very top position. Once when President Dwight Eisenhower was taking a stroll around the White House grounds, he stopped to inquire why the grass was torn up in a certain area. He was told that the squirrels had done it; it was the season to bury acorns and pecans. He mumbled something about, "Well, those little bastards." The next day from his office he saw a number of men busy in the yard and he asked what they were doing. He was informed that they were trapping squirrels. When he asked why, he was reminded he had ordered it be done during his walk the day before.

But the practice of reading the wishes of the boss in large organizations can have its sinister side as well. During Richard Nixon's presidency his anger about leaks of information to the press and his statements about wanting to get even with "enemies" he despised brought about the creation of a "Plumbers Unit" inside the White House. This group of enthusiasts committed to handling leaks then planned to break into the Brookings Institution to steal Morton Halprin's copy of the Pentagon Papers. And they did break into Daniel Ellsberg's psychiatrist's office in California to get dirt on him to discredit him with the press. Out of this hubris came the break-in at the Democratic headquarters in the Watergate office building and all that followed.

During President Ronald Reagan's second term John Poindexter and Colonel Oliver North broke laws by swapping arms with the Iranians for the release of hostages because they knew how desperately the president wanted to free the Americans kidnapped by terrorist groups in the Middle East. With that escapade behind them, they then used the profits they made off selling the arms to covertly assist the *contra* rebels in Nicaragua. They embarked on this venture because they knew how strongly the president felt about supporting the rebels even though Congress had explicitly prohibited any further assistance to them.

Not every unhappiness, frustration, and dissatisfaction griped about by the boss should be interpreted as a subliminal order that should be carried out. The boss you can put your trust in is one who communicates the idea, "Tell me what I need to know, not what you think I want to hear."

Once several years ago I was meeting with the staff of a division that I had just put under a new director. The new man was not familiar with our usual staff procedures for developing our positions on controversial items to be taken to our next board meeting. At the outset I stated the position I thought we would take on the particular controversy before us and I began to draw out the staff on this position and to itemize a few of the beginning arguments to support that position. A couple of the staff present began to lay out counterarguments to my position as well. I sort of subconsciously noticed that our new director had cut off several of his subordinate staff members as though they were out of line for disagreeing with me.

We proceeded for some time to lay out the arguments to support the position I had initially stated. I noted that the new director became more and more enthusiastic about where we were coming down on the case as it appeared we were all coming into agreement. Then I said, "Well, we've worked that position over pretty well. Let's see what arguments we can put together on the other side." The staff went at the new position with zeal and I joined in. Again I sort of noted that our new director slowly began to build increasing enthusiasm for the new position as I warmed to it and as I drew out the staff with their views and arguments. I realized later that it must have appeared to him at some point that I had changed my initial position on what we would recommend to the board. We put together a rather convincing new stand on the issue at hand. The new director then unnecessarily committed himself by saying that it now appeared this alternative was by far the better position for us to take with the board.

But I then had to disagree and I said I thought we could overcome these arguments and prevail with our first position. That would be the one we would present at the board meeting. This was the position we would build our case to defend. But we also now knew what the arguments against our position would be.

Our staff practice was to abide by John Stuart Mill's admonition: "He who knows only his own side of the case knows little of that." Unfortunately our new division director never recovered fully from his "whiplash" injuries. He was wedded to the belief that the boss always knows what is best. Under his approach to policy development all he and his staff would need to do is find out what I wanted and give it to me or do it for me. He took no position on anything until he knew exactly where I stood. Then he would permit no one on his staff to disagree with it. Although he had moved from halfway across the country to join us, I could not keep him in his job.

Sycophancy is like elephantiasis. The longer it goes untreated the more stolid and immobile it makes you.

You can learn from bad bosses too. The first thing you should learn from a bad boss is that you want to get the hell out of there. I watched one weak boss—from afar, fortunately—who managed to waste everyone's time and talents all week long and then measured the performance and commitment of his staff by their willingness to come in with him on Saturdays to do busywork he created. He had a unique ability to trivialize his organization's purpose through voluminous and meaningless activity. We coined a phrase for him, "If it isn't worth doing, it isn't worth doing well."

Our grievance committee is in the next room waiting for me. So I must sign off. We sent a disagreeable supervisor away for personnel training and "behavior modification," and the committee has now received new complaints. His staff says he's even worse since he came back, although he tries hard to be a better people manager part of the time. He only reverts to form part of the time, mostly when he's in a crisis or under pressure. They say he used to be just a son of a bitch but now he's an unpredictable son of a bitch.

After this meeting with the grievance committee I am due at the capitol to answer to a Senate chairman and a board of regents on why I am picking on their university. On occasion I agree with the younger Governor Adlai Stevenson when he said, "There have been a couple of times when I have yearned for the serenity I knew as a Marine Corp combat tank commander in Korea."

More when I can . . .

Your doting

Uncle Ken

re: *Dealing with unpleasant and difficult people*

Don't worry about your enemies. You always know where they are.
It's your friends you have to watch out for. They'll move around
on you. — *Presciliano M. Rangel, Kingsville, Texas*

A clever man is the one who finds ways out of an unpleasant situation
into which a wise man would never have got himself.
— *Dan Vittorio Segre*

JANUARY

Dear Kim

I ended my last letter on a note of levity. There *is* occasional
humor in these jobs but you often have to dig and sift for it. Much that
comes to be laughable after the passage of some healing time isn't all that
funny while you're getting through it. It still retains the pucker factor. Living on the razor's edge of the unknown future in fights about things you
care deeply about does not lend itself to high humor. It may become laughable later when the stress of not knowing how the fight is going to resolve
itself is gone. As one philosopher put it, "Life is fired at us point blank." It's
only after the bullet has missed that you laugh about it.

But my closing comment last month was about the probable imprac-
ticality of changing the behavior and personnel practices of one of our supervisors. Unfortunately, in my experience this turns out to be the case
about eighty percent of the time. The child is father to the man some poet
said, and somewhere in our early experience is probably where most of us
get our basic rules and practices for dealing with other people. So let me tell

you my theory on why some people we have to deal with are so disagreeable and difficult.

We all replay tapes in our heads that we encoded when we were young. I remember well when Governor William Clements yelled at me across his desk to sit down and then shook his finger at me and shouted, "As far as I'm concerned you get a zero for your performance in the last session of the legislature." For a moment I was back in the fifth grade. I felt I was in the principal's office being chewed out for bringing a bamboo pea shooter to school and using it to communicate my interest in Joan across the room.

But everybody is playing tapes based on their experience with life. In his analysis of the progress (or lack of progress) of the human mind, the French philosopher Condorcet described how we all preserve the errors of our childhood and our nation and our age long after we have seen the truths that should have destroyed them. One tape difficult people play is that they see other people, especially subordinates, as tools to get a job done or to get their way. Therefore, they see people as manipulable instruments. The result is they take away from others their single most important need for them to be at all happy in their work, that is, their sense of having at least some control over their job setting. These difficult people reason, "Well, it's worked before; I can make it work here. Other people have come into line, why can't these people? If I am severe enough they'll come around too. In time I'll have only people working for me who do exactly what I want them to do. Those who don't, we can run off." (He's thinking, "I'll know when I've got them whipped into shape when they all run like scalded dogs.")

Another tape rolling continually in the heads of some disagreeable people is like background movie music, somewhere between "Gaslight" and "Jaws." It is the constant murmuring of their lack of self-confidence. Diffident people are only four letters short of being difficult, and typically their subordinates can provide other four-letter variations concerning them. A primary characteristic of people who lack confidence is they like neatness, uniformity, predictability, and conformity. They are extremely uncomfortable with the unprogrammed, and that includes circumstances, people, and events. Give-and-take is extremely difficult for them because they can't control it or know ahead of time where it will end up. Improvisation is not among their skills. Response to outside criticism by such supervisors is "Circle the wagons. Here they come again. It's us against them."

These people will also not want to hire anyone who might cast a shadow or make them look less than competent or less than in complete control. Now pay attention, here's an irrefutable axiom: "First-class people hire first-class people; second-class people hire third-class people." Never be afraid to hire people smarter than you are. You're going to need all the help you can get to look good. Besides, it will amaze your friends and confound your enemies.

Now to the third tape disagreeable people play in their heads called, "Learn how to accrue power." They look at leaders and they see that leaders have power and they see leaders as being in control. Ergo, they deduct: Control and power are what make a leader. But they have it backwards. What they do not see is that power and control come to the leader by virtue of being able to lead, recruiting followers, and envisioning and enunciating a future that people want to help to bring about. Those who seek power as such do not recognize that power is an accoutrement or a consequence of leadership; they see power as a *means* to leadership. But power by itself is never leadership; power, taken alone, is primarily the ability to bestow rewards or inflict punishment. Power is not a convincing reason for people to follow a leader of their own volition.

Nonetheless, many people in organizations and bureaucracies are able to build their little centers of control and power. Typically they don't share information, know-how, or expertise. In fact many of them create arcane procedures, forms, and filing systems understood only by themselves and a trusted few. It is this type of people who give bureaucracies a bad name. In fact, the term bureaucracy is often used to describe precisely this kind of organizational behavior. Such bureaucrats often tend to be gossips and have networks for collecting intelligence and for spreading vitriol about rivals or those who will not pay tribute and conform to expectations of those in control.

Such supervisors are territorial and can tell you exactly where the boundaries of your authority lie, especially if you are in their jurisdiction. They tend to hire weak people and to make those people dependent on them. They also tend to make narrow specialists of their staff people and prohibit them from learning each other's jobs. All these devices concentrate control in such a supervisor's hands.

Every time you fill a vacancy you will face the danger of hiring such a person. How's that for a terrifying thought? Well, add this fact of life: The good people you hire will tend to move on and be hired away from you. Each time that happens you have a fresh chance to make a bad hire. On top of that the bad ones can't leave and other people rarely steal them away from you. Considering this sorting process, it is a real wonder that organizations don't all end up fully staffed by the worst employees hired over time. As someone said once, "We winnow the wheat and keep the chaff." But let me leave this thought hanging and return to my comments on difficult and disagreeable people. I'll get back to this.

We are a generous people in that we continue to indulge ourselves in the belief in the perfectibility of humanity. Our Puritan forefathers believed they could beat the devil out of children even though we are all born full of sin. We still reason today that we should be able to improve people who fall short of the mark, and not by beating them—although on occasion this has its own particular appeal. On the positive side it is fortunately true that some people can be improved. In dealing with difficult employees human resources specialists recommend trying "behavior modification." There is one problem with modifying behavior that is best summed up in an old Aggie joke. Question: How many Aggies does it take to change a light bulb? Answer: Five. One to hold the light bulb, four to rotate the ladder. But the Aggies have come up with the most meaningful response: If you want to change a light bulb, the first requirement is that the light bulb has to want to change.

The initial response by nearly all difficult people is that they are not in error or they are not doing anything wrong. What they do works—for them—or at least it seems to. Or if it isn't working, it's only because people aren't doing things the way they're told to do them. By the time corrective action is required with such supervisors often there has been a long exchange of words or self-justifying memos among all aggrieved parties with the principal player explaining why everyone else, inside or outside the organization, is wrong. It's the other people who are defective, not the difficult individual.

T.V. Smith, a largely forgotten Texas philosopher, poet, and political scientist, made a profound observation that will help you all your life to understand this strong sense of rightness and righteousness among difficult people. Smith discovered this remarkable social and psychological phenomenon: "No person is ever a son of a bitch to himself."

Bearing that in mind, it will become necessary for you (a) to have to try to change such people and/or (b) to make a record to dismiss such persons before they run off your best people or ruin your organization. We'll take (a) first. Here is lesson one in how to get started in your counseling with them: You will accomplish nothing in telling such a person what he is doing wrong or what behavior is not acceptable. (See T.V. Smith's notable discovery referenced above.) The first requirement is to get the person to admit he might try some corrective or different approaches. But this is a big problem.

Try this instead: "We're having some real problems in your division (low morale, high turnover, poor quality work, bad staff recommendations, a rash of suicides, whatever). Here are some specific examples. (Give him some.) Do you agree we have some problems here? Well, why is that happening? Is it possible your style or approach might be part of the problem?" (Work hard here; you must get an agreement of sorts.) Now we are at part two, your follow-up effort after you get acknowledgment that there *is* a problem: "Let's try to identify what the problem might be in how your people are reacting to your style and approach." Once he identifies or acknowledges any problem, ask for suggestions on how he might alter, change, or improve. Get him to *say* it. Don't *tell* it to him. Part three, the wrap-up: Recap verbally and make a big deal of writing down notes on the problems he has identified in his behavior and what corrective steps he plans to try out. Then set a timetable for you both to make a follow-up assessment on the list you have made. After he leaves prepare a memo documenting what he acknowledged about his behavior and what he has agreed to do about it. You will probably have to repeat such sessions a few times until he gets the idea that you are dissatisfied and expect him to identify changes needed in his supervision and to actually begin making them.

Don't despair. It actually works occasionally—maybe one out of five cases (optimistically one out of four). In any event, even if it doesn't work, you have started your documentation about what is wrong with his work and your paperwork for dismissal when that becomes your only remaining option. You will also find that often where this approach does not result in improving the employee, he gets the message and will leave of his own accord.

Harold Ross, founder and long-time editor of *The New Yorker,* used a simplified version. He'd call the person he intended to dismiss into his office and he'd say accusingly, "You're no genius." And the person would modestly and readily plead guilty to the charge, whereupon Ross would continue, "That being the case, we won't be able to use you any longer." And he would turn back to the work on his desk.

Incidentally, one of the chief work products of difficult people is to seek forums for their complaints. This is because many of them suffer from something called attention deficit disorder. Their disorder is that they suffer from a deficit of attention. The second work product of difficult people is to drive *other* employees to seek forums for their complaints. Here's my resulting advice for a young bureaucrat: When you come to head up an agency, establish a standing grievance committee to deal with complaints. Make up the committee mostly of members elected by the employees. Set up the committee to report their findings and recommendations to you. If you wait until after a complaint is filed to appoint such a committee you will be accused of "rigging" or "loading" the committee with employees opposed to the complainer or with employees opposed to the person being complained about.

As head of your agency or organization you must take action concerning such difficult people. T. V. Smith discusses in his autobiography the golden, silver, and iron rules for getting through life. You can look them up, but his iron rule is: "Don't let other people do unto you what you would not do unto them." Here is my Iridium Rule (the hardest element that I, as a nonchemist, could identify): "Do not let others do unto any of your employees what you would not have them do unto you."

The most important commodity you are attempting to get from your employees is their mental energies and creativity. A bad supervisor can do terrible damage to your best efforts to get the most from your employees. A punch-clock approach will get you far less than each employee's potentiality (at most an official eight-hour presence each day). Your challenge is how to extract the most of that mental energy and creativity. You might begin by permitting flextime. Control-freak supervisors will not like it. Show you trust your people and that you appreciate their devotion to solving the problems you face together. Listen to their ideas even if you can't use all of them. Involve them in the issues facing your agency or their division. Treat them as professionals. Grant them credit, give them face, and treat them with respect. Be available and practice administration by walking around. Go directly to your staff experts for their feedback and recommendations. (Some supervisors between you and their subordinates will not like this.) Find out what people are doing, what they are thinking about and concerned about, and encourage them to "keep after it." Again, your supervisors will have to learn to tolerate your direct contacts with their subordinates. But that's why you're the boss.

I alluded to hiring good people and having those employees hired away from you. This is not all bad. Having such good people stolen from you is one of your best ways to build a wider network of influence and information. And, after all, when you do your new hiring you often take people away from some other agency. Individuals hired away from you become a good source for references to find new people you want to hire. They know your standards and expectations.

But there still remains the broken synapse in your organization's feedback system, the bad supervisor who is depressing morale and productivity. To the extent my brief advice above helps you to deal with improving poorly performing employees or in running them off, part of your problem of dealing with bad hires will be rectified.

When you do make a bad hire, which I managed to do well over a dozen times during my career, it is your responsibility to do something about it. One mark of a leader is to be firm with nonperformance. Inappropriate, incongruous, and inept actions and judgments can be just as intolerable and unacceptable in terms of job performance as failure to perform or complete assigned tasks. It will not take you long to appreciate sustained and reliable performance as well. If anyone on your staff does fine work most of the time but does a half-assed job part of the time, you've still got a problem. You never know when she's doing one and not the other. This means you have to check everything she does to be sure her half-assed work doesn't get through undetected and uncorrected. At least someone performing poorly all the time is predictable; you know what you're getting.

You must clean up your own messes when you make a bad hire. You will be tempted to reorganize around your problems. This rarely works. Reform the bad performers or move them out. If you do not, you will begin to hear criticisms both from below in the organization and from above in your board or from others governing or monitoring your agency's activities.

Yet there still remains the high risk of making bad hires with each vacancy that occurs. It is not enough to tell you to check references. You have three strikes against you from the outset: The applicant will give you a selected list to contact; second, in these days of open records no one will provide you with a written account of anything bad or very frank about a job candidate; and third, if you were impressed enough with the interview to follow up on references you will tend to be looking for what you want to hear, to confirm that you have found the ideal candidate for this job. This is particularly true if you have a very weak pool of applicants to select from. You will be reluctant to have to go through the hiring process again and to leave the position vacant even longer. So you tend to gloss over your instincts that tell you a candidate is weak and you start to look for comments from his references that make him look strong enough to hire.

Written comments are often worthless, especially with the threat of lawsuits hanging over the heads of those writing frank assessments of candidates. You will need to learn to read between the lines for some of the code phrases. Try these for practice: "I cannot say too many good things about this person or recommend him too highly," and "I would urge you not to waste any time whatsoever in employing this candidate." Or "I can assure you that no person would be better for the job than so and so." Or another, "I am pleased to be able to say that this candidate is a former colleague of mine." One I have always admired read, "If this is the quality of candidates you are considering, this person will compare very favorably." Gone are the days of complete candor in written letters of recommendation or assessment. Gone are the days when someone might write, "Yes, Joe works for us and each time I encounter him I reflect on how we are depriving some village of its idiot."

Before the days of candid references passed entirely, President Abner McCall of Baylor University was once asked for a reference on a former law school faculty member who had worked for him when he was dean of the University's Law School. The man had been a continual thorn in McCall's side while he was dean, but the man apparently had decided that it would look good to list among his references his former dean, who had subsequently become a university president and a member of the Texas Supreme Court. When McCall wrote back he said, "You have written inquiring about my views on Dr. Blank. Let me put it this way. If you ordered a trainload of sons of bitches and this man was delivered, you could consider the order substantially filled."

Since you can no longer put much faith in written assessments, you must use the telephone or face-to-face appointments to elicit the candor you need in order to learn what kind of people you are actually considering. And you must go beyond those references listed in the candidate's application. Always ask among the references whom you call for the names of others you might be able to contact concerning the candidate. Or seek out other ways to identify objective references.

One of our boards of regents decided to hire a new chancellor based solely on his interviews with them. They acceded to his request that they not make any calls to the state where he was then employed. He told the regents that he was the second most important person in the state, second only to the governor, and any rumor that he might be leaving would be devastating to the state as a whole. He was a heck of a salesman; they hired him, references unchecked. Immediately when his appointment was announced by the regents, I received a call from the Arkansas commissioner of higher education. He said, "Can you hear me all right? I was concerned I might be drowned out by the noise of the parade and the bands in the background. They're celebrating after hearing that one of your universities just hired our esteemed president away from us."

I am due at a committee hearing on our budget in about an hour so I'd better head for the capitol. I need to get there early to see what line of abuse legislators have chosen for today. The theme this year is: "It is more blessed to ask permission than to seek forgiveness." This is a subtle prelude to a new round of micromanaging. They like us to display an appropriate aptitude for groveling and then to kiss their . . . holy rings.

Oh, I suppose you may wonder what I said to Governor Clements back across his desk after he shouted at me. I said, "Governor, I mean no disrespect but when you shake your finger at me and give me a zero for my performance in the session, I suppose at some point you are going to let me say something."

He reared back in his chair and grunted, "You got something to say, say it."

So I explained that while he had been giving the universities over $150 million he knew perfectly well they did not need or deserve for new construction in order to keep them from opposing his efforts to repeal their statewide ad valorem tax, I had been trying to get the legislature to restrict their use of that new money for rehabilitation and remodeling rather than have it spent on unneeded new facilities.

He backed off his attack and we parted amicably. But when I got out in the corridor my board chairman, former Governor Preston Smith, whom the governor had asked to accompany me, stopped me. He asked, "Did you have the feeling you might have been set up when we got in there?"

I should have known this foxy politician would catch it, but I acted naïve and asked what he meant.

He said, "My guess is that fellow sitting in there, his budget director, wants your job before the governor leaves office. He's the one who set you up to get you fired. That's why Clements wanted me to be here. I suspect I'll have a call from the governor waiting for me when I get back to my office."

Keep on keepin' on.

Your much maligned

Uncle Ken

re: *More on unpleasant people*

[Lawyers] must struggle with each other yet be friends the next day; make maximum claims as bargaining points but aim at a compromise settlement; satisfy most people somewhat, rather than a few people fully; represent diversity by uniting difference; be always more neutral than hostile; deal in increments and margins only, but deal constantly; always adjusting, hedging, giving in a little, gaining a little; creeping toward one's goals, not heroically striding there.

— *Garry Wills*

A scrub woman's prayer overheard at the front of a church: "Oh Lord, I know you don't give me more than you think I can handle, but sometimes I wish you didn't hold me in such high esteem."

FEBRUARY

Dear Kim

While I was telling you about disagreeable people in my last letter I could not help but think not only of those you will have to deal with inside organizations but those outside as well — aside from politicians. Now, I make a distinction between those with whom you have to be disagreeable because you hold different opinions or different positions on issues. It is the nature of jobs in the public arena that you are going to hold different views on public policy issues. In fact, one measure of whether you are in a significant line of work or in a backwater agency is whether you are intensely involved in disagreement over issues. If your agency is quiet most of the time and controversy is rare and hardly ever heated, you had better ask yourself whether you shouldn't start looking for more significant public work.

But back to my classification of unpleasant and disagreeable people. In the public sector people must assume different roles and positions and consequently must confront each other in the public arena, be it before a court, before a board or commission, or before legislative committees or executive review panels. Even those holding views contrary to yours may hold those views honestly and sincerely, hard as that may be for you to accept at times. So public fights are inevitable and to be expected. And as the old saying goes, all is fair in love and war and politics or something like that. But, in fact, all is not fair; there are forms of behavior and techniques and practices that are outside the pale of honest and open disagreements. Some of these include lying, backbiting, or backstabbing, misusing friendship, and insincerity. There are other personal characteristics not so egregious, traits that are merely annoying and petty such as pursuing personal aggrandizement, an aura of being "holier than thou," being overbearing, and impatience or a short temper. You just get used to accepting these latter personal deficiencies as part of the political landscape.

Personally, I think I may often be seen as part of the furniture. I simply have never had the confidence to be anything but modest. I haven't pushed myself forward. I don't fight unless I have to and I'm pressed into it. And even then I don't always like it very much. The result of my inherent modesty and my high ignition point has been that I am very frequently underestimated. And you may remember in *The Godfather* somewhere, somebody says the greatest gift you can make to your enemy is to underestimate him. Most of the time what they underestimate is your courage and your tenacity and your readiness to go to battle. As a result, if you are modest and quiet, your opponents will do a lot of bluffing.

But back to the behavior of unpleasant people. There was one campus president who flat out lied to me on three separate significant occasions. The circumstances were so outrageous that I could not actually bring myself to believe the first two situations were based on outright lies, but the third time I caught him out in a bold-faced lie, I finally woke up to the fact that this was his operating style. The old saying, "Fool me once, shame on you; fool me twice, shame on me," certainly applied. I was a slow learner and my consistency in administering public policy suffered as a result of my permitting this president to lie to me and get away with his gains in doing so.

The result of his lying had placed his senator and me at extreme odds. He was lying to the senator as well and misrepresenting me and my positions to the senator. This had caused the senator to attack me on the floor of the Senate and that put the senator at odds with the lieutenant governor. Finally I faced the question of how I was going to deal with a bill the senator had introduced on behalf of the president's campus. I decided, unpleasant as it would be, that I had to discuss the provisions of the bill with the senator directly.

His aide was clearly reluctant to call the senator out of a committee hearing to talk with me in the hallway on the bill, and he stood back as the senator and I approached each other to talk, expecting fireworks, I'm sure. When I explained what his bill would permit the president to do and I suggested two possible amendments, the senator turned to his aide and said, to his amazement and mine, "Fix my bill with these two amendments before the committee hearing on it." I could hardly believe it. Here was a case where meeting with my opposition paid off handsomely. Perhaps he had been fooled once too often by the same college president as well.

You might think in the future of setting up a couple of files: "Brickbats" and "Bouquets." A couple of subtitles used by one university administrator might help: "Read these when puffed up." "Read these when cast down." You will need a place for unpleasant letters from disagreeable people. Or from citizens who have just had all they want to hear from government or bureaucrats. One irate letter to me read, "Your whining and yapping for more tax money is an outrage to the taxpayers who have been bled white over tax increases. You'll be old and gray and on Social Security without any teeth before you get any more money out of me."

One day my secretary, Mary Allen, asked me how I was going to answer an especially irate two-page letter from a university president responding to an earlier letter of mine to him. He accused me in his letter of megalomania, egomania, presuming to tell him what he already knew, and who the hell did I think I was, in addition to other less constrained comments. I handed Mary the tape with my dictated response. When she brought it back, she said, "You're surely not going to send this." I signed it and handed it back. It said simply, "Dear Grover, Tell you what let's do. You send me back my letter and I'll send you back yours. Cordially."

Grover called three days later laughing and said, "My secretary *told* me not to send that letter. . . ."

It is difficult to know how to respond to irate and abusive letters. The anonymous ones are the best; they go directly to the file. For those we must answer, we don't have the privilege of the response Senator Stephen Young of Ohio used to use regularly. He would write, "My dear Mr. Blank: I regret to inform you that some idiot has stolen some of your stationery and is writing me letters on it. Knowing you will want to address this urgent matter, I am enclosing the letter for your immediate attention."

Those of us in career or appointed positions do not have that enviable luxury of elected officials, who can on occasion respond exactly as they feel. Another example is California Congressman John McGroarty's reply to a constituent. He said, "One of the countless drawbacks of being in Congress is that I am compelled to receive impertinent letters from a jackass like you in which you say I promised to have the Sierra Madre mountains reforested and I have been in Congress two months and haven't done it. Will you please take two running jumps and go to hell."

Speaker Sam Rayburn was known regularly to dictate, "Dear Madame or Sir, I have your letter of X date before me. [There was a pause as he read it.] Now it is behind me."

However, such responses are not the usual fare of politicians. They are often too concerned about every vote to risk offending a constituent. As the former speaker of the Wisconsin legislature said, "When you are elected to office you start to tolerate fools. It is because each opinion is supposed to count, and each caller or letter writer is a potential vote. . . . Think of Tinkerbell on your shoulder with a poll and a clip board."

A president wrote accusing me of crucifying his fine Christian college on a cross of bureaucracy and he went on for a page and a half berating our intrusions on his freedoms and our unfair application of rules to his school and our violation of the separation of church and state. This came out of our attempts to close his college, which consisted of a printing press for diplomas and a post-office box being run out of the back of this right reverend's small church. After much berating and maligning of us and our work, he came to the point of his letter concerning the court appearance set for the following week. He ended by saying, "I am writing to inform you that God has found us a better location in Arizona."

Churches wanting to become colleges and to award degrees are often creative in their arguments to us. They object that we are regulating religion by not letting them award degrees, even though the attorney general has ruled that we are carrying out our legislative directive and are regulating education, not religion. One protesting seminary cited scripture to justify their awarding degrees. "Surely men of low *degree* are vanity, and men of high *degree* are a lie: to be laid in the balance, they are altogether lighter than vanity." (Psalms 62:9) And "For they that have used the office of a deacon well purchase to themselves a good *degree*." (II Timothy 3:13) Or "And with them their brethren of the second *degree*, Zechariah, Ben, etc., the porters."

But enough storytelling. From time to time I get sidetracked, as you will note. Back to unpleasant people. Big people, good people, do not stoop to acting petty. They meet you face to face or even toe to toe, but they don't ambush you by spreading tales and gossip, by imputing dishonorable motives to your actions and decisions, by misrepresentations or by lying. Big people don't have time for this kind of immature behavior.

It is the little people who act shabbily. Sometimes they reach positions of authority and act small and set the tone for their subordinates to act small in turn. Harold Stoke, from his experience as a university president, warned us to wear the garments of dignity and authority only for the purposes intended and no others. Acceptable behavior is set from the top down by example. Cue-conscious subordinates learn quickly what is tolerated, maybe even encouraged, what is permitted, if only enjoyed in the telling or the repeating. This is similar to little boys sitting and giggling in a clubhouse as they pull limbs off a granddaddy longlegs. Smallness among little people engenders feelings of camaraderie they are incapable of finding through competency.

Here's another technique you will encounter because it is so pervasive. There are those who accrue influence by making little problems into big problems and then solving those "big problems" they have created. Politicians do this to make people indebted to them. Lawyers do it to increase the hours they bill. Bureaucrats do it because it is a way for a person to look good with his or her boss and a way to put down somebody else. The difficulty it can create for the person being "helped" is that it can make you look incompetent or unable to handle your own affairs.

I'll be specific. You might take a piece of proposed legislation to your boss's staff assistant and say, "This is ready to go but there are a couple of options I'd like to discuss with our chief honcho." The assistant says, "Oh, I don't know; these are major policy options. There are going to be all kinds of ramifications. Why don't you leave it with me? I'll work it over and get back to you." Or you might say, "It's come to the point I'm going to have to take disciplinary action against Joe. You know the continuing problems we've been having with him. I'm considering several different ways I might do it but I want to keep the boss informed before I proceed." Again the assistant says, "You know how sensitive the boss is on this kind of thing. With the lawsuits we've had and all that. He hates confrontation. I wouldn't jump into it. Just leave it with me. I'll find the best time to talk with him about it."

In the midst of a busy day, your first reaction is to be grateful for the help. And very often it is genuine help. But then later you may find that the assistant has taken credit for your proposed legislation. Or that he has taken your personnel problem to the boss and asserted that you have been unable to handle Joe yourself and he has worked out a solution for you. And what can you do about it? Is it worth causing a flap about and make an enemy in the front office—especially with one of the boss's gatekeepers? Most of the time you learn to live with it and be more careful about what you ask for his help on. Such a person does not engender trust in the organization. And there are a lot of them around.

On a bill amending our student loan program one year there was language that might possibly lead to ambiguity of meaning. The bill had passed the Senate, and we asked the sponsor and the chair of the subcommittee that handled the bill in the House if they would accept the minor Senate differences in the bill and then make some comments on intent of the legislation in connection with the House vote. This would establish legislative history and intent and would remove any doubt about what the legislature had in mind on the language in question. The bill sponsor agreed, but the subcommittee chair insisted that the bill would have to be amended in the House on the point we had raised and be sent back to the Senate for concurrence.

It was in the very final days of the session and we knew that this could become a major undertaking with all the procedural obstacles to overcome and the bottleneck of important bills pending for votes. For us it meant that if the subcommittee chair's new amendment did not get through both houses, its failure could later be interpreted as legislative intent *opposite* from the intent we thought a few spoken words on the floor could establish. The subcommittee chair overrode the sponsor and magnanimously offered to carry the amendment on the floor. He began arranging caucuses and conferences to get his amendment through. Frankly, as a relatively insignificant legislator he had nothing else to do. In the final days this gave him a chance to appear active in the midst of all the crises others were involved in. And it gave him visibility with the Speaker as he postured for a better committee assignment for the following session. The amendment squeaked through both houses in the final hours of the session. It was a perfect example of making a mountain out of a molehill and then bulldozing the mountain.

Incidentally, recalling this subcommittee chair reminds me: You need to know the difference between a cactus and a caucus. With a cactus the pricks are all on the outside.

We had one case of smallness which even we, hardened as we are to misrepresentations, found difficult to believe. An accusatory letter from a senator asked us why we were refusing to provide certain information to a constituent of his, a banker and a former member of the state legislature. The banker wanted the senator to sponsor a bill to permit him to buy our student loan program portfolio at a huge discount. The banker was also a lawyer with whom we had had several tussles in the past, and out of these we had arrived at a perfectly balanced mutual dislike.

The senator enclosed the banker's letter, which told the senator that our agency "would not provide the information I need." We studied the circumstances and we were able to respond to the senator that his constituent had never requested from us the information he was referring to. The banker's use of the word "would," we had to report to the senator, had to be, therefore, *conditional* use rather than *past* tense, speculative and not descriptive of something we had actually done. We heard nothing further from the senator.

Such are the games played by the small minds and little people who operate on the periphery of public policymaking. As another toiler in higher education, Harvard's Dean Henry Rosovsky, put it, "We do not know ahead of time that in reality life will be a roller coaster taking us from the sublime to the ridiculous five times a day."

And when in honest disagreement over an issue with a colleague, hope that you never hear him bring himself to say, as I have heard one president say, "But I thought we were friends."

Another president once pleaded at length with me to permit him to add the first ever doctoral degree program at his school. It was desperately needed. It would be his legacy to the school. He would never ask for another. This one degree program would make the university great and help him to take the school, to which he was dedicating his life, where it needed to go.

Two weeks later he called to ask me if he could use me as a reference for a new presidency he was seeking. Fortunately for the Texas school, he left to go to Illinois. Or was it Ohio?

Bosses can be disagreeable as well and this is not the place to deal with that at length, but I do suggest this. Don't let your boss shoot the messenger. When I was a vice president my boss blew up at me one day over an unpleasant report I gave to him on our failing to make progress in one area in opening our new university. When he continued to rail at me, I got up and walked to the door. He yelled where was I going. At the door I stopped and told him I needed a clarification. Was he merely mad at the problem I was reporting on or was he mad at me for telling him what he needed to know as president. Because if he was mad at me, I planned to begin looking for another job. He never abused me again, not that he didn't continue to lose his temper.

Sometimes you find yourself disagreeing and arguing against views that are so extreme that they take on the hues of implausibility. And then there may come a moment of epiphany.

An entrepreneur was operating a new private university in Texas at such a low level of quality and performance that we sought to force it to close. The president appealed. Our staff and several lawyers from the attorney general's office worked for weeks preparing for the hearing and getting our questions ready to lay out the basic facts to support our position.

At the hearing the school's attorney—a big name among lawyers in town—arrived late, leafing through his file folder. As he sat down, continuing to refresh himself on the case at hand, he began to lay out the facts with his client. He asked several background questions, stalling for time as he read the file.

He asked the president on the stand, "Tell us about your campus."

"Well, we don't exactly have a campus. We teach at various places around town. Right now we are leasing space in a shopping center."

The attorney looked up, a little startled, and asked as he went back to the file, "Then tell us about your full-time faculty."

"Well, we don't actually have any full-time faculty except my wife, who is also our registrar. We hire local people part-time to teach our courses when we need them."

"Then tell us about your laboratories and equipment." Still looking through the files.

"We only need several projectors and VCRs for the films we show for our classes. We don't have any laboratories as such."

The lawyer laid down the folder and said, "Well, then, you might describe your library for us."

The president brightened and replied, "We have two hundred books at present. But we are prepared to buy more to obtain state approval. If they will just tell us which books we need to buy, then we will buy 'em."

At that point our lawyer from the attorney general's office also laid down his file and folded his hands. Our case had just been presented.

On another occasion Maharishi International University tried to open several branch campuses in Texas. Their representatives simply could not understand how we could possibly not accept the legitimacy of their teaching physics and chemistry as well as other fields of study through transcendental meditation. They explained at length to our board how films of the Maharishi speaking on these subjects should constitute sufficient basis for awarding college credit and degrees. I had appointed Dr. Raj Thyagarajan, an outstanding professor of chemistry at one of our universities, to chair the review committee and to assist us in not being led astray in Asian philosophy and religion. In the process transcendental meditation was discussed at length.

Toward the end of the hearing a medical doctor on our board arrived late. He took his place at the table and looked mystified as to what was under consideration while the discussion continued. Finally he turned to a colleague and, not realizing his microphone was open and would send his question to the entire audience, he asked, "What kind of *dental* school did they say this was?"

You don't plan or pray for such manifestations that God does exist. But we are permitted to give thanks when they appear.

Among the disagreeable folk you have to live with there still remain those who prosper despite being uneducable and unconvincible, the ones you truly despise, those who will never come around, the primordial blockheads, the grade-A, certifiable, born-again sons of bitches. As one friend put it, the revolving sons of bitches, a son of a bitch from any angle you look at him. What do you do about them? How do you live with them while they continue to prosper and remain so undeserving? I have always found it immensely helpful to follow Samuel Goldwyn's advice, "I don't even ignore 'em." My approach is to feel sorry for them in their unfortunate, uninformed, contemptible state and to look down on them in their paltry insignificance. Even if it's only in my own mind and not theirs, it makes me feel better. And I doubt it can be called pathological, or even neurotic.

I don't know how much I have helped you with the topic of unpleasant people, but I hope you have been reading between the lines. Not only was I telling you something of the kind of people you will encounter, I have been suggesting something about the kind of public servant you should strive to become and personal characteristics and practices you should avoid.

Your long suffering

Uncle Ken

re: *Subordinate leadership, getting help from above*

The task of responsible leadership . . . is to avoid
irreconcilable positions.   — *Lyndon B. Johnson*

Change is inevitable. In a progressive country change is constant.
                                             — *Benjamin Disraeli*

Kings and bears often worry their keepers.   — *Benjamin Franklin*

MARCH

Dear Kim

Despite your idealism, which leads you to believe you can solve
all problems for the betterment of mankind, and despite your youth, which
makes you think you have *time* to accomplish all these things, you will learn
one thing early. You will need to seek help from those who can indeed make
changes happen because you will not have the authority, power, or position
to get them done yourself. And this will be true all during your career, regardless how high you rise in an organization or politics. A person's skill in
getting his boss or another superior to help him in a good cause I like to call
subordinate leadership.

Leaders have a sensitivity for discovering what other people want and
desire and then they find ways to fulfill those needs. This is one way a leader
creates followers. But my lesson for you today is a variation on that theme.
As a beginning bureaucrat you will certainly want to develop a keen awareness to the needs of others around you. This approach to building a cadre
of followers usually assumes that the leader is exercising this propensity to
fulfill the needs of others upon those *below* her or at the same level.

But let me assure you that it is possible to practice this trait on those above you as well, hence my label "subordinate leadership." Those above you in positions of authority, power, and leadership also have their own wants and desires that they like to have fulfilled. Even if you do not have first-hand contact with them it is still possible to learn or speculate on what their needs are. They frequently speak on what they care about. They have political agendas they promote. They accept accolades and awards and honors for the things they value and spend their time and energies on. Those who are po-litical figures are always searching for ways to look good with the voters and garner citizen support and approval. And if you have any imagination you should be able to conjecture about what might appeal to those above you in terms of what is right, fair, honorable, and in the interest of the general pub-lic, the city, the state, and nation. If you can delve the needs and wants of those above you, you will have found a key you might possibly be able to use to motivate them to act upon something you want to accomplish.

Perhaps my telling you a story or two will illustrate how subordinate leadership can work. Early in my public career I worked in San Francisco in the city's slum clearance and redevelopment agency. I was assigned, among other duties, the task of trying to breathe life into a project to clear some old wartime-era housing off a large hill on the south side of the city known as Hunters Point. Our goal was to rebuild the area with low-income and middle-income housing to serve those who would be displaced. The ex-isting prefab housing had been built quickly during World War II and was now overcrowded and falling apart. Without going into details, let me just say that through Justin Herman, my boss, and Mayor John Shelley, we suc-cessfully convinced Secretary Robert Weaver of the Department of Hous-ing and Urban Development to fund the project.

Then during the planning stage for the project my job was to work with the Hunters Point residents in the area to get their buy-in and partici-pation so we wouldn't have a rebellion on our hands when the old housing started to come down. It was even then a primarily black neighborhood and I spent months of evenings in the area, meeting with the working fathers and mothers, church leaders, and small business owners. We spent the evenings in a local church putting together an acceptable plan for relocation, demolition, redevelopment, and public subsidies.

Very quickly I came to accept Saul Alinsky's approach in working with the neighborhood. That is, I worked myself out of a job as the emerging community leaders bit by bit took control of the project and some of the planning. At first I could not understand why I had to hear and they had to replay the same speeches night after night when the participants and audience always remained almost the same. Then I finally realized most of these people had never spoken in public before and they were learning how to do it through their involvement in this project.

As the proposals for redevelopment took shape I gradually became a resource for the community on procedures and standards and an interpreter for the citizens to professional planners with my agency and the city. On one occasion when the neighborhood leaders met before the board of the agency I worked for they even referred to me as "harmless." Frankly, I have to admit even now, I was offended. This label demeaned what I felt I had been doing for them. But by hindsight I realize this only reflected how effectively I'd gotten them to take ownership for the rebuilding of their own neighborhood and how they were becoming self-sufficient and didn't need me to do anything for them. Alinsky would've been proud of me. But harmless? At the time it hurt.

In any event, the state division of highways finally announced it had decided upon the route for a new freeway from south of San Francisco to connect to the Oakland Bay Bridge. The danger to our project was quickly apparent. The federal agency funding our Hunters Point project had a very firm policy that if an urban renewal project is bisected by a federally funded highway, all of that agency's funding for the project would be terminated immediately. The relocation and housing problems in the project area would then become the responsibility of those carrying out the highway project.

A few weeks later at the public hearing for the freeway proposal I was dismayed to watch the Division of Highways lay out the route they proposed. It was over the top of our hill at Hunters Point, right through the center of the neighborhood. My fears for the federal subsidies for the new housing were realized. And all the hopes of the citizens in the area about their plans would be dashed.

At the hearing the highway planners discussed why this was the best of all possible routes. It was the lowest cost to build, because buying residential land rather than industrial land was much cheaper. It was the most direct bypass; drivers would save time, fuel, and money on this shorter course. And above all, future drivers would have a better view of the bay as they sped north and south on their appointed ways—through what would have been at one time a residential neighborhood. All the cost-benefit analyses and time studies supported this as the far best possible route of alternatives considered.

When the city's testimony to try to preserve the neighborhood was rebuffed by the highway commission members as being inconsequential, it became clear that the state Division of Highways was going to have its way

again. For decades throughout California the highway department had ignored or simply run over local preferences all over the state. They had become a power unto themselves, reckoning with no one else, and putting
their roads wherever they chose to place them. The agency received all gaso-
line tax revenues directly without even having to go through appropriations
procedures in the legislature. And the agency was independent of any oversight by anyone over budget, planning, design, or administration. The highway commission held supreme authority on highway routes, to the detri-
ment of parks, neighborhoods, and business districts across the state, and
they acted accordingly.

The hearing on the proposed route proceeded throughout the afternoon, and the commission members were obviously planning to finish it up
quickly and make their preordained decision. But at the end of the day, as
the residents of Hunters Point returned home from work, I began calling
the community leaders to tell them what was happening downtown to their
project. Within hours the hearing chambers filled with irate citizens from
the area, and the commission was privileged to hear the speeches I had heard
the residents in the area rehearse and replay and repeat and polish over the
months as I had watched the developing rivalry for community leadership.

All citizens were heard and the hearing was finally recessed after 2:00
A.M. Just before adjourning, the highway commission cynically voted unanimously to proceed with the freeway along their proposed route through
our project. The local testimony and citizen opposition meant nothing to
the highway planners.

Ever since the highway department had built the atrocious double-
decked and elevated Embarcadero Freeway in San Francisco over the objections of the city, people had remained furious with the agency. Anyone
living in the city sensed this. It was perhaps the single issue that could unite
such a diverse citizenry.

When I arrived in the city, I had been curious how the city had managed to stop that Embarcadero Freeway before the highway department
completed its planned course around the northern shore of the San Francisco peninsula. The long-term plan was unknown to the city when the elevated freeway was initiated. The state Division of Highways planned for the
double-decker freeway to go past Telegraph Hill, over Fisherman's Wharf,
around Ghiardelli Square, past Knob Hill, and around the Marina area and
the adjoining Yacht Harbor to connect with the Golden Gate Bridge. The
attitude of the highway planners seemed to be that the city of San Francisco
was just in the way of moving traffic north and south. But at this point in
1964, the Embarcadero Freeway had sat there for years, unfinished at North

Beach with only one exit at Broadway. How had the city disrupted the run-away state highway department in their plans? Out of curiosity, I read up on and studied this.

I also knew that the citizens, the board of supervisors, and the local media, along with the conservationists and the mayor, had all been up in arms for months since the state Division of Highways had proposed to cut down scores of towering redwoods in order to tunnel under part of Golden Gate Park with a new freeway. More importantly, the mayor was abundantly on record about his distrust of the highway planners. When asked by Governor Pat Brown to come to the state capitol to discuss future highway plans, Mayor Shelley played to the public and labeled the meeting "an effort to blackjack San Francisco leaders into supporting the Pan Handle-Golden Gate freeway." Knowing his inclinations on this topic, I thought I knew where he might be willing to lead the city on the Hunters Point project if given the opportunity.

The morning after reading the newspapers announcing the new free-way's route through our Hunters Point project, I called the mayor's office and talked with an aide I knew there to see how the mayor was taking it. He told me Mayor Shelley was angered and frustrated but resigned to the de-cision. There was nothing he could do. I told him, on the contrary, the mayor alone could stop the project if he wanted to. I explained that the mayor could use the same defense the city had used years ago to stop the Embarcadero Freeway. He could refuse to close the streets that the high-way department would need to use to move their equipment to their pro-posed construction sites. By refusing to close any streets to help the high-way department, the mayor could hold up their construction permanently until they agreed on a route acceptable to the city.

Mayor Shelley announced his defiance of the highway planners and how he was going to stop them. The next day he got highly laudatory com-ments from the media and the public at large. He had stood up for San Fran-cisco against the most hated bureaucracy in state government. Whether everyone in the city liked Shelley or not, they were with him on this one. Mayor Shelley called that afternoon to tell me if I had any more ideas like that to let him know.

Then the city's board of supervisors wanted to share some of the mayor's political glory in beating the highway department, and I helped to draft a resolution for them to endorse the mayor's position.

Another situation arose when I employed a little subordinate leader-ship just after I had become commissioner of higher education. There were 130 degree proposals pending for review and approval by the board, with over a dozen of those for new doctoral degrees, many of which would turn primarily undergraduate colleges into new doctoral-granting universities. The board had been stampeded during the previous two years into approving degree programs far too quickly, and the more they approved, the faster other colleges developed proposals in order not to be left behind in the largess. I asked my board to permit me, as my first act in office, to try to get the universities to agree to postponing approvals for six months to a year to give us time to develop a more thorough review procedure for such requests.

The board members told me to go ahead and try to get the schools to agree to a slowdown. They sympathetically wished me "lotsa luck." That should have forewarned me. I then approached the presidents and explained that I could ask my board, as their new commissioner, to support me at my very first meeting and to declare a moratorium on approving new degrees since their new proposals were so numerous. But I said I would prefer not to wear the hero's white hat alone and appear to put black hats on the presidents as I tried to slow things down. They finally all agreed that a short delay of less than a year would not hurt their programs. Never being at a loss to gain credits and put me in their debt, however, they made clear that they were doing this as a special favor to me in my new position.

Just as I had all the agreements in place and I started to turn to other matters for my first board meeting, I began to receive calls from presidents, then from regents, and finally from my own board members. They were having second thoughts. They asked me for exceptions for particular degree proposals that could not be delayed without serious injury to the faculties and to particular schools. I explained to those calling me that any exceptions I would agree to at this late point would break my pledges to all the other schools.

Several of my board members then said they could spare me that personal problem. At the board meeting they would merely move that the board override my recommendations and make those exceptions that the members chose to grant. I knew once such a movement began, the board would break ranks, and they would then swap favors with each other and proceed to approve programs without any staff analysis or recommendations of any kind. The burden would shift from the question, "Why can't this proposed new degree program wait?" to "Why can't we just go ahead and approve this one right now?" What I had devised as a plan to slow down runaway approvals would turn into a rout. It would be a disastrous way to begin my administration of the agency. I knew the presidents would feel they had driven a permanent wedge between my board and me. Having tried to be a nice guy, I was facing a debacle.

When I called the chairman and explained what was happening he said (leaving aside his expletives), "This is typical of the board, breaking ranks to look after their special interests and their alma maters. They're on the phones right now with each other, cutting deals and swapping votes to undo everything you've gotten the schools to agree to. And wait till the rest of the presidents find out what's going on. They'll all be on the phones too. There's seventeen other members to call. I guess I'll have to get on the phone and try to get them all back in the corral. But I know it won't work. It never has before. I don't know what would help."

I said I had a proposal. I reminded him that Governor Dolph Briscoe had recently said that higher education costs were growing so fast they would soon bankrupt the state. I suggested that the governor might like to send a letter to each of our board members, noting his great satisfaction with what he had heard about their good efforts to slow down the runaway growth in higher education. He could commend them highly for standing firm in the face of all of the pressures he knows they are getting to approve new degree programs. He could offer to stand firmly behind them in whatever they did to control runaway growth.

My chair said, "That might just work, but he hasn't got anybody over there smart enough to write a letter like that."

I said, "Let me read you a draft."

Within the hour he called back and said Governor Briscoe loved the idea. "Send him the letter."

At the next board meeting the presidents could not understand what had put the steel rod up the back of the board and the starch in their speeches.

At the social hour that evening board members were slapping each other on the back and saying they had never had so much fun. "Did you see the look on their faces when we said no?" "Not just no, hell no!" "We need to do more of this." "I'm going to ask the governor to reappoint me in September. This is the most fun I've ever had on this board." And the chairman did not neglect to say several times, "See what we can do when we all stick together?"

You can appreciate why I have never told this story publicly. But I knew it was a risky game I was in. The full danger of what I had done came home to me that morning just before the board meeting started. One board member took me aside and handed me a letter and said, "I want you to read this. It's the first letter the Governor has ever sent me. You need to know what's going on behind the scenes." Big lesson here: When you play for big stakes, learn to keep your mouth shut about how clever you are.

Another example comes to mind. The city fathers and legislators from a small town in central Texas had been trying for years to get a new state-supported university established in their community. After a long string of ploys, they had their legislator try one more time. They asked for another study of the need for their university, this time to determine whether the new school should be made part of the Texas A&M System of universities. It just happened that that university system had a chancellor anxious to expand his roster of universities. The city fathers managed to get authorization for the study for their new university put in the appropriations bill. The members of the Appropriations Committee decided that it would be best to have the study done by a disinterested third party and selected my agency to do the study. But at the very last minute the lobbyists for the city fathers got the bill amended to have the study done by the Texas A&M University System.

This was like asking the fox to design the security system for the hen house. After the legislative session was over, I drafted a letter to the chairman of our board from the governor. The chairman took the letter to the governor and he signed it. The governor's letter said he would be very interested in seeing the report to be made by the A&M System administration, but he directed our board to undertake our own study because he would like to see what our independent findings would be about the need for the new university. I knew from conversations with this governor that he wanted us to stop the creation of new campuses. Foiled again, the city did not get its new university. But, again, I did not go around advertising what I had done.

One example of overplaying your hand at being clever might help to illustrate this. William O. Douglas told a story in his autobiography about a conversation he had with President Franklin Roosevelt while he was on the Securities and Exchange Commission. A vacancy had just occurred on the U.S. Supreme Court. At a poker game a little later the president told him he was being inundated by letters urging him to appoint Learned Hand to the opening. And Douglas told Roosevelt he agreed that Hand was the most obvious successor to the opening on the Court and that he would make an outstanding Supreme Court justice. Although Roosevelt said he agreed that Hand was the best candidate for the position, he told Douglas he was personally offended by the vigorous letter-writing campaign being pressed on him. He said he knew it was all being orchestrated by Justice Felix Frankfurter. Roosevelt told Douglas that as a consequence he was going to refuse to appoint Hand and was picking Wiley Rutledge instead, even though he had never met the man. Rutledge had been suggested by another friend just at the moment FDR was particularly incensed by Frankfurter putting pressure on him. And the great Learned Hand never made it to the Supreme Court.

Appointments are always touchy with governors and presidents. President Lyndon Johnson had told a friend that he was considering appointing him to a certain post in the federal government. The friend made the mistake of leaking the probability of the appointment to the press in order, in his judgment, to keep pressure on the president. Since Johnson had never mentioned the possible appointment to anyone else, he knew the source of the leak. He appointed someone else instead.

One more short example should suffice to make my point about subordinate leadership, that is, getting your boss to do the right thing or getting your boss's help. Under the threat of being issued a court order, Texas negotiated a settlement agreement with the federal government to eliminate any remaining vestiges of racial discrimination left over from the days when the races had been legally segregated in colleges and universities. Texas was one of over a dozen states which at one time had separated the races during those decades when a Supreme Court decision permitted the states to do this and while the federal government was making grants to the states to establish separate colleges for black students. The new Texas plan negotiated with the federal government to increase the integration of the races in the public colleges and universities ran for five years, during which time our agency was the enforcement arm for the state. When the plan ran out we could have waited and hoped that the federal government would go away. Or we could have waited for the feds to order us to develop a second five-year plan under their direction and supervision, which is precisely what the Office of Civil Rights was doing in other states that had completed their first five-year plans.

It seemed reasonable to assume two things that would be pleasing to our governor. First, we could seize the initiative and prepare our own new plan and, in doing so, try to do it without federal interference—always a popular position in Texas. Second, the governor could take the high ground and say that we are going to continue on the road to increasing integration because it is the right thing for the state to do for our minorities—not because the federal government has ordered us to do it. Feeling confident these reasons would resonate with the governor, we were in a position to exercise a little subordinate leadership while advancing the interests of our minorities and the business of our board.

We drafted a letter (and a suggested press release about the letter) from the governor to our chairman, directing us to prepare a new five-year plan and setting forth the governor's reasoning. He signed the letter unchanged. It was one of the most popular things Governor Clements did in his second term. Later, when this second plan also expired, we did the same thing again with Governor Ann Richards, with the same popular public response. Even if increasing integration of the races was not the most popular idea with every faction in the state, the idea that Texas could determine its own future without direction from Washington was a universally popular position for the governor to take with both Republicans and Democrats.

There is one minor drawback to remaining invisible and anonymous as you exercise "subordinate leadership." At a national conference my agency was attacked (with me as the specific target in the audience) for dragging our feet on developing a second state plan for racial integration in the universities. The speaker said, "If Governor Clements had not *ordered* the Coordinating Board to go on with the desegregation planning, nothing more would have been done until we had gotten the federal government to force them to do it."

This smoked me out. In fact it steamed me. I could not sit there and take this imputation. I was forced to speak. I said, "Arturo, who do you think wrote that order from the governor to us? Check it out." Arturo apologized later, for he had never imagined we would do that to ourselves. He had given the governor the credit we had intended for him to get.

But I'd rather be smoked out than to be caught out for braggadocio.

Your avuncular counselor,

Uncle Ken

re: *Taking the initiative, or risk taking inside government*

I was proud of the youngsters of that day. . . . The sense of freedom, the feeling of power over people and events, the desire for an all-out effort, the excitement of adventure—all these and more made lawyers, sociologists, economists, and political scientists march to the beat of the new drum that was echoing across the land. . . . They were filled with idealism and fervor.
— *William O. Douglas*

You can't cross a great canyon in two small jumps.
— *David Lloyd George*

The man whose eye is ever on himself doth look on one, the least of Nature's works . . .
— *William Wordsworth*

A P R I L

Dear Kim

You will by now be hearing a lot about theories and models as to how decisions and public policies are made. And you will probably have run across some criticism of these conceptual frameworks, such as that they ignore the role played by opportunity and chance events in how things get done in government. Politicians are forever being criticized for being opportunists. I want to see if I can't defend to you opportunism as an effective approach to promoting government programs and policies.

In the first place, why would we believe that a person who feels strongly about a cause or goal should not eagerly take advantage of circumstances that can advance that cause or goal? Since a primary requirement for moving governments to address public issues is the political will to act and since a responsibility of public executives is to infuse that political will into policymakers, anything that can solidify or influence political will is too good to be ignored or discarded.

In the 1950s it was suddenly discovered that the popular use in Europe of thalidomide to ease sleeping problems of pregnant women was the cause of severe birth defects. With that the mounting criticisms of the Federal Drug Administration (FDA) as being too slow in approving new drugs immediately stopped. Those defending and wishing to reinforce the agency's rigorous review procedures for new drugs seized on the circumstances to strengthen the FDA's legal and regulatory position.

Since opportunities and chance events can have such an impact on policy development, government officials endeavor to find ways to shape and influence events to their advantage, that is, to create "opportunities." Odd as it may seem for a public administrator not to run from criticism, one way to create opportunities is to build opposition to an existing condition. For example, if you are convinced that a change in policy needs to be made, one sure way to get shot down quickly is to propose the change because you personally can look ahead and foresee its need. You can help kill such a good policy change by saying it is your personal sense that it is a good idea. This is particularly true when there is no visible or audible objection to the present situation or existing policy.

Politicians and many policymakers do follow the old adage, "If it ain't broke, don't fix it." And if you alone say something is broke, you are likely to be ignored. It is far better for you to propose a modification to a policy in response to vigorous criticism of the status quo. In other words, it sometimes helps to have countervailing opposition to how you and your agency are doing things at the moment. This may mean that you need to stimulate an opposition group, or even to create one, to attack you for doing nothing about their concerns. This criticism then allows you to modify your rules or to propose to your policymaking body a compromise position that moves away from the old policy. You aren't out on a limb by yourself. Rather you are trying to find a reasonable new policy to accommodate those people who are complaining.

When there was reluctance and hesitancy by the state government to move quickly enough in responding to minority underrepresentation in higher education, I appointed an advisory committee and arranged for the minority co-chairs (Hispanic and African American) to address our board on the committee's findings. They used this meeting as a public forum to present facts and projections that would have drawn yawns or tut-tuts if presented by our own staff. The emotional quality of the reports, presented by minorities, was essential to give the issue personal and human interest for press coverage and visibility. Much of the criticism was directed at our agency and some of it at me personally. This created a situation that demanded a reaction by us and by the legislature. In their zeal, the critics—those I had appointed as co-chairs—moved on in their enthusiasm to visit legislators and other state leaders as well. And in doing so, they were presenting data my own staff had put together. In the meantime we and our board were busy setting new directions and goals in anticipation of coming pressures from the legislature and the governor's office. Even if I were represented as unresponsive and dilatory in not taking action before the report, it was a small price to pay for the progress we were able to make afterward.

When the Federal Fifth Circuit Court ruled in 1996 that Texas could no longer take race into consideration in admissions and financial aid decisions, I appointed a committee of fifteen sociologists, consisting of a majority of minority members. Their task was to study the feasibility of identifying markers and social characteristics that we might use as a surrogate for race. When they reported their findings to our board, the committee told us that they had found that using combinations of all other sociological categories, but not race, would still result in a fifty percent reduction in minority admissions in coming years. But these negative findings were not useless. They were picked up by the legislature in drafting bills to ease the impact of the court ruling. The findings had a particular impact on the conservative legislators, who did not want minority enrollments to decline sharply because they recognized that Texas will soon become "majority minorities." They might object to favoritism of any kind based on race or ethnicity, but as a result of our study they suddenly became very interested in finding other approaches the schools and the legislature could still use to recruit and retain minority students.

I have always thought that Alice Roosevelt Longworth, Theodore Roosevelt's daughter, was talking about this approach to policymaking when she was in her nineties. A reporter asked her if she had developed a philosophy of life from her experience. She replied, "I have. Empty what's full, fill what's empty, and scratch where it itches." I think she believed in this definition of the primary responsibility of the public servant: "Comfort the afflicted and afflict the comfortable." I'll bet she would have been among the first to agree that from time to time you have to introduce a few gnats and fleas to start some itching.

Once when I was addressing an annual meeting of the Mexican American Legal Defense and Education Fund (MALDEF), I was commending them for how effectively we had been working together despite our apparent differences in public. We were getting results even if we were a long way from conspiring. They had been impatiently pushing the state to move off the dime to increase Hispanic enrollments in higher education, and our agency had been progressively making things somewhat better by responding to their pushing. As a metaphor in my talk I used Mark Twain's comment that every dog should have a few fleas; it keeps him from forgetting he's a dog. Several of them apologized later after some of their colleagues had left the meeting to report that the commissioner was now calling Mexican Americans fleas.

This reminds me of a blooper during a campaign for governor. The campaign staff of one candidate tried out the new capacity of computers to use first names in the salutation of letters to voters to personalize the governor's campaign messages. For example, you would have received a "Dear Kim" letter from this candidate whom you did not know at all. A friend from the Mexican American Legal Defense and Education Fund sent me a copy of a note he had written to a colleague with the African American Students Association at a nearby university. My MALDEF friend wrote, "I am enclosing a campaign letter I just received beginning, 'Dear Mexican.' It is with fear and trepidation that I wait to learn how yours was addressed."

The opportunities that come your way may be in small things, not big nation-shaking policies. In 1965, I was working with the U.S. Office of Education (before it became a department), running a grant program of several hundred million dollars for constructing college classrooms and laboratories. At the end of the fiscal year in June we had about $5 million left over that we could not commit because some states had not fully used up their allotted shares. I was in my office over lunch trying to figure out how to allocate these remaining funds among the other states. My division director, Jay du Von, came in and said President Johnson had just talked with the secretary of Health, Education and Welfare and the secretary had, in turn, called him to say the president wanted all federal agencies to do everything they could to help Topeka, Kansas, and Washburn University. Just the night before the city had been hit by a devastating tornado and the university had been largely destroyed. Jay said to let him know right away if I had any ideas on how we might help.

When he left I turned back to the problem on my desk, how to deal with the $5 million figuratively lying there awaiting my decision. I saw an opportunity and I quickly dashed off a briefing memo which made these points:

We have $5 million for construction grants left for the year.

Our rules say to divide it among states with remaining demand.

All states have received funds under the program.

Congress likes the program so much they have *doubled* our appropriation for next year.

With everybody counting on more money next year and Washburn U so badly hurt, I doubt any state or university president would want to appear a "dog in the manger" and complain if President Johnson were to announce that he has given the $5 million to Washburn University.

No bureaucratic delays here. As I recall, the White House announced the commitment of the funds within the hour. Our offer was the first to reach the president's desk since his directive to the federal agencies and departments. And when my direct boss returned from lunch and found out what we had done, he was livid at our having violated written rules and regulations in such a cavalier manner.

Lessons: (a) Learn to quickly write short and convincing briefing memos, and (b) when the big boss is in the stew with you, you'll probably survive being unorthodox. Incidentally, I will make a note to tell you in a later letter a few things about writing briefing memos.

The greatest fun in being a government executive is the ability from time to time to create a new program. One day I had to go to Corpus Christi to give a commencement talk and as I read over my speech before leaving my office I was not particularly pleased with it. So I grabbed a handful of my business cards. That night, after congratulating the graduates, I said, "But I'm talking to the wrong group here. You are sitting there in your caps and gowns all prepared for success. I want to address the younger people here tonight. To be successful you will need a network of influential people so in a few years you can also be sitting down there in your own caps and gowns. I want to be part of your network to help you get ahead. After the ceremony is over if you young people will come up here on the stage I will give you my business card. I want you to take it home and stick it on your mirror where you'll see it every day to remind you of our deal we are going to make tonight. Our deal is this: You graduate from high school and I will guarantee that you will get the financial aid you need to go to college."

Of course I ran out of cards, but I wrote names and addresses on the back of my speech and the next week we sent those students cards and letters as well. This was no big commitment on my part because the state already guaranteed student financial aid to needy high school graduates. Students and parents just don't always know this. Our agency turned what I did that evening into a statewide program. Today we still send a newsletter to the eighth grade students across the state as we try to reach the most economically deprived young people. We have received hundreds of letters over the years from students I have promised to help, calling on me to meet my end of our bargain since they have met theirs by graduating from high school. One letter I remember particularly. A thirteen-year-old girl wrote saying, "I have lost the card you gave me. Does that mean I can't go to college?"

The point here is that entrepreneurship is not limited to the business sector. You need to learn to be a risk taker in government too. You must learn to recognize opportunities when they come your way and be prepared to grab them. Often those opportunities are ephemeral and will disappear quickly. "Wild Bill" Donovan, chief spy and director of the OSS in World War II, frequently used to say, "The perfect is the enemy of the good." A perfect or better decision or plan of action late by a day or even an hour may prove worthless. A timely but merely good decision or plan of action may serve to seize an opportunity that will otherwise be lost. Of course you must learn to expect the Monday morning quarterbacks who will later criticize you for not having used a more perfect approach to the circumstances you faced at the moment.

There was an occasion when my entrepreneurship ran up against that of a major computer company. Our agency had over 100,000 accounts of loans due from students who had borrowed from the state loan program we administered. When the Y2K problem of computers not being able to distinguish between 1900 and 2000 as we would cross into the new century came to our attention, we faced a serious problem with those accounts. Due dates, interest computations, balances due could all go haywire if we didn't solve that problem in our computer system. The company that had won the state bid and sold us our computers told us they could work out our problem for around $300,000. We went to the legislature as did all agencies with similar problems for supplemental funding to handle the problem.

In the meantime two of our own employees in our computer center found a glitch in the computer hardware. Through that chink in the overall system, our staff was able to solve our problem ourselves. It was done. No more problem. And we turned back over $270,000 to the state that had been appropriated to cover our staff and contract costs to overcome the problem.

When I was told about this, we acknowledged and thanked publicly before our board the employees responsible for saving us and the taxpayers a bundle of money. I suggested that we approach the company with the solution we had found to see if they might like to have it. I told my staff also to find out what kind of a discount they might give us on future purchases and services for our discovery. The computer company's reaction was, "We're not interested. We already know about that approach."

So they were going to charge us over $200,000 for a solution they already had in hand? And they weren't interested in giving us any reward for finding the answer to our problem they already knew about? I instructed my staff to be certain that every other state agency with our kind of computer knew about how to solve their problem without having to go to the company for assistance. Furthermore, I told my staff to put the solution to the Y2K problem for all owners of our kind of computer on the Internet as worldwide public information—free of charge. The word came back to me from the company that I seemed to "have an attitude." Only when it's thrust upon me.

I have been telling you about opportunity and the role it plays in government decisions and policies. But there is a corollary and that is patience. When I first took on higher level positions I constantly worried about how to be ready for every problem that I saw coming at me or likely to come. I spent enormous amounts of energy and time trying to develop responses and to be ready for those eventualities. Then in time several things became clear to me. I have gained confidence that I can handle the problems when they actually arrive. Second, I have found that some of the problems never came to full bloom and I was wasting my time planning ahead too far. Third, that the problems, when they do come into full bloom, are so different from what I had imagined and spent time preparing for that an entirely different response is often required. And last, I have found I can be more effective in trying to influence the circumstances and conditions related to the developing problems rather than focusing on the imagined problems to come. I have learned I can sometimes shape the development of the problem more to my liking. I look constantly for opportunities to change the way problems come to me. I have discovered this is a better and more effective use of my time and energy than worrying about detailed solutions and responses for possible use in the future.

Another point about patience. There was a time when I became convinced that I could not survive in my job because the governor wanted me out. The governor appointed one-third of my eighteen-member board every two years, and the new governor had just appointed six who seemed committed to questioning my every move and recommendation and to make my job as agency executive miserable. I reasoned that with his next set of six appointees he'd have the two-thirds necessary to have me removed. I considered, metaphorically speaking, turning off my engine when I saw a flat, green pasture ahead and gliding down to an easy landing, that is, taking a job in one of our universities, from whence I had come to this job. But the more I thought about it the more I came to the realization that I had come into the public service to have at least one really good fight someday, and this might be it. I decided, to continue the metaphor, I'd rather be shot down in flames. So I was unremitting in my staff recommendation to the board and refused to quit. Then two years later, when the next six appointees arrived, I found that I had underestimated the educability of the governor's first six appointees. I still had twelve solid supporters on the board, who immediately set out to educate the new, entering freshman class of board members that the governor might be wrong about their executive.

I have had the impression that every new governor wanted me fired. It is not so much that the governors have disliked me—and several of them truly have—but because I have worked for the previous governor and because they would prefer to have their own person in the commissioner's position. There is clearly a good argument to be made for the cabinet form of government, wherein every new governor should be able to appoint his or her own people to all top state agency positions. How else can the new governor carry out policies and be responsive to the voters who elected him or her to do certain things and change government in accordance with the platform if he or she cannot put his or her own appointees into the key jobs?

On the other hand, I can argue, with a strong personal interest, that the higher education commissioner's job should not be politicized and that it should remain nonpartisan. Under a cabinet form of government, the commissioner and other offices filled by a governor become lame duck positions when the governor is in his last term. Moreover, there would be a great loss of continuity and expertise with frequent turnovers in the office. This argument can be made for other specialized fields in government as well, such as health, the public schools, and the state police. The structure wherein governors appoint boards which, in turn, hire and fire commissioners and agency heads seems to me to provide sufficient accountability to the governor and the voters, even if there is a time delay during which the governor is not able to force immediate turnover in all agency executives. In any event, you can see why I like this system better than the cabinet form of state government. This is the principal reason I have survived in my job for over twenty years.

One lesson I learned is to have patience and to keep on working and playing the game. I gained an appreciation for the Arab story about the camel driver caught in the sheik's harem. When he returned to the prison yard from his scheduled execution, everyone was amazed and asked how he had managed to survive. He explained that he had convinced the sheik that he would teach his horse to fly. They all exclaimed this was impossible, why bother to try? To which he replied, "Perhaps. But while I am teaching the horse to fly many things might happen. The sheik might die. The horse might die. I might die. And, who knows, I may teach that horse to fly." Keep your options open. Keep playing the game.

You asked in your last letter for me to write to you about leadership. I have been, haven't you noticed? Everybody wants the formula or the secrets or they want the books and instructional tapes that reveal the formulas and secrets. In any event, I will think on it after I've written you on several other topics I've jotted down—if there's anything special left over to say on the topic.

Your transgressive kinsman,

Uncle Ken

re: *The kinds of pressures and influence used on you*

Let a judge take but one bribe, but once execute a justice purchased, and all his words and actions forever after may justly be suspected, though never so uprightly done or spoke.   — *Sir Edward Coke*

If you put a fish in a can of milk, it will never be the same can of milk.

                                                              — *Backwoods wisdom*

Behold the ships, though so great, are turned about with a very small helm.   — *St. James Epistle*

M   A   Y

Dear Kim

You will hear these arguments: Humans are social animals in that they flourish in groups and relationships. Humans are economic beings in that they seek personal gain and benefits. Humans are political creatures in that they attempt to influence and persuade fellow beings on issues of import. Once you reach a position of authority and public responsibility you will become a target of influence and persuasion. This is because you will have the power to bestow favors and penalties, to grant approvals and denials, to authorize and to prohibit, to facilitate and to hinder, or perhaps only to endorse or to annoy. However mild or severe your favors and sanctions may be, you will get worked over by people who want you to see things their way or at least to let them have their way. Those efforts to influence and persuade you will play on your being a social animal, an economic being, and a political creature—the full gamut. This goes with the territory of being involved in politics and the making and administering of public policies that affect economic interests and social relationships.

So let me alert you to some of the ways you will be approached. One way to attempt to influence you is to threaten you with harm or punishments. "Do this or I'll cut your budget," is the way a legislator may put it to you. Or, "Keep your mouth shut on this, or your agency reauthorization bill will never see the light of day." Or as a board member said to me once, "The governor has asked me to give you this message: He wants you to stay quiet and keep your mouth shut on this bill. He says if he hears you are opposing it or working behind the scenes to kill it he will get you fired."

Or the threat may be more indirect and subtle. A college president came to me and said, "I want to give you a 'heads up' on something that's happening. Senator Jones and Representative Sadler are going to introduce a bill to create a new campus for us in Marshall. There's nothing I can do to keep them from doing it. I just don't want you to get blindsided." On the surface this would appear to be a thoughtful and considerate step for him to take. Of course he did not have to explain the positions of authority the two sponsors of the bill held in the legislature. Nor did he deign to tell me what I already knew: that he and his staff had for several months been presenting to local service clubs and the chamber of commerce in Marshall plans and drawings for their proposed first new building.

It was a classic case of a college president covering his ass with me and trying to have it both ways. He was telling me I was going to have trouble if I opposed these two legislators, but he was also claiming "Me no Alamo" on going around our agency and directly to the legislature to promote his expansion plans. In dealing with presidents I have always held in high regard the comment Woodrow Wilson made when he stepped down from the presidency of Princeton University: "I don't want you to suppose that when I was nominated for governor of New Jersey I emerged from academic seclusion, where nothing was known of politics."

Another approach to influencing you that you need to be prepared for is outright bribery. Once when we were holding a large bond sale to finance our student loan program I was on my way to lunch with a couple of bankers who had unsuccessfully bid on the sale. Since they had lost the bidding, there did not seem to be any favors I could bestow on them or any appearance of favoritism. I was anticipating a friendly and relaxed meal. I remember the exact corner on Congress Avenue in Austin where we stood waiting for a light to change when one of them said blithely, "Sixty million dollars is a lot of money to move around before it goes into the state treasury. Why, if it sat in a bank three or four days or even just over the weekend before it got moved that could be worth what?" When his colleague just shrugged his shoulders, he answered himself, "Probably worth a new car for somebody."

The offer was on the table waiting for my move to pick it up. If I expressed outrage, they would have shown shock and alarm and denied they were suggesting a bribe to me. I let it pass but it was a very unpleasant and cold lunch. That ended our relationship forever.

There was a time we on the staff were vigorously opposing the creation of a new branch campus of a university. A politico from a public relations firm tried to persuade me to another view. Over lunch he described the prestigious neighborhood developing around the area where the new university would be located and how all the property in that area would then sharply appreciate in value. Then he explained that he was sure arrangements could be made for me to acquire some nearby property "for a very good price." Again, nothing to prosecute, just a casual comment and an understanding on both sides about what was being proposed and that at this point the ball was in my court.

Perhaps by hindsight, in both cases I could have acted interested and gone to the attorney general and set up an entrapment for those attempting to bribe me. Frankly, such an approach just did not occur to me at the time. Now that I've had more experience, that is what I would do.

You may think of bribes as being made more forthrightly than these two examples. But that is rare. They need to check you out, see how you react. The offer is usually made offhandedly and ambiguously to permit you to refuse it graciously or ignore it altogether and, more importantly for them, to permit the person offering the bribe to deny that any such abhorrent intent ever crossed his impeccably pure mind.

But such offers are not limited to coming at you from those outside of government. The head of the budget office of a state agency disbursing substantial federal funds wanted to help a friend to place his mother-in-law in a state job. He offered to increase a federal grant to our agency if I would create a position and hire this woman. Another agency head agreed to a similar proposal from this same individual and ended up being convicted, losing his job, and serving time. Ironically, the perpetrator won his own lawsuit, defending himself successfully against the charges brought against him.

He made out that the case was nothing but political vindictiveness growing out of bureaucratic displeasure with his rigorous administration of grants.

Of course, the first consequence of accepting a bribe is to compromise yourself. You put yourself at the mercy of those from whom you accept the bribe.

I faced a touchy situation once in the line of my regular duties. I had made suggestions to a board of trustees and a particularly inept president of a community college in a very poor taxing district about how to improve their applications for federal grants. In the next round of competitive grants the college received two large grants for facilities. At the groundbreaking for one of the new buildings I was taken aside by several of the college trustees. They proceeded to thank me profusely for my assistance on the project as they walked me over to a nearby car. They then thanked me for rigging the rankings of their projects in their favor. I denied I had done any such thing and they all smiled. One of them opened the trunk, where there lay four beautiful, expensive shotguns. They wanted me to accept one as an expression of their appreciation for my having given preferential treatment to the funding of their projects. I told them they had been funded on merit and need, not preferential treatment, but they refused to believe me and urged me to accept a personal gift from them.

To this day I believe they genuinely wanted only to thank me, but their local practice and bona fides could not overcome my resistance to accepting a gift for merely doing my government job. They had no idea how they had shocked and offended me, but I tried not to let them see it as I turned down their offer.

When I mentioned the episode to my board chairman later, he laughed it off and then said, "But don't forget they think they owe you one. You may still find a way to use the chit." And he was right. Months later I saw nothing out of line in asking for their help in making a couple of calls on legislators on a bill I was pursuing. But there was a difference. That was not bribery or unlawful; that was at the most a small political favor. The difference was there was no personal gain in it for me. I was pursuing legislation beneficial to all higher education institutions, including the community college they governed.

Another form of compromising public officials can come in the form of offering sexual favors. These are nearly always made even more subtly or indirectly than offers of money. But the purpose is the same—to compromise you.

What is it the Greek philosophers said about the values that mankind pursues? Wealth and pleasure are two of them. And these are the very desires which can become any person's weakness. It's no wonder that bribery works on some people or that sexual favors corrupt others.

And the third human need according to the Greeks, to find fame or honor and prestige, is also something public officials are especially suscep- tible to. This is so because we are social animals. As a prominent public of- ficial you will be flattered and honored. You will be cajoled, kidded, made to feel you're one of the insiders, included among those of stature and sig- nificance, and praised for your dedication and service. They will make it a cozy place to be, somewhere you may very much want to be. And then there will come a time when those of importance and fame and consequence, among whom you have been made to feel a part, request a special favor or privilege or ask you to look the other way on some "minor infraction." Will you be corrupted from your public duty of equal treatment for all? Will you be willing to become the outsider again? And perhaps be despised to boot?

Whatever your greatest personal need and desire is, there will lie your greatest weakness and temptation. Acknowledge what it is you want and de- sire most and take warning from that knowledge. Oscar Wilde's sarcasm was right: There are some temptations it takes great courage to give in to. There will lie the entryway for others to try to use to persuade and influence you in your public trust.

It is no wonder then that the philosophers conclude that the only wor- thy goal is, therefore, not wealth, honor, or pleasure, but to seek the truth. It is not so evanescent as they say it is. To me that means to keep yourself and your personal wants out of the picture and to be governed by your social val- ues and by actions that uphold the principles of our democratic society.

Now I've come close to preaching, something I promised to avoid. So let me end with advice on another approach to persuasion that will be used on you. You will not be able to refuse to meet with people who want to dis- cuss new proposals and plans with you. Often they will use such meetings to discuss a topic in broad, general terms, not coming to specifics or even avoiding them. They may say they merely want your impressions on the di- rection they are headed.

People do this for at least three reasons. First, they are indeed inter- ested in your views and ideas. But the other two reasons are more suspect. If they can get you to agree to their general plans they can extrapolate that into specific proposals that they can later remind you they have already dis- cussed with you and for which they have already gotten your endorsement. The other reason is if they can get your approval or okay from the top, they won't have any subsequent problems with your staff and subordinates and their analyses. If you reach agreements without consulting with your staff, you have not only excluded them from the meeting where you make the agreement, you have excluded them from future involvement as well. There's an old military saying, "When the emperor is in the field, all the generals become privates." Be careful you don't permit this to happen. You will continually have to deal with the efforts of constituents to separate you from your staff and to try to get your approval before you have consulted with your staff.

To be certain you are not misunderstood in these kinds of meetings, you might quote to them Eleanor Roosevelt's comment to Winston Churchill. She said, "You know, Winston, when Franklin says yes, yes, yes, it doesn't mean he agrees with you. It means he's listening." On occasion I have made it clear that when I am nodding my head it means only that I am listening, not that I am agreeing to what my visitors are saying.

Or when the glittering generalities glitter but do little else, you might refer to what the poet Robert Burns said when he was asked what he thought of marriage. He replied, "Show me the woman you're talking about." It may be "politically incorrect," but it does make the point that you want to see specifics before you commit yourself. There are ways to be understood without being disagreeable. Your visitors know very well what they are trying to do, and you sometimes have to tell them you understand what they are up to without offending them.

And you need to learn the price of asking for help from some politicians. Mayor Robert Wagner warned a friend Paul Screvane about dealing with Robert Moses, the great dictator of public works projects in New York City. He said, "Paul, my experience with Moses has taught me one lesson, and I'll tell it to you. I would never let him do anything for me in any way, shape or form. I'd never ask him—or permit him—to do anything of a personal nature for me because—and I've seen it time and time again—a day will come when Bob will reach back in his file and throw this in your face, quietly if that will make you go along with him, publicly otherwise. And if he has to, he will destroy you with it." Good advice to anyone near any proposal that smells of taint.

The chairman of our board is on the phone for the second time and I must go. He has promised something to the governor without checking with his staff—or worse, without conferring with the rest of the board. I will be telling you about working with a board—and with chairmen—next fall when you return. But from the pickle my chairman has gotten himself into I am prompted to give you a last quick bonus lesson to wrap up this year: There are two sides to every argument, and it helps immeasurably to hear them both before committing yourself to the first one presented to you.

You will be taking your exams in the next week or so and then heading out for your summer internship. I will take a break in writing you, but I'll have a letter waiting for you when you return in the fall. Best of luck and good interning.

Your much humbled

Uncle Ken

re: *Relations with a governing board*

Men who always do as they're told do not know what to do when they're not. Without the thoughtful habit of decision, they decide . . . thoughtlessly.
— *Milton Mayer*

Be ashamed to die until you have won some victory for humanity.
— *Horace Mann*

To serve the public faithfully, and at the same time please it entirely is impracticable.
— *Benjamin Franklin proverb*

SEPTEMBER

Dear Kim

Welcome back to another year. I hope your parents have become more reconciled to your commitment to a public service career. I presume you must have told them I am encouraging you in your decision. Why else would they have stopped writing or calling me? Well, on with my aiding and abetting.

There is so much I need to tell you about working with a governing board I hardly know where to begin. So I'll start by telling you about two competitors for the commissioner's job and how they inadvertently helped me with the board that hired me. I knew the vice president of another university desperately wanted the job. I knew she had been hard at work trying to find out who else was after the job. Still, I was entirely taken aback when she called and said, "I have been talking you up and pushing your name for the commissioner's job and it suddenly occurred to me I should check with you first." I began to get the drift. She went on, "So I decided I ought to find out if you really are interested in the job before I push you for it anymore."

If she could be coy, so could I. I said, "Gosh, June, I don't know. What do you think? Should I look at it?" And I got a thirty-minute dissertation on all the reasons why this would be a terrible idea, how it would wreck my career, how it was the wrong job for me, how many enemies I would make, and so on. With friends like her you hardly *need* enemies.

A president of another university who applied for the job never really made any pretense at being my friend. The morning the board interviewed five candidates I was scheduled to be first and I was waiting outside their conference room while the eighteen board members met in private to get organized for their day of interviews. This president stopped in the hallway long enough to say to me, "I don't understand why you even applied for this job. You're not strong enough for it. But I guess doing the interview will be good experience for you." Then he turned on his heel and went straight into the board meeting without knocking.

In a few moments the chairman came out and said, "Arleigh has another appointment and he's asked if we can put him on first. I hope you don't mind."

I told him to call my room upstairs in the hotel when they were ready for me. As I sat waiting for the call, I said to myself, "Arleigh's down there right now telling them I'm not strong enough for this job."

Sure enough, the very first question was from a woman member, "What makes you think you're tough enough for this job?"

I replied, "The real test of this job is to *win*, not to look like you're tough. You know from your own experience with presidents, as I do, that they all have huge egos. They're used to having their own way and doing things on their own schedule. The trick is to win every fight you possibly can and then back off and let them save face. There's no need to antagonize them unnecessarily for the next fight." I could thank my good counselor, Arleigh, for warning me to prepare for that question. The chairman told me later that this first answer I gave to the board got me the job.

At the end of the interview the board asked me how I planned to work with them. I said I knew that I would need to have a recommendation and to take a position on every issue they would face. I told them I would never lay a problem before them without an analysis and a recommendation for a solution. I said, "I think it is my job to bring you the toughest position I can defend and to document my recommendation on every issue. You may want to soften my recommendation or modify it sometimes, but if I bring you weak positions, you can't toughen them up because you won't have the research staff and the data I will have." Then I ended on a light note, which I meant for them to consider seriously. I told them I hoped they wouldn't soften my recommendations too often because I might come to read that as a message that they wanted me to start bringing them softer positions.

A couple of years later one of the presidents asked me if I knew why so many presidents had supported me for the commissioner's job. I said it had to be the poor quality of the competition. He said, "Well, there's that. But we'd known you for ten years as a mild-mannered, soft-spoken, easygoing guy. We figured if we couldn't persuade you, we'd run over you or go around you to your board. Now, to a person, we all think you're the meanest son of a bitch we ever met."

He was kidding—I think. They beat me regularly with the legislature and with my board. Bill Johnson, one of our better presidents, appeared one day with a hang-dog look and an unaccustomed slouch in his stride. I asked what was wrong and he replied, "For the first time in thirteen years my board voted against a recommendation I took to them."

I couldn't help but laugh. I pointed out that my board overrules me at least four times a year and sometimes more. My view has always been, besides bringing the toughest position I can defend to the board, that I need to test the board's willingness to move into new policy areas. Sometimes board members will say, "By god, it's time we drew a line in the sand on that," or perhaps, "Bring us a hard recommendation on that." Then when I bring them my proposal and they hear the opposition to it, the board will sometimes say, "We didn't mean *there* is the sand," or, "Not *that* hard a recommendation." They often act as though that is the ugliest baby they've ever seen and deny paternity. But they more often modify my policy positions than rejecting them out of hand because they recall that they have asked that something be done on the issue.

It is by testing a board or commission, even while getting overruled from time to time, that you can move policy toward where you feel it needs to be. And times change and major shifts are sometimes needed even though the easy thing would be to leave everything unchanged. One such shift in higher education occurred across the country in the mid and late 1970s. For the previous two decades and more, higher education had been continuously expanding. First it had been the veterans using the GI Bill, and by the 1960s it was the baby boomers going to college. Expansion was not just a need, it became a habit of behavior. Everybody was marching in ranks in the same parade to enlarge colleges and universities and add degree programs and faculty and research and buildings. All were in step, the governors, the legislators, the presidents and their trustees, the public and businesses, and the state agencies established to coordinate the growth of higher education.

Then among the first to break ranks were the higher education coordinating agencies. They could see the slowdown in college-age students coming along in the pipeline. Others saw it too, but these higher education coordinating agencies *talked* about it and began to shape public policy to address the coming change. They were about as popular as the family bastard at the reading of the will. Responsible coordinating boards tried to slow down the parade or take it down a side street. In the context of the times there were many battles because the slowdown was painful. Unproductive activities had to be discontinued as a condition for starting something new. It was no longer possible to ignore some earlier effort that was failing and merely leave it in place and try out something new. Habitual and easy-to-do, add-on planning had to give way to substitutive planning, which required setting priorities and making hard choices. Aspirations had to be nipped, ambitions frustrated.

But enough history. The point is this: In whatever field you work there will be times when existing policies will need to be reconsidered and fought over. The old debenture holders and coupon clippers of the status quo will object. As an agency head, it will be your fate and duty to be defeated from time to time as you push to redirect policies.

You are not an official member of your board, yet you are the most important member of your board. You are a part of the staff, yet you are more than a member of the staff. At board meetings and in discussions with members, your views, your position, your voice will often have more import than any other member of the board. As the agency head you will lose the privilege of not having a position on every issue. In looking at any issue they at least start from where you tell them to begin. You can reason but you can't make a motion, you can argue but you can't decide, you can persuade but you can't vote. You are first among unequals. You have influence but you can be overruled, given instructions, handed assignments—and replaced.

As part of the staff, you present and represent staff findings to the board. But while your board considers you separate from your staff, they will judge you by the quality of your staff. In your position between the board and your staff you are the principal "reader" of your board and interpreter of the board to your staff.

Your board expects you to lead them. Your staff expects you to lead them. You are in the opportune position to do both. To sit still, to be satisfied with the status quo, to be only responsive to outside pressures is to fail in both these expectations and duties. As I have said in earlier letters, inherent in any effort to lead is the need to have others follow you. That requires instilling in potential followers confidence and trust in you and an understanding of where you are taking those who consider following you. A prerequisite to this will be your ability to communicate to both your board and your staff your vision on each issue and on the mission of the agency as a whole.

One of my colleagues who held a position similar to mine in another state took an unusual view of his job. He asked his staff to develop recommendations to their board on critical issues before them and he had his staff present their recommendations. He would sit with the board and decide whether to support or oppose his staff's recommendations, depending on how he felt his board was leaning. Earlier I described the agency head as between the board and staff and being part of both. This man was definitely between his board and staff but was of neither. Surprisingly he survived almost two years. And then, alas, he moved on to a job to train and prepare mid-career government employees for advancement. In universities we have a saying: When old deans lose their faculties they can at least serve as bad examples.

The understanding of respective roles is not always clear to everybody. A newly appointed board member was inordinately interested in how we developed our recommendations to the board before each board meeting. After I had been through our procedures in increasing detail to address what I thought were his concerns about thoroughness and research, he got to his point. "No," he said finally, "what I want to know is when do *I*, as a board member, get to go over your recommendations and put in *my* preferences and changes before you send your recommendation to the board."

Now, stop right here and think about how you would respond to him. Ready? Now I will tell you what I said.

Very gently I encouraged him to call me on any issue we are considering and to feel free to let me know how he feels. But I explained that the board has always made clear to me that they want my own unadulterated views and recommendations. They pay me for my expertise and respect me for my independence. I explained that the board feels it can then, in open meeting, with all members participating, discuss my position and then accept it, reject it, or modify it. I also gently explained that the board does not want me to try to find out how eighteen members feel about an issue before I develop my recommendations. I told him the board does not want me to bring them a mishmash of what I think is the way all the members feel about the matter. He said, not too enthusiastically, that he could work with that but it was not the way two other public boards he had served on did their business. Not good news, in my view, for how some agencies conduct public business.

There will, of course, be occasions where the board will appoint a special committee to look into a specific topic and bring a committee recommendation to the full board. In such cases you will need to offer to staff the committee and help them present their own recommendations. You might also be prepared to be asked by the full board if you agree or not with the special committee report. Unless it is a really important issue on which you feel you must part company with the board, in such cases it is advisable to stand by the committee findings and recommendation as closely as you can. But unless the committee is very partisan, single-issue focused, or at open odds with the agency head, this should not be a problem. Even if you can't appoint the committee, you should offer to do the staff work and supporting studies for the committee. Remember the old advice on having your way: Call the meeting, prepare the agenda, write the minutes, publish the recommendations. It doesn't always work, but it sure beats being left entirely out of the loop.

Staff relations with your board are worth looking at. Your best staff will also be reading your board with you and trying to figure out where the board might be led or where they might be leading or where the members are saying they want the agency to go. You are all reading the board to try to see if they are dissatisfied with the advice and direction they are getting from you and the staff. Your staff will watch with special interest how you and your board accommodate to each other.

You may find a staff member occasionally who decides he can help you in your relations with the board by tempering his staff work and recommendation to favor what he reads as board preferences. There are a number of dangers to you in permitting this to happen with a staff member. You are not getting his full and unadulterated analysis and recommendations. Second, he may very well be reading the board differently than you. Third, something I said earlier about my first interview with the board applies to you and your staff as well. Your staff has the data and has done the research and it is harder for you to toughen up a soft position they give you, based on your more limited command of the data and findings, than for you to temper or ameliorate a tough position the staff brings to you. So you want your staff's toughest analysis and recommendations. And fourth, you may prefer to take a recommendation to the board that flies in the face of palpable board preferences. That is, you might prefer to get shot down on a particular position with the board than to accommodate to their apparent predisposition. You may be playing to a minority group on the board whose position you respect or whose support you need on something else. You may feel any softening of your position will erode your credibility on a broader issue or with a constituency you feel is more important at the moment than the favor of your board on this one topic. You may be staking out a position for the future even if you lose for now. You may prefer to take a position to your board and have them modify it to where you know they will come down than to take that position to your board in the first place. It rarely hurts you to appear tougher than your board.

Your staff cannot know these things and it is dangerous to let a staff person jump to conclusions and try to pander to the board. Just as there are certain political considerations your board may take into account when they modify your recommendations because they operate in a different political arena, there are your own considerations you will need to exercise in evaluating your staff's recommendations. Just as you should not very often exercise the prerogatives of your board in making your recommendations to them, your staff should not be permitted to preempt your privileges as the head of the agency in relation to your board.

There are agency heads who hold a very tight grip on their position of standing between the board and the staff. They insist on being the hole in the hourglass; nothing flows from either compartment to the other without passing by him or her. Another label for that approach could be called "bottleneck control." This approach is followed by those who fear that someone below them on the staff might build a special board alliance that could lead to his being undercut in authority or even displaced by the subordinate. Someone else on the staff might begin to look too good. Remember what I said in my third letter about second-class people hiring third-class people and their fear of having people around them who cast shadows? People who are control freaks about communications with the board usually lack complete self-confidence.

Personally my approach to this question has been ruled by my own way of dealing with staff expertise. I prefer to talk directly to the person who has done the research on the topic I'm concerned about than to have that person's work filtered to me through several levels of intervening supervisors. I've often had to say to such a subordinate after a consultation, "Now, be sure to tell your boss I've been down here talking to you about this."

If it works for me, it should work for board members. I have always encouraged board members to talk with anyone on my staff without asking or telling me about it. This is a point I make when I orient every new board member. However, I do expect my staff to inform me if they have been working with a board member. And if there is a follow-up required or an assignment of work proposed, I ask that the response to the board member usually be made through me—or with a copy shown to me, just to keep work assignments under control and to let board members know that I am in the loop.

In all my years I have had only two disloyal subordinates who tried to build a personal base with the board in hopes of succeeding me. Very quickly several board members told me what was up. As you might guess, I encouraged them both to find another position. But I did watch a chancellor be undercut by a scheming deputy, who orchestrated their board and the demise of his boss in order to succeed him. This usually takes more collusion than can be kept secret unless the top person is already in some disfavor with the board.

There's lots more I need to tell you about what it will be like working with your board, but let me finish for now on what I've been talking about—dealing with recommendations and your board. When you stake out a position on an issue, remember the mother-in-law's advice on disciplining children, "Start out like you can hold out." You are in a position of selling, persuading, and negotiating. You hope your board will buy your plan as you lay it out, and you have to persuade them to do so. But if they won't buy it whole-hog, you will need to sell what you can and salvage as much as possible as they formulate and set agency policy.

In the beginning I used to feel sorry for some board members as they anguished over some unpleasant choice I was forcing them to make. During the break or in a social setting I made a mistake, maybe twice or three times before I caught on. (But, hey, I never said I was a fast learner.) In sympathizing with them in reaching a difficult decision I left the impression that a slightly softer position might be acceptable. This was definitely *not* of help to the board members. It only confused them. Or made them angry about why I was putting them through this distress if an easier choice had been acceptable to me from the outset or was an adequate response to the problem we were dealing with. Why hadn't I just said so and saved them all this discomfort? If a softer position was okay with me, why was I defending this one with such vigor? From those early mistakes I have learned to feel no remorse in the cruelty I inflict on board members by posing difficult and painful choices. Nobody promised them a rose garden when they signed on.

Let me take you to a board meeting now and show you how a controversial recommendation can play out. Let's say for two years we have been administering a test to all entering freshmen to determine their academic readiness to do college level work. We started out with standards that were far below the level that would be expected of entering freshmen nationally or abroad. We did this because we did not want to flunk an exceptionally large portion of the entering classes just because they were testing far below the expected skills they needed for college. We knew there would be serious political consequences if we started out too severely. Another purpose of the test was to identify those students who would be required to take remedial classes in the areas they failed, and if our standard was too high the cost of those basic classes would become exorbitant, an outcome that also would have political consequences.

But now, after two years of experience with the program, we are recommending that our board begin to ratchet up the required minimum standard for passage so that our entering students will be more competitive with students in other states and workers elsewhere in the world. Our arguments are that our present passing standards are so low as to be an embarrassment. Our students are eventually going to have to meet a higher standard in the marketplace to compete economically with workers in other countries. With such low standards we are sending a message to the high schools and the students that they do not have to take hard courses or study hard in order to pass the test that says they are ready for college. With such low standards we are also neglecting to upgrade the skills of large numbers of students who ought to be taking some remedial courses, that is, those who can't do real college level work but yet can get by the present low standards of our test. Many of these students will continue to do poorly in college and large numbers of them will continue to flunk out if we don't identify and correct their deficiencies.

Consequently, our recommendation is to raise the standards, and we reveal to the board and the public the probable results in terms of numbers and percentages of students who will fail the tougher test if the board raises the required performance as recommended. We also show the impact on students by race and ethnicity.

During testimony we hear from minority groups who object to the disproportionate effect of the test on their young people. We hear from business people who want tougher standards, who want college degrees and high school diplomas to mean something in terms of certifying minimum learning and skills. We hear from mathematics faculty members who complain that even the new standard will not require competence in basic algebra or geometry. We hear a rebuttal that the higher failure rate of minority students is not a criticism of the colleges but is a condemnation of the lower funding level for the state's predominantly minority school districts. We hear a proposal that the high costs of remediation should be billed to the school districts sending the colleges unprepared students. We listen to a group that says the test, intended to improve retention, is actually discouraging minority students who enter college and then are told they not prepared to do college level work. We hear from a legislator who accuses us of having decided we want to fail 25,000 more students and we have intentionally set the new standard to do that. And on and on. The board listens and considers and agonizes over the options I have put before them.

This is only one case but it illustrates the tough choices and decisions a public board has to make. In a situation like this, and you will be in many, you will need to deal with the delicate balance between not weakening your position and recommendation too early in the deliberations and watching for the point where you will need to start helping your board fashion and shape an alternative to your recommendation. If the board hangs tough and appears ready to adopt your recommendation, you have only to stay your course. Or very often the board can find its own way to an acceptable compromise position through an amendment or two. But in some situations you will begin to see that the board is either going to reject your position in toto or they want to try to find another different way out of the mess you have put them into. If you sit there and continue to be uncompromising and stand by your recommendation, at some point the board will leave you on the sidelines and design its own solution. When the board undertakes to do this they are about to embark on a time-consuming process in most cases because they will have to find their way to agreement without staff support and advice. And if you stay intransigent in your position, who knows where they may end up?

At some point, which you will have to learn to sense, you need to begin to help the board to formulate its consensus. If you do this well you can still gain something toward the goal you set out to reach, even if it is not everything you sought. You might hand a note to a member with a suggested motion or amendment. Or you might suggest a solution to the chair that he or she can propose to the board to see if it is acceptable. Or you might ask the chair to direct the staff to work during a break or over lunch or overnight, perhaps with a couple of board members, to bring back a new proposal based on the sense of the board discussion. Or if the board is at a complete impasse, you may want the topic referred back to the staff for a rework for the next meeting. You might need to suggest a motion to table the matter. The point is that even when your board won't accept a staff recommendation, you are still their staff and you need to continue to try to help them reach decisions and keep the agenda moving.

You will quickly encounter another consequence of your helping your board to find a new position different from your recommendation. Those in the audience who strongly support your original recommendation will very often see you a traitor to their position. They will feel betrayed because you have abandoned them and are now working with your board to settle for less than your original recommendation. Not being where you are and not being aware that it is better to achieve something incrementally in the right direction on the policy issue than nothing at all or something totally unpredictable, they can become very critical of what you have done. Why did they bother to come and support your position if you are just going to abandon them when the going gets tough?

One of my new chairmen called me to his office one day soon after his appointment and said he had been visited by a delegation of college presidents complaining about me. He said they accused me of differing with them too often, fighting too hard to defend my positions, and winning the board's support too much of the time. My new chairman wanted to know how I would respond. I pointed out they disagreed with me exactly as many times as I disagreed with them. On the second point I said that I fought hard only on the issues that I didn't negotiate away to the schools over the phone or in my office. I pointed out that the board expected me to settle at the staff level as many problems and requests as I legitimately could under authority delegated to me and to bring to the board only those problems I couldn't agree to or reach a settlement on at the staff level. I explained that this meant that what I couldn't agree to I had to fight about before the board and make my case against that presented by the universities involved. And if I wasn't going to fight hard in that confrontation before the board, then why not just give it away at the staff level? How could they expect me to fight half-heartedly about something I didn't have to fight about at all if I felt only half-hearted about it? On the last point, that the board supported me too much of the time, I said I thought the presidents were actually criticizing the board and not me. The chairman laughed and said he had just listened to their side; he merely wanted to hear mine.

So I've ended where I started: Always take your board the toughest position you can support and let them deal with it. At the same time, don't fall on your sword on every recommendation you make. Learn to back off. Learn to take what you can get and don't fight for the whole loaf when your board is drifting away from you. You will come to understand that the making of public policy is the result of the board and you working together. If it were acceptable in our democracy that each public policy should be set as you alone recommend it, then there would be no need for your board. But if you hold very tenaciously to that view, your board may come to find there is no need for *you*. So get used to compromising and making incremental gains. And get used to losing.

This brings me to my last thought at this writing. When you win, don't gloat. When you lose, bleed profusely. By that I mean study the wounds of your losses closely. Why did you lose? What can you learn from it? What would you do differently? What long-term loss, if any, did you suffer? Did you maintain grace under fire? Are you still credible? Are you still respected? Did you lose graciously? You will learn far more from your losses and defeats than from your wins and victories. This is because we rarely examine our victories; we feel exuberant and then move on.

But when thinking on the lessons of your defeats and mistakes, you might wish to recall the exchange between an interviewer and the football coach of the University of Texas. It went like this:

Cactus Pryor: "Coach, you came from Oklahoma, you are our savior, the Messiah who was going to lead us out of losses, but you've lost three consecutive years to your alma mater, Oklahoma. How do you feel about this?"

Darrell Royal: "You know, I've been thinking about that. Looking for solace. And I've turned to the words of Oliver Wendell Holmes, who said, 'As I look back on my life, I value my mistakes more than my victories, because I learned more from my mistakes, my defeats, than I did from my victories. My defeats were more to my advantage than my victories.' You know, I've been thinking about those words of Oliver Wendell Holmes, and I'd just like to say: 'Piss on Oliver Wendell Holmes.'"

Many of my colleagues suffer deeply and inconsolably because they can't make everybody happy in their decisions, or because not everybody likes them. Some get ulcers or get sick over the continual conflicts and confrontations and unpleasantness. They sometimes feel if they were only a little more creative and effective they could find solutions that everyone could agree to. Remember my version of Murphy's Law: "Any solution devised to please everyone will be objectionable to somebody." Some even feel they are to blame for the problems they are dealing with. Some quit. Their biggest problem is they don't understand the nature of these kinds of jobs. We are not put here to make everybody happy or have people like us. We take these jobs to try to find what is right for the people and to establish and administer public policies.

Your grandmother was wrong. The secret to success in this world is not to make people like you.

Your oft-besmirched antecedent,

Uncle Ken

re: *More on governing boards*

You cannot order people to think. You cannot order people to cooperate. People have to want to do these things.

— Admiral Arleigh Burke

The truth that is suppressed by friends is the readiest weapon of an enemy.

— Robert Louis Stevenson

If I agree with you, it's administration; if I disagree, it's policy.

— A board member's comment

OCTOBER

Dear Kim

As I said in my last letter, there is more I need to tell you about working with a board or commission. So I'll get right to it.

When you get some new members to your governing body, try to meet with them one on one. Go to where they live, visit them in their offices if you can. Get them to tell you about themselves and their interests and what they value most. This will help you to understand them, and by going to them, not having them come to you, you also show them the respect they are entitled to. Let them know you want to meet with them alone to permit them to ask you any questions they might not feel comfortable asking in a group as new board members. Most new board members are a little intimidated as they come on a board that has more seasoned members. They will appreciate the chance to talk with someone privately about the responsibilities they will assume.

I have never failed to learn valuable things about my board members by doing this. One member told me a story over dinner about her family that she later wrote into a book at my urging. Her father, at the age of two, had run out into the streets of New York City when his father was murdered. He was lost, and since his father had just brought him from Germany and he spoke no English, the police could not locate his family. Consequently, he was raised in an orphanage and moved to Texas when a teenager. He had nearly grown children when a colleague sorting mail with him on a train suggested he run an ad in a Chicago German-American newspaper about his childhood. I had goose bumps when my board member told me how an elderly lady in Indiana opened the paper one day and exclaimed, "Ach, Himmel, I think we have found Otto."

Your first goal with new board members is to gain their trust. You will recall how I told you that I had underestimated the educability of a bloc of new members whom the governor had appointed with instructions to fire me. Perhaps equal to their ability to learn was the trust they grew to have in my staff and me. I've sort of been guided by a categorical imperative: Never treat another human being as a means to an end but always as an end in himself. (Kant said something close to that.) I have found that if I always respect my board members, they will rarely if ever use me or abuse my staff or me. And a byproduct of this is that when an occasional member does attempt to abuse me in any way, the other members quickly discipline that member and let him know he is out of line.

You might ask, "But where does this disciplining take place?" It is extremely important for you and your chairman to arrange your board meetings so that there is time for the members to get to know each other socially and to know each other's spouses, if possible. They cannot get to know each other exclusively through board meetings, for conducting business and making difficult choices and disagreeing with their colleagues in public are not conducive to coming to work together effectively. There needs to be a bonding, a sharing of common interests and backgrounds, a building of a common view of where they are going in shaping public policy issues. The socializing of all members and the disciplining of errant members get done very subtly in these social gatherings, ranging from frank comments to the degree of warmth or coolness shown by colleagues to each other. I've seen board members turn away from a conversation when a member who is out of line walks up. Or they may show their distaste by sitting at a different table at dinner. Or they will not include the member in the kidding and joshing that takes place socially or during board meetings. Or such kidding as does occur becomes sarcastic, tough, and unkind. I have seen these kinds of treatment bring troublesome members into line. They want to be accepted as part of the group and the board as a whole can bring most aberrant members into line with the way the bulk of the members prefer to do their business. I have seen it work often, and I don't know who is the happier when the errant member comes into line with accepted behavior—the individual member or the rest of the board.

One member came on our board for the specific purpose of obtaining a new nursing program for the college in his city. He set out at his second meeting to present to the board the case against the staff's recommendation for denial of the request. He orchestrated the testimony of the city fathers and the college representatives and he spoke at length himself. Then after his presentation he confidently made a substitute motion to reject the staff position and to approve the new proposal. The board had listened politely for a couple of hours, even asking a few questions, but when he made his motion, they let it fail for lack of a second. I thought it was excessively cruel of the board not even to give this motion by a new member a vote. But they were sending a tough message. The new member was a quick learner and he set out afresh to gain the respect and camaraderie of his colleagues on the board. And within a year he was fully accepted and liked. But he never got his nursing program—nor did he again propose it.

I witnessed one member put his arm across the shoulders of a colleague during a social hour and say, "Why don't you let me make the motion tomorrow to approve that new building at your alma mater. That way people won't think you're on this board just to look after the business of your school." The new member got the point and thereafter went out of his way to take a more statewide view of the board's work. Of course, some just never learn or remain obtuse even though the other members continue to work on them.

Odds are that you will get a real turkey on your board from time to time. Turkeys take many forms. One common variety is a member who may be smart but just can't effectively relate to the rest of the board, the board's constituents, or the staff. A German general named Schlieffen once said in his experience there are four kinds of officers: category I, bright and ambitious, an able officer but possibly dangerous politically; category II, stupid and lazy, a harmless officer all around, the kind that fills most of the ranks; category III, bright and lazy, the best officer because he will find the easiest way to do the job and yet create no political problems; and category IV, stupid and ambitious, the most dangerous officer of all. This last one will get into everything and can wreck an organization.

I'm not saying turkeys are stupid nor that one can wreck a board, but when you get one you'll find he or she can really make life difficult for everybody. They tend to think they know more than the other members and the staff and they point this out to everyone as often as they can. They sometimes alienate the public you deal with because a turkey shows an inborn suspicion that there is some hidden motive behind every constituent issue brought before the board. Turkeys may be perceptive and work to master the subject matter of the agency, but they tend to have an uncanny ability to be abrasive in how they ask questions and in the way they constantly imply that only they are capable of really understanding the difficult issues at stake. It will not take you long to recognize a turkey when he or she appears. He quickly makes himself known by his call. And his plumage is not meant for concealment. If he is to be brought into line, the board will have to do it. I can't give you much advice on how to deal with turkeys. Be nice and be tolerant. This too shall pass. The really sad thing about turkeys is that they sometimes have good ideas and recommendations, but they somehow just don't connect well with other people. They alienate everybody so often that they run into opposition even with their good proposals.

Another kind of board member who is particularly difficult to deal with is one who takes personal credit for actions of the board. We had a member who used his committee chairmanship to claim credit with universities for each of the items the board acted on coming out of his committee. Without anyone on the board knowing about it, he was making clear to the universities that they needed to be nice to him and treat him well since they would have items coming to the board through his committee. By the time we discovered what he was doing he had enticed two universities into making him an honorary alumnus and another had bestowed a very special recognition upon him. The board chair reprimanded him for the way he was misusing his authority, and he may have tempered his behavior but he did not entirely stop. He had to be removed from his committee chairmanship.

If the chairman, on the other hand, is the member getting out of line, that will be a more serious problem for you. He may become overbearing or dictatorial or take positions for the agency without consulting with other members or by capriciously setting meeting dates or agendas or bullying other members. He may have his own "enemies" and "friends" lists that he works with. Such a situation can become very touchy, and if the other members will not confront the chairman about his misuse of authority or his dominating the board too strongly, there is very little you can do about it as the board's "hired hand." You will know from body language, facial expressions, or voting patterns which members are most upset with the actions of such a chairman. You may have to ask one of them to put together a group to meet privately with the chair.

Our board once had a chairman who was so obstreperous, vindictive, and troublesome that the universities went to the legislature to complain vigorously. Fortunately his obnoxious behavior became apparent early in his chairmanship, and his gubernatorial appointment was rejected for confirmation by the Senate. When the legislature adjourned he had the audacity to go to the governor and say, "If you will reappoint me chairman now, the legislature won't be back for over a year and I can fix all those sons of bitches who got me busted."

There was one occasion when my chair and I parted company in a board meeting and there was no time for me to arrange for help from the rest of the board. I believe what happened was as big a surprise to many of the other members as it was to me. This conflict occurred in those years when inflation was running in double digits. We had determined that faculty salaries in the state had eroded by over thirty percent in the previous several years. Consequently, I recommended that our board send a request to the legislature for a twenty percent increase in faculty salaries for the next biennium. The day before my chair's surprise move, our salary recommendation had passed by a vote of eleven to four. But unknown to me, overnight the governor and his aides had been on the phones to our members objecting to this level of increase. On the day of our board meeting when we arrived at this item, which had so easily passed the day before, most everyone in our audience of university presidents expected it to move quickly to final adoption. But after the committee's motion from the day before was on the floor for approval, the chair handed the gavel to the vice chair and made a substitute motion for an *eight* percent increase in faculty salaries and vigorously urged its adoption.

I had about 30 seconds to decide what to do, and I asked to speak against my chairman's motion. It failed eight to seven. Then the action of the previous day also passed by the same one-vote margin. You might understand why I was unpopular with this governor—and this chair.

One of the most difficult situations an agency head can face is constant intrusion by the board into administrative matters. Some board members simply do not feel there is any area of agency business that they are not free to interject their opinions and preferences into. For example, I have been told whom to hire, whom I should fire, where I should cut the budget, how I should make assignments of staff time, what appointments I should make to committees advisory to me, and even how to reconfigure space. But fortunately these were not *board* directions but suggestions from individual members. Several such directions were from a chairman and instructions from a chair are a little more difficult to deal with.

However, compared to many college and university boards of regents, my board was quite self-disciplined in maintaining distinctions between policy and administrative matters. College and university trustees and regents tend to get into details such as building design and decorations, which architect to hire, what kind of fiber optics should be used on campus, degree program content, faculty hiring and tenure appointments, the priority of athletic facilities over academic buildings, and all sorts of details in student services, bookstore administration, food service contracts, and parking arrangements. Former alumni on a board often want to keep the campus the way it was when they were there or remake it into an earlier, usually illusory and imaginary, memory from the past.

Our agency was asked several times over the years to hold orientation and training conferences for boards of regents and trustees to help them, among other things, to recognize the difference between administration and policymaking. At one such conference we brought in a long-serving regent and business executive to talk with the regents about what they ought to stay out of and leave to the administrators and how they should better spend their time on real policy issues. The speaker drilled away at this topic relentlessly and we were pleased to see six of the nine members of one particularly interfering board sitting in a row listening intently. At the end the speaker said, "But I know there may be some of you who feel I have overstated the case. . . ."

As if on cue, the six in a row all nodded in unison. At the end of the meeting one of those six regents, a former speaker of the House, who was most egregious in his encroachment upon the authority of his president, approached our board chair and said, "I am so glad I came to this meeting. Everything I have heard here underscores the way I conduct myself as a regent." So much for the educability of regents. (You might also refer to T. V. Smith's discovery described in my letter last January.)

I have had my own share of fights over keeping board members out of my prerogatives to manage the agency. Perhaps an example will give you a feel for what it can be like. One of my chairs was especially insistent that we cut the size of our agency to comply with the directives of the new governor and his budget director. Over several months I managed, with great difficulty, to eliminate ten percent of our positions, primarily by eliminating a federally funded program and several state-supported positions related to it. But the cuts hurt and we were very tight in staffing to cover the duties assigned to the agency. Then as I began putting together my operating budget for the next year, the chair was constantly after me to cut ten more positions from the agency budget. I kept explaining that I could not do that without harming the effectiveness of the agency. She kept insisting. Finally she called a meeting with the vice chair and me a couple of weeks before our next board meeting. I thought I knew what was coming so I invited one of my assistant commissioners to sit in with us. I thought it useful to have a witness.

At the meeting the chair again insisted that I cut ten more positions from our budget before I submitted it to the board for approval. I again explained that I could not in good faith do that. She then said, "You aren't listening to me. This is not a request. It is an order. I am telling you to cut ten more positions." I explained that the budget we were discussing was *my* budget, not yet the board's budget, and that I would present my budget to the board at the next meeting. At that time the board would adopt some kind of budget, mine or a modification of it. Then it would be my duty to administer the board's budget for the agency or to choose to leave. She again said she was directing me to send a budget to the board with ten fewer positions in it.

At that point I said, "If I had known how important it is to the board to take credit with the governor for cutting positions in our budget I would not have cut the sixteen positions I have eliminated. I would have talked with the board and let you direct me to do it." With that, she got up and told the vice chair to come with her. As he left, the vice chair told me to calm down, that all of this could be worked out. My assistant commissioner was pale, sitting stunned in his chair.

As they closed the door he said, "I've never seen anything like that. Do you realize what you just said?" I said I did; I had thought long and hard about it the night before. Then he asked me what I thought they would do. I said, "Go to see the governor—and wait until he has six more appointees to this board and then cut the budget." Incidentally, at the board meeting two weeks later my budget was adopted in the form I submitted it.

When a former governor agreed to accept the chairmanship of the board, it gave our agency a strong endorsement and raised our visibility. At the first meeting after Governor Preston Smith took over as chair of our board, we were working our way through a long agenda. Then on a matter dealing with his alma mater he called for a voice vote. There were audibly only two ayes and a dozen or more nays. He banged the gavel and declared, "The ayes have it."

There were gasps and a stunned silence, and in the weeks ahead there was much grousing about this vote to me and among the members. Governor Smith asked me one day, "Why didn't the board call my hand on that voice vote at the meeting? I was really surprised they didn't." I explained that the members had told me they would never let him get away with that again, but they let this one pass out of respect for him as former governor. They said they did not want to embarrass him at his first meeting as chairman. Governor Smith replied, "They wouldn't have embarrassed me. I would have called for a show of hands and then I would've said, 'It looks like somebody changed his vote.'"

For a while I worked with a deputy chancellor—and later chancellor—whose style was to try to co-opt every new member appointed to his board of regents for his own uses as quickly as he could. He would fawn over them, call them frequently, and try to identify some special thing each new member wanted and then find ways to give it to him or her. I've mentioned before that identifying the wants and desires of others and fulfilling those needs is one way a leader develops followers. But the kinds of wants and desires this man was trying to find were not public objectives, academic goals, or principles or abstractions related to the universities' advancement—the kinds of wants that a true leader attempts to satisfy. He was looking for special favors he could do for his regents to make them beholden to him, little projects, short-term undertakings. And he usually found them. I recall once a new member said he would like to create several special fellowships in his own field of study at one of the medical schools. I was greatly surprised that the chancellor, who oversaw billions of dollars of investments, did not immediately agree to pursue such a modest request. But instead he said he would have to look into it. It would be very difficult but he would see what he could do.

At the next board meeting the chancellor took the member aside and said, "I have looked everywhere to find funds for those fellowships you asked about. It took some creative accounting but I managed to scrape together $150,000 to do this for you." The regent expressed eternal gratitude. This paltry amount had bought the regent and the chancellor what they each wanted. This chancellor was forever looking for ways to bolster his own position and to extend his power and control, and he relied heavily on the regents for this purpose.

This approach of co-opting members can be dangerous. One day I received a call from a former regent who had been replaced by the governor the previous month when his term ran out. The regent thanked me graciously for taking his call and said, "Don won't return my calls. He kissed my hand for six years and now he can't find ten minutes for me. I'm not going to forget this." And then he joked and added the old Australian adage, "One day a peacock, the next day a feather duster." In time, that chancellor was pushed out by his board. But since he had earlier worked so assiduously with a group of regents to force out his predecessor in order to succeed him, it seemed fitting. Live by the sword, die by the sword.

Now I am going to tell you the most important thing I have learned about working with a board. Typically, board members are treated by agency heads as a sounding board and as a group to provide oversight and to monitor the agency. Many executives keep their boards informed but they use their boards to set policies and make decisions only so far as the law says they must. Some executives even go so far as to keep as much as they can away from the board or they obfuscate the topics they must take to the board. A subtle message is sent that the principal job of the board is to support its executive officer and to trust him or her to do the right thing.

One board member unhappy with such treatment repeated the old adage, "He treats us like mushrooms. He keeps us in the dark and periodically covers us with shit."

A typical board meeting under these circumstances consists of reports, presentations by the agency head and his staff, and action items laid out and described by the agency head and his staff. Although avowed to keep the board informed, such meetings are in reality not even very informative. Most of all they are boring. Board participation is curtailed. Initiative rests almost entirely with the executive. Attendance becomes poor.

From my experience a far better approach is to work with the chair to organize the board into committees to cover all its areas of responsibility. The chair of each of these committees then should preside over the board while it meets as a committee of the whole for his or her committee. Under such an arrangement each chair then will present the agenda items to the board and present supporting material, which is usually prepared by the staff, whether reports, findings, or recommendations for action. Staff members assigned to work with each chair may be called on by the committee chair to assist in presenting the reports and recommendations. The important point is that the chair of each committee conducts the business and takes the votes on items before his committee.

Following all of the committee meetings, the board can then come back together under the board chairman's direction to receive the committee reports on which the board members have already acted in order to take formal and final board action on each of the agenda items. Our board always takes the final votes the following day. A consent calendar on each committee's work can be used to avoid having to go back through each committee's materials item by item. To be certain that no board member feels actions are being rammed through to a final vote at the formal board meeting, any item on any committee's consent calendar may be made subject to additional discussion at the request of any one member of the board.

Consider the dynamics at work under this approach. First, rather than one chair, the board has in addition to the board chairman as many additional chairs as there are committees, and these chairs actually have a chance to preside, to perform, to take votes. Second, no committee chair will want to be embarrassed in making a presentation so he will master the material he must present and preside over. Third, as a result, he will closely scrutinize the staff material and position on each item before his committee from the point of view of what he knows about how the other board members feel. The staff gains an early review of its recommendations from an influential board member. Fourth, the other board members will very often give more credence to a colleague's presentation and the position she advocates than to one laid out by a staff person. Fifth, board members love to show off for each other. It is natural to want to look good and to want to participate rather than sit and listen and be talked at. Sixth, this approach will turn a quiescent and passive board into a true working board that is involved in the development as well as the presentation of materials and recommendations. Finally, every item gets thoroughly discussed to everyone's satisfaction since any item acted upon in the committees can be reopened for further discussion and reconsideration with the replay when the board chair convenes the formal board meeting for committee reports and motions. Staff and board relationships under such an approach become a two-way street, and the staff receives quick feedback and suggestions from the board on agency business.

Odds are that in the different jobs you hold you will only have a board or commission to govern your activities in a few of them. But what I have described is highly transferable to other settings. For example, you will certainly want to use advisory committees from time to time. Such advisory boards or committees are notorious for their poor attendance and participation. The approach I have laid out on how to get them involved will make them much more effective. Incidentally, creating a strong and active advisory committee is an effective way to draw attention to your program with your bosses and governing bodies above you. Advisory committee members can get an audience for your ideas that you often cannot and they become your advocates. In addition, if you make it a fun place for members to serve and to perform and be visible spokespersons, you can attract and retain out-standing people.

Now the approach I used with my board is not without a downside. One wealthy university that fell one vote shy of approval of a request at a board committee flew in from New York City the next day a member of our board who had been absent for the committee vote. The school also flew back to the formal board meeting another member who had returned home after his vote the previous day in support of the university's proposal. The school won its proposal by one vote as the previous day's vote was reversed, but then the chancellor could not resist bragging to everyone how he had beat our board by doing this. He did not endear himself to the other universities, nor to our board members whose committee vote he managed to reverse.

In my last letter I said you will learn as an agency head that you are sometimes the first among unequals. Let me tie that to the "wit and wis-dom" of the board. Someone said that democracy is a quaint experiment in government where some people are more equal than others. Never forget that your board members are always more equal than you. Cockiness, ag-grandizement, grandstanding, and posturing are out of place in a career where you should learn early to have a "passion for anonymity." Incidentally, Louis Brownlow, a lifelong public servant and advisor to presidents from Woodrow Wilson to John Kennedy, gave that title to his autobiography. He told me the review of his book he liked best was the one by a lady who chided him for the incongruity of calling a book of 500 pages about him-self *A Passion for Anonymity*.

You need to give way on the stage to your public members. There will be more than adequate opportunities for you to have visibility. And while I think of it, a passing point of advice. Never call your board members by first name in a public setting or meeting. That implies an equality that does not, in fact, exist. It also demeans the formality of meetings that deal with seri-ous business affecting individuals and constituents. Your use of first names implies to those affected in your audience that you have a special privileged position they don't have with your board. I think your own board members will sense this. Most importantly, board members will prefer to be addressed formally by their staff, but they probably won't say anything to you about it if you aren't sensitive to it yourself.

Give as much limelight as possible to your board. I remember an ap-pointment when two of our members accompanied me to meet with the chairman of the Senate Finance Committee. The board member explaining the matter of concern was having a little difficulty articulating our request and I spoke up, thinking to help him out. He said, "That's right, speak up at any point. Pitch right in and help me out." But I heard what he actually said. He really meant, "Keep your damned mouth shut. This is my chance to shine." And he did just fine without any further interpolations from me.

On this subject of active board participation, I could not understand for some time why bankers and brokers, lawyers, and businessmen and women, many of them quite wealthy, were willing to give so much of their time and energy to serve on public boards, commissions, and advisory committees like ours. Of course, they do it in part out of a sense of public service and as payback for their education and privileges in society. Then I came to understand another motivation. These men and women have usually become very successful at what they do and part of that success comes from mastering their specialty by doing the same thing over and over. Their professional jobs often become routine and repetitive and fairly predictable. Ours never do, not in our carrying out public policies. Believe it or not, making money and being successful in a narrow field at some point turns dull. Our public business never does. They want to give something back to society, to pay their civic rent, as one of our members called it, but it is also exciting for them. You need to think about ways to make their service on your board rewarding to them. Consequently, let them shine at your board meetings, and create opportunities for them to do it.

So much for wisdom, and now to wit. There are indeed some people who cannot resist a witticism. They are so taken with their own wit that they cannot pause to assess the consequences of their sharp remark. I have certainly been guilty of this and on occasion wished dearly I could retract some facetious or stupid comment I uttered. Humor should be used in your public meetings with great caution. Leave the jokes and laughing to your board members. Levity by you can offend constituents or clients against whom the board may be ruling based on your recommendations. To those affected it's never something to be made light of by you and your staff. You need to maintain a serious demeanor even as the board and the audience may find humor in a situation or their repartee. I have found that my mistakes and misspeaks usually provide sufficient laughter to cover my part.

If you must use humor, use yourself as the butt of the joke. Governor Preston Smith was the best at that technique I have ever witnessed. At least one example is a must. He went to visit his good friend and long-term political colleague, former Senator Dorsey Hardeman, when he was recovering from a stroke. To make conversation he asked Hardeman what he thought about the new governor. Hardeman replied, "Well, he's sure better than that son of a bitch Preston Smith." The governor said, "Now Dorsey, I *am* Preston Smith. We served in the House together and in the

Senate together and fought lots of good battles together when I was governor. Surely you don't mean me, do you?" Hardeman thought about that
for awhile and then said, "You're right. . . . Name some of them other sons
a bitches."

No one can be offended if the joke is on you and not them. But offend
someone else and you may make an enemy for life. Speaker Sam Rayburn
once warned, "You say something mean or sarcastic about some member—
humiliate him in public—and he'll never forget it. You probably will, but he
won't. He'll lay back of that log for twenty years if he has to, and some day
he'll pay you back with compound interest."

A legislator told me she had sounded off to the Texas House parlia-
mentarian, Robert E. Johnson or "Big Daddy," about how mad she was because a particular senator had promoted and found financing for an opponent to her and how much she wanted to get revenge. Big Daddy told her,
"Don't go out of your way. Just hold steady and watch over the sights of
your gun. Eventually every member of the legislature will wander smack dab
in front of your cross hairs." Sure enough, a year later the senator got a favorite bill of hers out the Senate. The offended legislator managed to let it
die in the House committee she chaired.

There is one form of humor you should never ever use in public meetings. That is sarcasm. It literally means "flesh tearing," and so it is, for it is
intended to be cutting. It reflects bitterness and petulance. You cannot use
it without reproaching someone, and you show acrimony and appear to try
to elevate yourself self-righteously above your victim. If you ever use it, expect to be booed.

Now for a few words about your demeanor with your board members
in private. Never say more than you know. If you do you will probably end
up having to say still more than you know or have to backtrack on what you
have already said. If you start opining about things you really don't know
much about, you may be asked some probing questions by the person you
are talking with if the subject you have picked is of any interest at all. And
if it isn't interesting you shouldn't be talking about it. More on that in a moment. I'll give you an example. I was sitting in a business lounge at an airport recently and a young man was talking big with a person who was an
obvious client for some computer service the young man was providing.
After they had pretty well settled the deal, the young man started talking big
and knowledgeably about a small company, and as his client showed increasing interest, he said he knew the company had just been bought. His
client then said, "Is that right? I've been watching that company for over a
year. I've been considering buying it. Did you hear what it sold for?" Then

the young man began to crawfish, saying he didn't know the details of the sale—or if it had actually been finalized. The client asked who had bought it and again the young man had to backtrack from what he had talked so informatively about a few moments earlier. It became clear he had no idea what he was talking about. During the ensuing long silence the client may have been reconsidering his future with his new service provider.

When I was still younger than you and I was a Navy musician, I was beginning to listen on the periphery to some of the "intellectual" conversations taking place among some of my brighter and better-read colleagues in the band. I said to a friend how frustrating it was not to be quick enough or informed enough to participate. He quoted a line I have heard dozens of times since. It is good advice. He said, "Better to be assumed to be ignorant than to speak and remove all doubt."

Someone said once that what makes great music is often the rests, the space between the notes. The same is true in conversation. Every moment does not have to be filled with words and comments. In fact it is the idle chatter and meaningless fluff that accompany efforts at good conversation that detract from contemplation and the flow of connected thoughts. Do not become a chatterbox, feeling compelled to make continual smart asides, cute comments, and witticisms. To pull it off and be truly witty, you have to score one hundred percent of the time and the odds are very heavily weighted against you. Even if you were successful, you would only have established that you are a wit. Continual witty interpolations make you appear flighty and unconnected to what is significant and important because you will be addressing what is superficial in the conversation or you will be trivializing what is meaningful. You should never sacrifice thought for the satisfaction of your wit. Such comments, even when truly witty, quickly become distracting and irritating. And your purpose in conversing with colleagues in setting government policy, in any event, is not to become known as a wit but to be taken seriously for your thoughts and views. Better to be thought too serious than to speak flippantly and reveal yourself to be quite the opposite.

Let us now assume you have an ideal board that has socialized each other to an admirable level of expected civility and objective deliberation. It is in addition a working board that serves, when needed, as a bridge to help you communicate well with the world at large and as a moat to defend you when unjustly criticized and attacked. Moreover, you and your board have found a perfect balance between them expecting and you providing recommendations for board actions and the board providing and you expecting guidance and direction for changes in existing policies and practices.

When, in this perfect world, would Dr. Pangloss advise you to back off and leave your board to decide a controversial issue? One of the greatest temptations in the heat of a board debate among the members is for you to get back into the discussion too soon and to try to influence the outcome. Your task is to put before your board in writing (which they may not have read) and in your oral presentation to them a clear description of the issue, your recommendation and why you make it, alternatives considered and rejected, and your assessment of the consequences of their taking the action you propose. Opposing views will often be presented and argued. And typically there will be some give and take and back and forth among you and those who differ with you as the board is getting their minds around the issue and the opposing sides of it. Then there often comes a point when the board has all the information it needs to reach a decision. You can sense this from the quality of the debate and discussion they are conducting. At this point it will take great personal discipline to stay out of the discussion until asked for an opinion or for additional information. And you need to be in control of your staff so they do not get back into the discussion while you are restraining yourself.

This is not just a matter of courtesy or style; you need to remember those in the audience. They are watching you work with your board. Your opponents in the crowd will see your reentry into the debate as taking unfair advantage of your position to influence the board. You will be seen as too eager to have your way with your board. And the board at this point will probably not want to hear further from you any more than they want to call the other side out of the audience for more arguments. If they get hung up and find they need more information or a clarification, be assured, they will ask you for it.

While telling yourself to remain quiet, you might console yourself with having done your job well. You should try to keep the faith that if you have done your job really well, they should work their way back to your recommendation. In any event, someone on the panel will probably say at some point, "Before we vote I'd like to hear again from our executive director about what he thinks about what we are about to do."

I told you earlier about the moratorium on degree program approvals I had obtained when I first took the commissioner's job. There was one near crack during the board hearing despite the commendatory letter to our board members from Governor Briscoe about slowing down runaway growth. The regents and chancellor of a university system were pushing very hard for an exception to the moratorium and for immediate approval of a new bachelor's degree in horse management. It would be "free." The industry would pay for it. The degree was essential. Students had been waiting for years for it. The industry needed it desperately. It would provide a boost to the state economy. Resources were already in place at the university to start it. Why should such a stellar program require any further study? Approve it now. Rush. Rush.

A motion for approval was made and the board was about to vote when I showed enough discomfort that a member asked for my views. I said, "I would only remind the board as you vote on this horse management degree proposal that this morning you already heard arguments to exempt three new nursing programs from the moratorium, and you denied all three of those requests and called for further study." The motion on the horse management request also failed.

Occasionally unfair arguments have to be answered by unfair responses. A university was requesting board approval of a new campus on land to be donated by a developer. It would, of course, attract new developers and increase housing demand to the area and enhance land values. But of all the places in the state that might need a new campus this one was low on the list, other than politically. The principal argument made by the university wanting the new campus was that the area had the lowest college-going rate in the state. True. The reason was that practically the only people who could afford to live in the area already held college degrees. And we told the board that.

Nonetheless, there were a number of our board members who favored approving the new university, and the president was very persuasive and insistent. In pressing forward with the motion for approval one board member asked me if I had ever been on the proposed site for the campus. I said, "No, not exactly." "Aha," came the reply, "so you haven't even been on the proposed campus. Then I don't see how you can oppose this plan. Mr. Chairman, I call the question and I urge a vote of approval." Another member interrupted, "Just a minute. I found that a very strange answer. What did you mean you weren't on the site *exactly*?" I replied that I had been *near* the site, but that it had been raining and the swampy conditions and the dirt roads in the area prevented us from getting to the actual site. Entirely truthful. Perhaps a tad unfair. The university president was furious. The motion failed.

Let me end this letter with an example of board courage in defending an agency head. The principal players were Governor William Clements; T. Boone Pickens, the notorious Texas millionaire and corporate raider; and a Dallas businessman and a former four-term speaker of the Texas House of Representatives. The Dallas businessman was serving as chairman of the board of regents of Texas A&M University and the former speaker was a

member of that board. Pickens was chair of the board of regents of West
Texas State University.

A bit of background: Pickens and his board had hired a new president
and between him and Pickens the campus was in constant and prolonged
turmoil. The president and the chair were highly authoritarian and overbearing to faculty, students, and staff. There was also outrage over a million-
dollar new home for the president. The easy way out for Pickens was to unload the whole mess on somebody else.

The senator from the West Texas University area introduced a bill to
move that university to the Texas A&M System of universities and disband
the existing board of regents for the school. With the support and political
persuasion of such a phalanx of influential leaders, the bill passed to amal-
gamate West Texas State University into the Texas A&M University System.

However, this decision came with a provision added by the Senate that
the proposed merger must first receive the approval of the higher education
coordinating board. Remember I mentioned earlier how the governor had
added a similar provision to a bill creating a new campus he had doubts
about? Well, now the same provision had been added to a bill he *favored*.
As they say in politics, what goes around comes around. The shoe was on
the other foot and walking with it was not comfortable for the governor and
his colleagues in this endeavor. Again, this put our agency in the unenviable
position of being authorized to veto the intent of a bill passed by both
houses and enacted into law by the governor.

One day a couple of months later my chairman, Hal Daugherty, called
me from his bank in El Paso to pass on a message from the governor. He
said the governor had heard that I was fool enough to take that provision in
the statute seriously that would permit our agency to kill his proposed
merger. In fact, he was correct. Our board had held two long public hearings on the proposed merger and there were some serious staff and board
concerns about the wisdom of the idea, other than to transfer Boone Pickens' problems at his university in west Texas to another institution.

Hal said to me, "The governor said he does not want to see your tracks
anywhere around that proposal. He wants you to take a dive or he says he'll
get you fired." When I laughed, Hal said the governor was serious. He had
made that abundantly clear. I told Hal I was only laughing at the choices this
left me. I could do what the governor ordered me to do and never again
have any credibility with any university or college administrator in the state
because everybody knew this was strictly a political deal and it held no educational merit or justification. Or I could stand my ground and get fired. I
told him the choice was actually easy to make. I needed respect more than

I needed a job where I could not be effective. Hal told me to think about it real hard; the governor was dead serious.

My wife remembers that I called her that night in Washington, D.C., and told her to stop packing for her move to Austin; I might not have my job much longer.

The governor began calling board members whom he had appointed and told them how he wanted them to vote on the merger. Mary Beth Williamson from San Antonio called to tell me she might have a very short tenure on the board. When the governor called her for her vote, she told him that she had been at the two hearings and had not seen him there and that she thought she could serve him best by making up her own mind based on her consideration of the merits of the proposal as she assessed them. She reminded me she had not yet been confirmed by the Senate and she thought that the governor might withdraw her appointment. She said she had enjoyed her few months on the board. I told her to rest easy. The governor might be mean but I had never known him to be small.

When our board met to take up this issue, Boone Pickens chartered a plane from Amarillo and flew several hundred people to Austin to pack our meeting and to impress and influence our board. Both boards of regents were present, as were the sponsoring senator, the local house member, the mayor, and countless others. Our board listened at length and then I made the only presentation in opposition to the proposal. When the board voted, the tally was eleven to seven to approve the merger. It was a done deal. I was very much surprised at the seven votes.

About three weeks later Hal phoned me again from El Paso. He told me the governor had just called to tell him that since he and the vice chairman, Cipriano Guerra, had voted to support the commissioner's recommendation to disapprove the merger and it was obvious that they would not now fire me, the governor was now firing them as chair and vice chair. The governor's further message was that he was going to get the commissioner fired next.

I asked Hal what he was going to do. He told me he and Cip had told the governor that it was wrong to fire the commissioner for disagreeing with him and not following his orders. They told the governor he might have the statutory right to fire them from their positions as chair and vice chair but he could not remove them from the board. They told him they planned to stay on the board and work full time to see that he couldn't fire the commissioner.

By the next board meeting there were rumors that the governor was beginning to get his votes lined up on the board to carry out his threat. At the meeting everyone thought that Hal was pouting about losing the chairmanship because he sat silently through several committee meetings. Then when Cip Guerra took the chair as head of the academic affairs committee, Hal said, "Mr. Chairman, I request the privilege of making a personal statement." Of course, no one objected.

He then said, "Everyone knows how difficult it is to serve as commissioner in this state even under normal circumstances. And the commissioner's job will become impossible if the rumors continue to go around that there are members of this board who do not support him. We need to clarify where the members of this board stand. Therefore, Mr. Chairman, I move for a vote of confidence in our commissioner."

When he got a second for his motion, he then asked for a roll-call vote. The secretary to the board began to call the role. As Hal had said cryptically to me at the beginning of the meeting, "I'm goin' to smoke them sons a bitches out."

The result was that I received a unanimous vote of confidence from the board. Then the former chairman said, "And I request that a copy of this board vote be sent to the governor." This was the only time I saw our board receive a standing ovation from an audience made up primarily of university presidents and administrators.

The epilogue was this: The governor did not withdraw Mary Beth Williamson's name from nomination to the board after she voted against the merger. Senator Teel Bivins won his case, never forgot the position I took or missed an opportunity to chide me about it, and remained forever a gentleman and never sought retribution of any kind. And a story came back to me that T. Boone Pickens, the multimillionaire, sent a bill for reimbursement to those from the Texas panhandle who had flown to Austin on his chartered flight.

Your wayward uncle,

Uncle Ken

re: *Bona fide bureaucratic behavior*

I like bats much better than bureaucrats.   *— C.S. Lewis*

The law should not be a huge and weighty slab which falls upon a man and squashes him into a uniform shape, for men are not uniform. The law should be a gentle sheet which falls over a man and shows his unique shape beneath its blanketing sameness.

— Colleen McCullough

People are tired of dealing with multiple bureaucracies. They want to deal with *one* bureaucracy.   *— Florida legislator*

NOVEMBER

Dear Kim

Most people think it is the general public who has the greatest problems with foot-dragging bureaucrats, those people in government who put procedures ahead of substance, people who forget that their expected service to citizens is why they hold their jobs, people who see change of any kind as the first step toward disorder and chaos. Actually it is those *inside* government who encounter the most frequent problems with such colleagues. The typical citizen has an occasional brush with such bureaucrats, but career civil servants inside government live miserably close to them every day.

Perhaps an example will help make my point. The very first job I had in government was in Washington with the Treasury Department. My assignment involved reviewing all letters, memoranda, circulars, and notices issued since the Civil War to banks and the regional offices of departmental

agencies by the secretary of the U.S. Treasury. The stone-vaulted room assigned to my colleague and me in the old Treasury building overlooking the
conjunction of 15th Street and Pennsylvania Avenue was filled with these
documents. We were told that banks and Treasury offices across the country had all or parts of these same files. No one dared to throw any of them
away or disregard rules and instructions contained in these papers because
no one knew for certain which of them might still be in effect. Our assignment was to make sense of this mess. We decided our job was, first, to identify those documents that were clearly defunct but still with us in the here
and now and to get them declared dead and buried by the current secretary
of the Treasury. The remaining less-than-five percent of the paper we would
deal with later with more deliberation. The additional job we saw was to recommend that the Treasury Department establish a document control system
so that different kinds of notices, rules, and orders would thereafter get issued under appropriate categories and classifications. And obviously a num-
bering system would be helpful to facilitate future cross-referencing of documents. But back to that later.

My first lesson in bureaucratic foot dragging came after months of reviewing the documents when we prepared the letter for the secretary to issue
to rescind the obsolete documents. The standard procedure for submitting
such a proposed letter to the secretary was to get each affected branch of the
Treasury Department to approve and sign off on the letter. In other words,
they were asked to lend their endorsement to our recommendation or at
least to indicate they had no objections to it.

Although we took a copy of each defunct letter, order, or circular to
be cancelled to the offices and branches concerned, we found great reluctance to join in our scything through masses of obviously obsolete records.
First, our document would lie for weeks unattended and neglected in offices
around the Department. Second, when we sat down and went through the
archaic and arcane documents with staff members in the branches, we could
not get others to agree readily with us, for example, that a letter issued on
August 4, 1903, directing closer coordination between the Coast Guard and
the Bureau of Engraving on counterfeit twenty-dollar bills should be included in our list of documents to be officially rescinded. Although the term
"CYA" (cover your ass) had not been coined in 1959, we soon concluded this
was the problem we were encountering everywhere.

Eventually we had to confer with the secretary personally and show
him examples of what we were trying to cancel. When we suggested he send
a memo (which we had drafted in advance) notifying all Treasury employees that he was fully behind this effort to clear all files of old Treasury orders,

he signed it with alacrity. Immediately everything changed. Employees throughout the Department formerly reluctant to assist us now signed off on the secretary's letter to revoke the old documents. It was as though our proposal had simply never been explained to them before. It became clear to us they had been waiting for a cue from the secretary about what he really wanted them to do. They were not about to be led to sign on to some plan proposed by a couple of new, young employees that might get them crossways with the secretary.

There are a couple of things you can do in your career to reduce this tendency toward protecting the status quo and being bound by established procedures. First, keep in mind *why* you are carrying out the government function of your agency and *who* it is you are ultimately serving. This will help you to avoid thinking of your agency as an end rather than a means, that is, to focus on program content rather than procedure. This applies to support areas as well as to program administration. It is somehow preferable for those running a personnel office (now more fashionably called "human resources"), for example, to see themselves as existing to serve the staffing and training needs of the agency, rather than to believe the agency exists in order to justify having a personnel office.

The second thing you can do to make your agency a more interesting place to work and consequently less bureaucratic is to enable those under you to feel they control their own areas of work. In this way they acquire a sense of ownership in what gets done and how they do it. Contrary to common misrepresentations, people in government do not take a job to do as little work as they can. But if your employees assume that you, their supervisor, think this is why they work there or how they spend their days, some of them will manage to sink to your level of expectations. Treat all employees as the lowest common denominator you can imagine for them and you will have to fight hard to get people to rise above it.

If you are challenged, involved, and given responsibility for how you get your tasks done you know you are happier and as a result more productive. The same is true of every person who will ever work for you. Nurture in them the same qualities and attitudes toward work you would like to seek for yourself, and most will thrive. You might even reward a little democratic insubordination occasionally. When people feel they can speak up freely to make suggestions or disagree with proposed assignments or procedures, you will get a lot more brainpower applied to your problems.

Years after that first job in the Treasury Department I watched out of my office window a metaphor for habitual bureaucratic behavior. Behind the building where our agency was located there was an apartment complex.

When we moved the agency into the office building, the garbage dumpster for the apartments was located on a median in the parking lot between the apartments and our office building. There were prominent yellow cross stripes painted in two parking places to denote "no parking" in order to permit access for the dumpster truck. Later the garbage dumpster for the apartment complex was relocated, but each of the three times the stripes outlining the parking spaces in the lot were repainted, the no parking cross stripes in those two spaces were brightly refurbished.

When a group of university administrators complained that they could not obtain certain public information about their schools from our data processing department, I was appalled. As I tracked down the obstacle, I confronted the head of the office, who said he was carrying out my orders. He showed me a dog-eared memorandum I had sent to him nine years earlier. Of course when I saw it I remembered it. At that earlier date the university presidents had been so suspicious of each other that I had had to agree not to share information on their universities with other schools as a condition to get them to agree to provide the information we needed for our data system. But after close to a decade the attitudes of the presidents about sharing information had changed. Most of the presidents had moved on as well. Ah well, my data processing officer was right. So I had to give him another set of instructions. A case of stripes in the parking lot.

Oh, I need to get back to the Treasury Department control system for issuing new documents. The secretary approved the system we recommended and it was installed. Several people I had haggled with to get them to sign off on the letter to bury tons of dead paperwork now encouraged me to take the new job as head of the document control office. To them it looked like a great opportunity—a secure, long-term job with permanent career status. Just think, your aging uncle might right now be writing these letters to you from somewhere in the bowels of the Treasury Building—if, after a career in such a job, I had anything to write to you about.

So, out of all this I have two words of advice. First, don't get locked into some early job just because you are good at it. During my early career I took two pay cuts and once moved my family across the continent at my expense to avoid getting locked into a career too soon. When you're young and haven't gotten to be too expensive yet, take a few risks and move around, change jobs, and get some varied experience.

Another characteristic of bureaucrats abundantly criticized is our propensity to propagate (or, to use one of our most favorite words, promulgate) rules and regulations (to say nothing of our passion to disseminate). This tendency to write rules and regulations is not in our DNA as public employees. Most rules come about in response to repeated abuse of people, power, or position. Rules and regulations have the positive quality of defining how the different parties involved will behave in specific circumstances. Often the purpose of a rule is to provide predictability. "If you do such and such, so and so will respond in the following way and the penalty will range from yea to yon." The difficulties with government rules begin when those who do carry a "rules and regulations gene" get carried away with jargon and decide they must define every conceivable eventuality, circumstance, condition, situation, and behavior, or combination of the aforesaid appertaining thereto that might or will arise or heretofore have or has arisen.

Another misapplication of rules occurs when those in authority try to find an impersonal way to deal with a poor performer or a malefactor or two. Rather than face the issue head on, some regulators will develop a standard or a rule to bring the few nonperformers or abusers into line. This means everyone else—those who are performing appropriately—is also subjected to the same rule and all of the associated data collection, reporting, scrutiny, and supervision as the actual target of the new rule. This is like requiring all the soldiers with the clean uniforms to wash and press them again in order to be certain those in dirty uniforms wash theirs.

But experience shows that the malefactors are often the first to find a way to evade or avoid a rule, leaving the burden of the rule upon those to whom it doesn't really need to apply in the first place. This is what happens when your rules focus on the lowest common denominator, the worst malefactors, the most base expectations of human behavior. Unfortunately a few doctors, for example, who pad their incomes by falsifying bills, who require unnecessary tests, and who overcharge patients or insurers, bring about a need for detailed regulations for all doctors. Brown University president Henry Wriston got to the weakness of this approach when he said, "Every time a formula is substituted for responsible judgment, there is official defeasement. Rules make decision easy but rob it of wisdom." Yet governments must deal with decisions in the mass and cannot individualize every judgment. Many of our critics may not believe it, but we don't have enough bureaucrats to adjudicate and deal with each separate case specifically.

When I was working for a university, a delegation from the major schools visited with the commissioner of elementary and secondary education about new complex requirements and procedures he was about to impose on all higher education institutions in connection with our preparation of public school teachers. For about an hour we debated with him why it was necessary to put all of us through the costs and miseries of what he was proposing. Finally he said, "Look, here's my problem. There are nine universities whose graduates are just not performing adequately to be certified by our agency for teaching in our public schools. This has been going on for years and I've got to put a stop to it. These new procedures will show them up and we can stop certifying their education graduates." We then, of course, asked him if he had known for years which nine universities were the poor performers, why didn't he just stop certifying their graduates right then and leave the rest of us alone. He said they were all small private schools or predominantly minority universities. While we could empathize with him in his problem, we did not think his solution justified the tremendous burden he was about to impose on the entire higher education community.

Now let me comment on another species of internal bureaucrat. To some extent these are the drones of government. Their job is to monitor, criticize, evaluate, report on, and, supposedly, improve program operations. The surprising fact is that many of these people often have little or no management or program experience. Yet they are quick to suggest how things can be improved or they are ready to criticize why things could have been done better. They stand above the fray but they second guess your decisions. They shun responsibility but they have perfect hindsight. They have no shame about using what you have learned in the meantime from your own decisions and actions to criticize what you did before you were a sadder but wiser executive. They profess that they are there to help you, but they report on your most minute failings to make themselves look good and to justify their existence. They claim to see the big picture, but they get bogged down in trivia and minutia.

Let's name names. These are the auditors, planners, sunset agency staffs, comptrollers, budget agency staff people, and legislative or review committee staffs. Not all of these people are as bad as I have described them, but there can be no question that the responsibilities for oversight that these people have and the kinds of autonomy and political protection given to them put them in a safe position to frustrate and enrage program administrators. It is easy to see the perfect solution when you do not have to experience the reality of the scrap of resolving a complex issue. It is easy to devise a formula for making certain decisions when you don't have to live with the consequences of your position or you never have to work amidst the subtleties of individual situations. It is easy to criticize the high costs of consultation with constituents when you don't have to live through the hostilities and resentments of a constituency you have neglected. It is easy to find a numerical or engineering solution to a problem if you ignore the personal interests and contrariness of human beings.

After you experience much of this you may come to appreciate the outburst by General "Vinegar Joe" Stilwell when he said about Washington, D.C., "Someone with a loud voice and a mean look and a big stick ought to appear and yell, 'HALT! you crazy bastards. SILENCE! you imitation ants. Now half of you get the hell out of town before dark and the other half sit down and don't move for one hour.' Then they should burn up all the papers and start fresh."

One of the problems for program administrators is that they usually hold very demanding jobs that keep them busy full-time to manage their program responsibilities and staffs. The in-house critics, on the other hand, spend *their* full-time efforts trying to find things that are not done properly or done perfectly or done efficiently in their view. They are provided full-time capacity to cause trouble and the more time they spend, the more likely they will find something of some kind to report. And the more time they spend investigating, the more important it becomes that they must find *something* to report on—in order to justify the time they have spent evaluating you. What chafes agency administrators is that they have to take time from their other work (1) to educate these critics to what the agency does so they can then turn around and credibly criticize the agency and (2) to respond to the Monday-morning quarterbacking of these critics and those to whom these critics have reported their findings.

This is not a new problem to government. Try to guess when the following statement was made.

> Commanders should be counseled chiefly by persons of known talent, by those who have made the art of war their particular study, and whose knowledge is derived from experience, by those who are present at the scene of action, who see the enemy, who see the advantages that occasions offer, and who, like people embarked in the same ship, are sharers of the danger. If, therefore, anyone thinks himself qualified to give advice respecting the war which I am about to conduct—let him not refuse to be of assistance to the state, but let him come with me into Macedonia.

Sound contemporary? This practice of criticizing actions after the event and of giving gratuitous advice is not new. This statement was made by the Roman General Paulus 200 years before the birth of Christ.

But back to a truly contemporary example. After a team of auditors completed one of their six-month reviews of our agency, I was invited to a private exit conference to hear their astonishing findings. I was told that the principal item in their report to the legislature and the governor would be that our staff had driven one too many cars to an out-of-town board meeting. I was assured, however, they would include a comment about possible mitigating circumstances since our board members had had to be transported between two university campuses thirty miles apart for the two-day meeting. I was simply underwhelmed.

I reminded the auditors that I had asked them at the outset of their audit to be certain we had no employee anywhere in the agency who was ordering checks for the agency for student loans or for any other purpose from the state comptroller and then receiving the checks himself. Oh . . ., they had forgotten to look into that.

There is no question that agency activities must be monitored and evaluated, and a good bit of it is done professionally and expertly. Some of the findings are helpful and do result in improvements in program management. Knowing you are going to be scrutinized helps to keep the agency honest and focused on efficiency. But it is not the inexperienced and presumptuous young people who "rush in where angels fear to tread" with their unrealistic opinions who are most resented by program executives and their staffs. The most despised are those who misuse their positions as monitors and critics to aggrandize themselves.

For example, the Texas state comptroller gained a national reputation for his recommendations for improving government operations. The way he did this was to send his minions out into all state agencies every two years to discover what ideas for improvements the agencies were considering or had underway. He then compiled these ideas he had stolen from the agencies into what he called performance reviews and would release them at public press conferences. Never one to hide his light under a bushel, he gave his color-printed reports such catchy titles as "Breaking the Mold," "Against the Grain," "Gaining Ground," and "Disturbing the Peace." Of course these reports never gave any credit whatsoever to the work going on elsewhere in government all across the state. The reports made it sound as though the comptroller was the only person in all of state government with any ideas or even any interest in ideas for making government more efficient and cost-effective. The rest of us were troglodytes still trying to find the exit from the cave.

Another person who misused and leveraged the authority of his office to monitor and oversee state agencies was the head of the sunset commission. He expected sycophancy and obsequious obeisances from agency heads and their board members when it became their unfortunate turn to ride the sunset trundle to the execution block. Without a recommendation from him for continuation of their agency they might be abolished by the legislature. His board consisted of legislators and a few citizen members. He co-opted his review panel by promising to find ways to make them look good in saving money and improving efficiency in government. Any agency head who disagreed with what the sunset commission director planned to do to his or her agency could be punished in provisions he could write into the legislation that had to be passed in order to continue the life of the agency. A favorite, nagging punishment was to require follow-up studies of an agency or reports on specific changes that were to be made. Again, the sunset commission staff worked full-time on their evaluation and oversight while the agency under scrutiny had to continue to carry out its usual duties and deal with the commission director as well.

It was the imperiousness of the staff and the peremptory notices of what was going to be done to agencies that most irritated agency heads throughout government. The broad, general dissatisfaction with the process went unnoted because no one dared to complain while under active sunset commission review. After the ordeal was finally over, there was a sigh of relief at not having to go through that again for another decade. Those who completed it would commiserate with the new flock of sheep scheduled for shearing—or worse—but they were not prone to make unnecessary enemies by criticizing the system.

Yet most agency heads agreed privately that the major deficiency in the sunset law was that it did not require a sunset review of the sunset commission and its staff.

When you've had sufficient experience with government's in-house bureaucrats, you too may come to empathize with the public servant somewhere who came up with the definition of an auditor: "A person who arrives on the field after the battle and executes the wounded."

Perhaps you will find your way to an organization that is entirely positive in its mission, one that builds and promotes and expands and is founded on optimism and boosterism. Foundations, universities, government grant programs, and agencies to extend opportunities fall in this category. But even these organizations reach a point where they must regulate and set standards and ration benefits or access because their resources are not unlimited. They must often define who is in and who is out in terms of eligibility for benefits or government favors or public sanctions. But on the whole such organizations are forward moving and less involved in regulating the actions of others.

These organizations are in contrast to regulatory agencies, which are seen by those affected as being negative, as staffed by naysayers, as interfering with what people want to be free to do. Many citizens will agree society needs such regulators; they just want the regulating done to those people who really need it, those *other* people. For example, in higher education each president will readily agree that every other university needs coordinating—but his or hers doesn't. It's good for everybody else. As one president of West Texas State University in Canyon, Texas, was reported to have said, "If it weren't for that board, I could make this university into another MIT." Regulatory agencies are about as popular as referees and umpires. But in a world where exploiters take advantage of the unwary and outright crooks prey on the defenseless, somebody has to try to level the playing field.

Both of these kinds of roles—regulatory and developmental—are essential in government. You need to understand which kind of job you have. One will be more popular than the other and perhaps easier to serve in. The expectations of the jobs are very different. The constituency pressures on a person in a regulatory job will be to try to make you a tool of those you regulate. And in some jobs you will, indeed, be expected to speak at times on behalf of those you regulate. Critic or cheerleader? Advocate or adversary? Jeremiah or drum major? Cassandra or mouthpiece? This is what I was talking about in one of my first letters when I referred to your having chosen a life of bifurcated expectations.

Just remember this about all the rules you will administer. A rule is a momentary solution to a constantly recurring problem; it is not an inviolable law. Most of the time it is "policy" on a small scale. A rule is not engraved in stone; it is a temporary agreement on how a particular set of circumstances will be dealt with. And it is far better to change a rule than to constantly be making exceptions to it.

Besides, I discovered that some of the rules we tried to administer were about as effective as half a pair of scissors.

In almost any job you take that has significant responsibility associated with it you will be required to deny requests and pleadings put before you. It will not take you long to discover that "no" is never a final answer. Pleaders keep coming back, often with the same arguments, but usually with some new wrinkle or with a more carefully organized polemic, or they will contend that the times have changed sufficiently to justify that their request now be granted. Then when you finally relent and say "yes" they will then take encouragement and quickly consult their "wish lists" and return to request something new that they find to be desperately needed.

Another technique you will find used on you is for your opponents to reluctantly agree to conditions and limitations you place on them as stipulations to your granting their request. They will promise anything to get their foot in the door and then they will find that circumstances have changed and they will plead that you must remove the provisos you attached. As soon as they receive such conditional approval they will work assiduously to have the conditions and limitations removed. Or they simply ignore your conditions and challenge you to stop them. When I have a proper forum I plan to offer to social scientists a label for this particular form of institutional change. I call it "creeping incrementalism."

This role of constraining unrestrained ambitions and aspirations of institution builders has occupied much of my public career. In Scotland I came across a tombstone that bears my epitaph. It reads, "Here lies Sarah McTavish. Bless her. She tried to say no." It is a depressing thought, but perhaps my greatest legacy in my jobs in higher education has been to say "no" and to try to make it stick.

Which reminds me of a not unrelated story. Governor Clements despised the Texas attorney general, Mark White, who had been elected to his post by the other party. The governor did not trust him in addition to disliking him. It was galling to the governor that the A.G. would not take orders from him. Consequently, on a matter on which our agency needed legal advice, the governor directed my chairman and vice chairman and me to hire our own lawyer and ignore the attorney general. I knew there was no way we could do that under state law. I waited for my chairman to object and then I knew I would have to speak up. I decided to start with the simplest argument against his instructions. I explained that we did not have money in our budget to hire an attorney. The governor said, "Then hire one and divide up the bill and send it to the universities. Make them pay their share of it."

I explained that from my experience they would not pay for our agency to employ an attorney and we had no authority to force them to do so. The governor insisted, so I turned to the argument I should have started with. I explained that it would be unconstitutional for us to hire an attorney. "The hell you say," he responded. I pointed out that no agency could recruit an outside attorney without the prior approval of the attorney general. The governor glowered at me a few moments and said, "You sure are a negative fellow." He probably wouldn't have liked Sarah McTavish either.

You might think there is a certain insecurity to working for regulatory agencies, all of which are so unpopular with the legislature and the constituents they must regulate. But you need to recognize that, complain as they will about you and your agency, legislators and governors need you. Without you, all the headaches you deal with would come directly to them. Most regulatory agencies that are abolished are recreated or reinvented very quickly in a new form after legislators discover how much flak they are going to have to deal with themselves.

I've got just enough time to tell you one more vignette to illustrate how true bureaucrats, in the bad sense, can behave and use the power at their disposal. Such career bureaucrats sometimes come to believe their agencies belong to them; they don't like to share them with anyone else. That includes the politicians who come and go as secretaries, undersecretaries, deputy secretaries, assistant secretaries, agency heads, or chairs of boards or commissions.

A secretary of a federal department became interested in information a freelance writer might be able to provide him on a policy issue his department was concerned about. The secretary decided he could use this writer's work, and he directed his staff at the department to contract with the writer for a brief report on his research.

Although it was a small contract, the secretary's approach was unorthodox and, not being sympathetic to the secretary's needs or his frustration with an unresponsive department, the staff handling contracts set out to teach the secretary a lesson. The staff either did not want to get someone outside the department to gather the information or they did not want the secretary telling them whom to contract with. The difficulty was that it was not the secretary—after all, he *was* the bureaucrats' boss—but the writer who would suffer the learning experience at the hands of these bureaucrats.

The first delay was in executing the contract. The next delay was with making the first partial payment. As a condition for receiving his second partial payment, the writer was subjected to several accusatory and impertinent letters and abusive telephone conversations, all implying that he was shirking his commitments and not meeting the specifications of his contract. They were obviously trying to discourage him and run him off. Eleven staff people handling contracts attended a conference with him in order to determine whether to release his second payment. After the supervisor in charge of the meeting listened for a few minutes he simply said, "Pay the man," and left in apparent disgust at his staff's unjustified foot dragging. Yet when I last heard, the researcher had still not received his final payment, even though he had submitted his final report six months earlier. Hell hath no fury like that of a bureaucrat whose procedures are scorned.

Bureaucrats have coined phrases to describe such behavior among their dilatory colleagues who are reluctant to carry out orders or get on with their assignments, such as "immersion in refining capability," "creative foot dragging," "masterly inactivity," "imaginative itemization of fearful consequences," "absorption in planning for action," and "inordinate preparation for readiness."

A Unitarian minister in Washington one Sunday waxed eloquent on the kind of world we live in. He said, "There are some people who still trot out the trite canard that loving our neighbor means what we do in direct relationship with him and that we cannot love him through acts of Congress. This is just tired platitude. In the modern world we cannot even do our ordinary duty to our neighbor except through acts of Congress."

Nor can we, one on one, address the needs of a vast society made up of winners and losers, haves and have-nots, and of people whose needs change over the seasons of life. Those kinds of needs and the conditions of a changing and progressive society can only be addressed through large organizations. And all large organizations are shot through with bureaucracy, in its best and its worst aspects. Your job will be to try to influence for the good those small pieces of those bureaucracies you touch.

Have you been paying attention? There's a lot here you want to avoid becoming or doing in your own career.

Your assertive

Uncle Ken

re: "Walking with kings"

People are always blaming their circumstances for what they are. I don't believe in circumstances. The people who get on in this world are the people who get up and look for the circumstances they want, and, if they can't find them, they make them.

— *George Bernard Shaw*

Make the most of your yard of space and your inch of time.

— *Robert Shaw*

There are no uninteresting subjects, only disinterested people.

— *Unknown sage*

DECEMBER

Dear Kim

When a friend of mine, a former presidential adviser, was describing the kind of person needed to fill a particular high-level position, he said, "We're looking for somebody who can walk with kings." That summed up so much of what you need to aspire to if you are going to get to the top. Anyone who has worked with top-level public officials knows exactly what he meant. He meant someone who is comfortable, or at least not obviously uncomfortable, associating with people in positions of authority; people used to making decisions; people who grasp situations rapidly and who take in information quickly; people who don't suffer fools easily; people who know they need advice and are constantly sizing up advisers as to whose counsel and judgment can best be relied on; people who keep their eye on the big picture while they concentrate for the moment on the issue at hand; people who can unbend while they deal with critical problems but who can turn serious and be tough in the midst of being relaxed; people whose time must be assumed to be precious but who can string out a discussion when they choose to; people who know you may hold them in awe but expect you to communicate clearly and completely what you need to tell them; people who want and expect you to say what you believe, not what you think will please them; people who must live their lives and find interest and enjoyment while making critical decisions and giving direction to aides and supporters; and people who are used to having their views and opinions carry more weight than those of others.

You cannot expect to "walk with kings" more than very occasionally if all you know is your area of specialization, regardless of how thoroughly you may know it. If you wish to be involved in broader levels of advising and policymaking and you want to be consulted and brought into higher level discussions of policy, you must know far more than your area of expertise. You cannot allow your special knowledge and area of government activity to become a mere crust on your small piece of all of government, for when someone breaks through it, you will quickly be discovered to be perhaps profound on the surface but down deep actually quite shallow. Your area of special competence should be as the part of an iceberg showing above water, with a far weightier bulk supporting you from below.

Now how do you acquire the necessary skills, how do you learn to walk and converse easily with "kings"? Through experience and exposure and maturity mostly. But I would say the first requirement is to grow the bulk of your knowledge below the iceberg's water line, outside the field of your expertise. Never forget that what you aspire to is the top of the ladder in the public service. So don't be misled by the narrow specialization your first employers may seem to want. Let me illustrate.

On one occasion at a conference of educators and business people, I amused myself by conducting an informal poll. The first afternoon I asked several business people attending what they wanted most to find when they hired new college graduates. They identified things like these: "I want an engineer who can design a span that won't fall down." "I'm looking for graduates who can reliably titrate a solution." "I want someone who can audit a set of books and who knows the latest tax code." "I want architects who can do their design work on computers and can access the supply catalogs for specs and ordering." In the parlance of our own field they would probably want somebody who can draft a bill, prepare a budget, write a grant request, or do a cost-benefit analysis of alternate policy choices.

The next morning I found those same business people and probed with them what they found to be the greatest deficiencies of our university preparation of their people for supervisory positions. Their answers and expectations were entirely different from the day before. They said what their middle-level employees lacked most were human relations and interpersonal skills, organizational understanding, competence in personnel management, and mastery of communications, especially in writing. "They can't think on their feet or defend a position effectively." "They can't get along or they don't know how to deal with people who can't get along."

That afternoon, continuing our conversations about what they really wanted to get from higher education in their employees, I asked them what they searched for most in going over their company rosters for people to promote to top-level, policymaking positions. Where were the universities letting them down? One said, "I hate to admit it but sometimes I'm almost embarrassed to send some of our people to meetings like this. Somebody might find out they work for us. They can't talk about anything but our company or what they do with us. They're just plain boring." Another one said, "Our mid-level people don't seem to know how the world works. They don't see how things are connected. They don't think internationally. They don't even think nationally." Still another woman said, "We make people so specialized and so cost conscious they can't recognize the kinds of investment opportunities we have to make if we are going to continue to grow. They don't know anything about the history or culture or politics of places we're looking to invest in. They don't seem to have initiative or ideas. It really puts a burden on the few of us at the top."

Of course it was unfair of me to milk them for the different answers to the questions I put to them. I was not surprised by their responses. I knew they would be looking for different qualities at different times in the careers of their employees. But it illustrates what I am telling you about what you need to plan for if you want someday to hold a top-level job. You should always be planning and working toward fulfilling the expectations associated with the next level of responsibility you aspire to. It's like that fashion advice for ambitious women, "Always dress for the next position you want to hold."

When you get into your early work and relate to those around you, including those above you, it might seem to you at times that you face the choice of being totally immersed or remaining totally aloof. Let me explain. You will need to do your job but you also will need to evaluate how you are doing in your job. Too much emphasis on either of these approaches will diminish your effectiveness. Total immersion in your day-to-day activities to the extent of losing yourself completely in your work will deprive you of information essential to your incremental improvement in your profession. Loss of yourself in your work with no "standing back and looking at yourself" will keep you from judging your performance or seeing how others are relating to you and judging your actions. In addition, total, unthinking commitment might also mean you have made no judgment as to the morality of the tasks you are being given to carry out.

On the other hand, maintaining too much distance from involvement to observe how you are doing and how others see you can make you so self-conscious that you will probably be less effective in your work and seem artificial or stilted in your relations. Everything you do may appear to be rehearsed. You cannot devote the greater part of your attention to constantly observing yourself as you do your job. The ballet dancer or an athlete or a skater or diver must be partly aware of how they are being seen and judged in their performance, but only partly. If they think too much about their each and every move and how they are being evaluated, they will lose spontaneity and the concentration demanded in their presentation and performance.

You might not think this is a matter that will be of any concern to you when you go to work. But it should be. If you are to walk with kings, you will have to grow immensely from where you are at the moment. Like it or not your middle name is Tyro. And you are not going to get many lessons along the way, except those you create for yourself. It will be up to you to discern at the different steps of your career what changes are occurring in what is expected of you, what new standards are being applied, what new skills you will need. With your head down in total immersion you will be seen as a good staff person or a good line officer capable of carrying out orders. With excessive self-awareness you may be seen as insincere and self-promoting and perhaps a little out of touch or odd. You will encounter people who suffer from too much self-awareness and you will see what I mean. They are often quite ambitious but they remain self-aware navel gazers. You must seek a balance between being both inside and outside your career, between commitment and involvement on the one hand and critical self-analysis on the other.

Right now you need to concentrate on your studies on acquiring those entry-level skills you will need to get your foot in the door and get your career off to a sound beginning. In doing this you will need to stay in touch with some of the literature in your field and the specialized areas you work in. But you can't stay specialized. You shouldn't get bogged down in your specialty. For example, you should start immediately upon graduation to broaden your knowledge about the larger world. Take at least one *great* general newspaper and start reading the editorials, syndicated columnists, and the op-ed pages as well as the news. Subscribe to two or three good journals that are read by thinking people and learn what the people who shape public policy are concerned about. The people who make policy are always aware of a bigger piece of the world than their subordinates, and those they rely on most are also more broadly informed. Narrow specialists only get called on when there's a problem in their area. You don't call a utilities expert when you're planning to redevelop a city. You don't call an expert in the printing and distribution of currencies when you're dealing with international trade policies and favored nations privileges and human rights violations and the resulting congressional politics.

A perfect example of the kind of complexity you will face are the multiple ramifications related to the European common market and the establishment of a common currency. Imagine the contingencies they must study. Consider among the many nations involved the issues of different taxes, competing labor costs, varying welfare policies, retirement benefits, resulting corporate migration, existing debts of different countries, deficit spending attitudes among different countries under a common currency, and questions of interest rates, to say nothing of concerns over national sovereignty and language barriers. How would the computer billionaires or top-level heart surgeons or award-winning engineers or architects deal with such questions? Yet many of them will have opinions on issues like these, most of them simplistic and uninformed. Some of these professionals and business types and other celebrities will become the politicians or board members you will have to educate and work with on complex public issues during your career.

If you are going to be an effective leader of opinions and policymaking, you will have no choice but to become more broadly aware of the whole world and how the pieces relate to each other. You will need broad, general knowledge to meet your responsibilities for whatever your own small role is in promoting a civilized world and protecting our democratic processes. For it is inevitable that some of the specialists from the private sector who make bundles of money and who rise to positions of honor and prestige and authority will acquire political influence. These are the ones who can become the most dangerous. Some of them come to believe that from all the adulation and fawning respect they receive and all the money they have accumulated that they must also know how to answer the big questions of all of humanity. They don't yet know what they don't know. But all too often they can tell you in a hurry what is wrong with the way things have been done and how to straighten out public policy. They are impatient with the rest of us mere mortals, especially those of us incompetents relegated to public service work. The thought rarely occurs to them that they hold a very narrow view of the world and their place in it. Their success and the application of their intelligence, even though narrowly put to practice, often mislead them to think that they can solve any problem of any breadth in any setting. As one of my colleagues puts it, part of your job as a public servant will be to "desimplify" the world. You will have to stand up to these kinds of people and their often simplistic solutions to complex social and economic issues. And you will have no choice but to learn to help them to acquire the understanding they will need to take on political responsibilities.

A great Spanish philosopher described this dangerous trend he saw coming in modern societies even before the Spanish Civil War and before the rise of Adolph Hitler. José Ortega y Gasset said that man has had to wait until the twentieth century to see "how brutal, how stupid, and yet how aggressive is the man learned in one thing and fundamentally ignorant in all else." He went on, "This new barbarian is above all the professional man, more learned than ever before, but at the same more uncultured. . . . With his friends he will emit thoughts that are monstrosities, and opinions that are a torrent of drivel and bluff."

Part of your task as a policymaker will be to deal with this new form of R and D, rot and drivel. And you will be able to do this effectively only if you yourself acquire an understanding of our times and our culture, meaning the world culture.

As to your reading to prepare for this role of walking with kings, I agree with Sam Rayburn's advice to those who want to be leaders. Read biographies. Through them you can see how the people who made history lived and thought and acted. Biographies come closer than any other record to giving you a sense of the myriad range of events and issues a leader has to deal with at the same time and make some progress on most of them.

Read history and the social sciences and the humanities. From these you will learn to make connections, see relationships, judge consequences of alternative courses of action. If this, then what? If we push here, who pushes back or who gets pushed out of shape? What precedent are we about to set? What parallel situations or circumstances are going to be affected by this, and who else is going to insist on being given the same exemption we are about to grant? Is this departure from policy so important that consistency should not bind us? Is this the time for a pause before taking the irrevocable step? If so, how do we do it?

And don't tell me after you get on your job you don't have time to read. You must make time from whatever else you do. "Do you long for the conversation of the wise? Learn to understand it, and you shall hear it."

Once when I was giving a group of graduate students this same gratuitous but stellar advice, a young woman asked me was it *really* so necessary to read? She said she had never liked reading but she watched the history and discovery and biography television channels. Wouldn't this substitute for reading? I may have offended her. But I said, no, there is no substitute for reading if you expect to get to the top in your field or be an effective leader. You don't want to spend a large part of your life reading? Forget your public career; it will go exactly nowhere. I can tell you one thing with certainty, if you don't want to read you will soon be working for somebody who does.

You may see the surface actions of figures in history dramatized on a television screen, but you can never know what is going on in their minds and the alternatives they are considering. You can never know from a dramatic presentation of an historical figure what you, as a future decision maker, need to know about what it is to face the requirement to do something, to decide, to act, or not to act. It is not the *action* or a representation of it or its consequences that we need to observe, but what causes and motivates individuals to act as they do, what mental processes and anguish they go through to make decisions, what other pressing issues are occurring at the same time the crisis at hand is being handled. No movie can capture like a good biography the intense feelings of being on the cutting edge of the unknown future, on the precipice of the unresolved outcomes of a decision. And isn't this the principal conundrum faced by every public policymaker? This is the practical value of such reading, aside from the knowledge you will gain—and your improved writing. And watching television is nearly a total waste. Imagine having sat through 1,000 hours of commercial television. In that time you would have wasted 350 to 400 hours listening to people try to sell you things you don't need. And you can't possibly spend that much time in the bathroom.

This letter is sort of devolving into advice for your personal development so I might as well continue with my preaching. Enough on filling your mind with the right things and ideas and information, except to say this: I will send you a list of some of my favorite books when you get closer to graduation.

On to communications. A few years back a fellow named Pericles summed it up. He said that a person who has knowledge about proper policy but has no ability to express it might as well have no idea at all on the matter.

I'll come back to writing. Speaking first. Seek out opportunities to speak in public. You might join Toastmasters International or another such group. Speak professionally every chance you get. Take positions in organizations where you can observe and learn from those who hold offices just ahead of you. This way you can ease into taking on speaking and leading roles. And study other speakers.

If in your early public speaking you feel rattled and excessively nervous, let me give you some personal reassurance. It doesn't improve. Well, maybe a little. It is not a question of whether you get nervous; it is how you learn to handle nerves.

Communications experts have discovered the reasons for the nervousness we all feel when we speak. It comes from the age-old, inherited fight or flight syndrome. The fear that triggers such a response in us is that we are afraid of humiliating ourselves before an audience. We fear the judgment of the people who are all watching and listening attentively as we might forget what we are planning to say or somehow otherwise screw up our presentation or stand there in catatonic shock. And it can be a truly debilitating fear. Still, all of what happens to you has an explanation in how your body is preparing for battle or to bolt. The shaking of your hands and arms and the weakness in your knees results from the large muscles pulling against each other in readiness for the release of fighting or running away. The increased heartbeat and faster breathing are also in preparation for combat or flight. The sweating and paleness of your skin are a physiological readying for struggle. The blood leaves the skin so if you get wounded you will bleed less. Your hair stands on end to make you appear larger to your opponent. And your mouth turns dry so you won't strangle on your own spittle in the middle of battle. I tell you all this so you will know the sacrifices I make every time I give a speech.

Debilitating is hardly an adequate word for the suffering many speakers undergo. Experience helps some people. Yet there have been outstanding, world-famous opera singers and actors and actresses who have thrown up before every performance out of fear of doing poorly or being unable to perform. Then they almost uniformly go out and do a superb job. You will learn to do so too, without throwing up, hopefully. So welcome to the club. Start getting used to it. This is something else that goes with the territory.

Now to the importance of writing well to your success. Harry Golden, editor of the *Carolina Israelite*, has underscored the point I made above when he said, "I advise everyone who asks about a career of writing to get himself all the books he can carry before he buys a typewriter. Library cards are more important than pens." But the only way to become master over words and to control them and make them do what you want them to do is to practice writing. The best advice I ever had was from my friend Tomás Rivera, an Hispanic writer who went on to become president of the University of California at Riverside. He told me to write short stories, setting down descriptions of events that happened in my childhood. He said this was a topic I should know something about and I could go straight to writing and not have to develop plot lines or do a lot of research or preparation.

I soon came to experience the interplay between what I had put on paper and what I was planning to write next. On occasion this give and take between what was already written and what still remained as potentially to be written proved beneficial in stimulating me to develop something I wouldn't have considered until I had actually started writing about the episode I was describing. Other times it was vexing to have the writing I had done suggest that I run off down some rabbit trail. So I had to learn to make judgments about my writing and to take control of it and to direct it to go in the direction I wanted it to go.

And producing poetry is an even more disciplined approach to writing. It adds the dimension of form, the need to capture meaning in tight phrases or single words and in limited space due to the dictations of meter, the consideration of alternative words to round a rhyme or attain an alliteration. All that you do in any kind of writing will prepare you to write better in your professional role.

And you will come to appreciate Mark Twain's advice on finding the exactly right word and not a poor substitute. As Twain said, in part satirically, in criticizing James Fenimore Cooper's literary sins, the author must "say what he is proposing to say, not merely come near it; use the right word, not its second cousin; eschew surplusage; not omit necessary details; avoid slovenliness of form; use good grammar; employ a simple and straightforward style."

The point is, you will need to write and to work seriously at writing. This will be a principal tool of your trade and you must learn to write with precision. Inadequacy in writing skills will hold back your rise to leadership positions.

For example, your first briefing memo could make you or break your early career. Well done, and your boss may take note. Poorly done and she may at best ignore you or at worst suggest that you not be asked to do another, which means, "Don't involve that person again in our policymaking work." And that's why you've entered this field, to be in the midst of policymaking.

So, a few words of advice here. A briefing memo is not a mystery, so you don't have to build your case first and then amaze your reader with your surprise denouement. Put your position up front. Get to the point. Marshal your arguments and make them march. Stay business-like; don't fall into the chatty style of e-mail. Incomplete sentences are often okay. Maybe boldface your major points.

Here are a few faults often found with a briefing memo: It is not *brief*. Key issues are missed or ignored. It is rambling, not focused, poorly organized. It is obviously an unadulterated first draft. Remember the old adage that it is harder to write something short than long. Work your writing over carefully.

Put yourself in your boss's shoes and ask what you would want from this memo you've been asked to write. Is this something she wants to read only once or to use as an outline? Is this just a starter memo on this subject with a research paper to follow or is it a summary of research already done? Does she need talking points for a presentation? Does she need to be warned of possible surprises—or questions? If she's appearing on a panel or giving testimony, what does she need to know about the audience or panelists? Don't put more than one subject in the memo. Think hard about what to leave out as well as what to put in. And remember: She who has the numbers wins. Perhaps a few hard facts and data might help your boss in her presentation.

A further few words about what is called an op-ed piece. This is short for "opposite the editorial page." Typically this page is used for syndicated columnists, but most papers also use it to place opinion pieces by public officials, public-spirited citizens who want to sound off on something, and experts and professors. The pieces usually run from 700 to 1,200 words. The purpose is to persuade, not to explain or analyze. And your topic should be something of contemporary interest to readers. You need to practice using style, creative phrasing, playful use of words, metaphors, and thought-jolting expressions or points of view to capture and hold your reader. You should begin to try your hand at an occasional essay on a topic you have strong feelings about, and after you have done a few, see if your local paper would be interested in publishing one.

You should start trying to publish, no matter how insignificant the media. Study your professional journals and the kinds of articles they are printing. I still recall my first article. It was in the Toastmasters International magazine and nothing I have published since ever gave me such pride and satisfaction. I glowed for days.

So, I say about communicating what I said about reading. If you can't communicate, you will end up working for someone who can.

As I leave this advice on preparing to "walk with kings" and other personal development, the Duke of Gloucester's comment comes to mind when he accepted the second volume of *The Decline and Fall of the Roman Empire*. He said, "Another damned thick, square book! Always scribble, scribble, scribble! Eh, Mr. Gibbon?"

Yes, always scribble, scribble, scribble! Keep at it.

Your uncle, the scribe,

Uncle Ken

re: *Delegating, or working for your subordinates*

I don't want you fellows sitting around asking me what to do. I want you to tell me what to do. — *General George C. Marshall*

It is not hard work which is dreary; it is superficial work.
— *Edith Hamilton*

The willing horse is ridden to death. — *General George S. Patton*

Half the failures of this world arise from pulling in one's horse as he is leaping. — *Julius and Augustus Hare*

JANUARY

Dear Kim

I must disabuse you of a commonly held idea, that when you get to be boss everybody under you works for you. You will get far more done if you figure out a way to work for *them*. My idea of a well-organized shop is for the next level of managers below the boss to be delegated responsibility for their program areas with the clear expectation that they are supposed to move their programs ahead and get their work done. They are to ask for the boss's help when they need it and to keep their boss fully informed about their programs and activities and plans. But their main responsibility is to move their business forward.

This way you get more initiative and your organization gets more done, and self-starters don't get held back. There will be more ideas in the pot because program managers don't have to wait around for ideas to come down from above.

The idea is to give up some power over programs in order to get more done. You can apply elsewhere for the good of the agency the power you give up. I'll come back to that.

When I first became head of my agency I decided that I needed to make all of the staff presentations to our board myself. I wanted to do this to establish a single standard for presentations, and I was so reluctant to lose any initial battles before our board with our opponents that I felt I had to be in the middle of the fray on every issue. This was especially important to me because the college and university presidents had decided to fight nearly every issue tooth and nail with me before my board. The presidents were very resentful of my efforts to apply more rigorous standards to their requests for expansion of facilities, campuses, and degree programs, and they wanted to make clear that they had always had their way with our board and they intended to keep it that way. After about a year and half the battles had been resolved more in my favor than theirs, although they were still seeing me overridden often enough by our board to encourage them to challenge at least three or four of my recommendations at every quarterly meeting.

After we had fought out a couple of intense issues at one board meeting I sat down to go through my papers to get ready for the next squabble. The chairman was speaking to the board and stalling for a few minutes to let me get organized. Suddenly I realized I was about to pass out and fall out of my chair. I found I was hyperventilating in preparation for our next assault. I got myself under control and went ahead with the meeting. But I knew right then I had to find ways to use my staff to assist me in these fights we were having at every meeting. By being so tense and by overloading myself, I had given myself a clear message: I needed to delegate more to my assistant commissioners.

The result was an immediate boost in staff morale. They had seen and helped me and suffered with me in my presentations long enough to know what I wanted, and they were eager to show their stuff. And they did. I began to divide the issues in my mind as to which were the ones I desperately wanted to win, and I let the assistant commissioners cut their teeth on the others. The staff presentations as well as mine were being made within the structure of the committee meetings of the board I described in an earlier letter, whereby the committee chair presides and makes the basic presentations to the board. But when it came down to the jousting with the presidents over data, facts, and rationale, the staff was still needed by the committee chairs and the board before they could adjudicate the differences between our positions.

The result of my delegation of responsibilities was we could take more fights to the board at each meeting. Another result was that I could concentrate my attention on the most contentious issues. A corollary result was noted by one of the staff, "The commissioner loses more fights before the board than all the rest of us put together."

This kind of delegation of authority, however, will require more consultation by you with your staff, and perhaps even dress rehearsals, before staff members make presentations to your board. In our case we needed to review each presentation as to time allotted, clarity, content, organization, and focus. You quickly discover that if you lay an issue out before a board without a clear definition and a focused presentation, the board members will quickly undertake to discover the issue for themselves hidden amidst your muddled exposition. This may result in several of them or the entire board going off down some rabbit trail. Worse yet, they get interested in sniffing down that rabbit trail and you play heck trying to get them all back on *your* trail, the one you wanted them to be on in the first place before you lost them.

As you delegate in this way you will have to make some accommodations for your program managers. You have to be more accessible to them for advice and counsel. They may need to try out ideas or see if you agree with where they are headed or check with you on precedent. They may need to ask you about a board member's views or consult with you on the institutional memory or agency history or ask your opinion on their plans in a broader context. Or they may need the help of other units of the organization over which they have no authority. Or they may just need reassurance that you both are still "singing out of the same hymn book."

And you have to make time to help them quickly when they need it. In these ways you will be institutionalizing in your agency something I advised you on how to use earlier: subordinate leadership, that is, how to get someone at a higher level to help you to go where you want to go. You will be working for your subordinates in helping them to lead their programs to where they want to take them. Your subordinates will be working to try to lead you to go along with them. When you begin to find them scheduling your calendar for you, then you will know you are indeed working for them. A price you pay for running your organization this way is to lose some control over your time schedule and your own agenda.

And once you delegate, try to *keep* things delegated. When I was executive vice president at a university, deans and department chairs would often come by to ask me to help them do something unpleasant or to get me to do it for them. It was usually a personnel action or a reallocation of space or an additional workload assignment, and other such things. I used to tell them that every time they asked me to do part of their job for them they were giving me part of their authority. They were giving up power entrusted to their position. All too often the dean or departmental chair would drop their shoulders and say, "Gosh, I know that's right. I really shouldn't. . . . But would you do it for me just this one more time?"

When you run an agency through delegating authority you then take on a different kind of job. You must be certain that you coordinate what all your divisions are doing. You must become the communications information center (CIC) for your agency. On a warship, the CIC is where everything comes together: speed, course, vectors with the enemy and other vessels, kinds of shells or missiles loaded for firing, kinds of bombs to load on planes to dispatch to the enemy, information on incoming bogies or unidentified aircraft, and data from radar, sonar, and screening vessels, in order to centralize in one place, CIC, the control of accurate and timely contact with the enemy.

Your new CIC duties in an agency will not be so dramatic, but they entail the same principles. You need to know what all parts of your agency are doing and how they relate, that is, how they support or conflict with each other. You also need to have a sufficient "intelligence system" to know how those constituents you affect most and the public out there are reacting to the activities of your agency and all its subparts. And if the individual managers are to be most effective, they need to know what others in the organization are doing. Of equal importance, they need to know what their colleagues are about to do or are *thinking* about doing. You must use your position of coordinator to be certain that information is cross-shared among the divisions and not just communicated to you.

It is through the consultations and sharing of thinking and ideas that individuals become prepared for those occasions when they cannot check back with you or with others, when they have to make an independent decision. The more sharing, discussing, and melding of ideas toward a common agency goal, the better chance you have that those independent decisions will be congruent with the agency mission and long-range plans. In other words, the greater will be the likelihood that those decisions will be correct.

My deputy and my legislative liaison can't always check back with me when a committee chair or a legislator is negotiating a deal for us or they have to give a quick response to a proposed accommodation that the politicians are ready to act on. Our guideline is that given by the Israeli Army to its officers: If you can't reach your superior officer, do what you think he would order you to do in the circumstances. At Trafalgar, Nelson was joined in time for the battle by ships whose officers had independently sailed there from many distant locations by imagining where Nelson would order them to go.

I have always respected Lord Salisbury's reply to a young consular general from Zanzibar. He telegraphed home for instructions as he faced mobs in the streets and an endangered English colony. From the British Foreign Office Salisbury answered, "Do whatever you think best. Whatever you do will be approved—but be careful not to undertake anything which you cannot carry through."

Although there are times our staff representatives at the legislature can't get back to home base to check in, we do try to keep the lines open. On our digital pagers and cell phones we enter not only the number to call back, but certain codes: 800 for "please check in"; 411 for "I need information fast"; 911 for "emergency, return call immediately"; and 666 for "get to the capitol—the devil's at work, all hell's breaking loose."

Now back to the point I left hanging: what to do with the time and power you have given to your top managers to run their programs. You should use this freed-up time to periodically reconsider the mission of your agency. This is absolutely essential for you to do for the simple reason that no one else will do it.

The job of any government agency or even a quasi-public organization is not merely to identify problems, devise solutions, find money, and then implement or enforce programs. Of course doing those things is important, but they can cause you to lose your way. You can forget what you stand for, why your agency exists. We can grow so accustomed to noting the pitch and volume of a scream that we don't hear it as a cry for help.

It is the boss's major job to think about and establish and talk about the mission of his agency. It is the mission that should guide planning and motivate action. And having defined the mission once at some point in the past is not sufficient. Nor is it enough to state it once. Not only do times change, but the citizenry changes in the ways they hear about and feel about conditions they used to think of as being tolerable. And your employees turn over and the rest forget and need to be reminded about the agency's mission. What is it we do? Why is it important? Who is it we serve? Again, why do we do this?

August 27, former President Lyndon Johnson's birthday, was a state holiday and when I arrived at the office I found dozens of cars in the agency parking lot. It was encouraging to see such staff dedication but a little dispiriting to realize so many people were having to give up a day off to do our work due to inadequate funds for staff. Inside I found that all the telephones had been redirected to our main switchboard outside my office, which was not staffed during the holiday. Several lines continued to ring incessantly. I finally answered to see what could be the problem. I learned quickly that while this might be a state holiday for state agencies, a hundred and fifty colleges and universities were open and today they were in the midst of their fall registration. The financial aid offices and multitudes of students needed to know what our staff had decided about their loans and grants for the coming semester.

All of those dedicated employees in our loans and grants division had given up their holiday to catch up on their backlogged paperwork. They had shut down the phones to get a little peace and quiet to get some work done.

Talk about mixed feelings. I had to get us focused again on our mission. We quickly got back on track as to what took priority. We opened the phone lines and served the schools and students the rest of the day. I gave compensatory time off for the holiday and we ensured this would not happen again on LBJ's birthday holiday.

I'll give you another personal example. At our opening registration at a new university where I was executive vice president, I came out to the mall to discover chaos. There was a line of several hundred angry students at one table manned by one person. It was a station reviewing evidence whether each new student had been inoculated as required by state law. Most students registering with us for the first time had no idea they were supposed to have inoculations as a condition of being admitted—or *which* inoculations. Staff at other tables sat idly by while this bottleneck slowly was bringing all registration to a dead stop. Understandably, students were refusing to be denied admission and were arguing with the sole person at this table. The registrar (whose principal qualification for his job was his Prussian DNA) informed me that no one could waive the requirement of state law that students show evidence of inoculations before being enrolled. His view was they would just have to wait until next semester to start college.

I took the registrar's pad from him and drafted a new form for him to reproduce and hand out immediately. It read simply: "I, _____, do hereby certify that I will submit evidence of the required inoculations within one month of this date. If I fail to do so, I agree that I may be dropped from university enrollment. Dated: _____."

The line was gone in 10 minutes. We were back to our mission of enrolling students.

The job of the boss is to speak about and act on what the agency stands for and to speak for those it serves. What standards do we want to apply? Is it quality? Is it access? Is it equity? Fairness? Assistance? Some or all these? In what mixture? Is it responsiveness and service? Who is our client? Are there other standards?

In addition, it is the mission that defines for the agency the standards that can't be compromised or mediated away. When a federal court ruled that the coordinating board for higher education could no longer practice affirmative action or assist colleges and universities in affirmative action programs as a way to achieve larger enrollments of Black and Hispanic students, the agency had to obey the law. However, this ruling could not stop the agency from suggesting legal ways to get around the law or from working with the legislature to find ways to promote minority representation in higher education. This commitment to stay on course came from the mission of the agency.

When a student challenged a minimum standard of performance for advancement to junior level status in one of our universities, that standard of quality and readiness for college would not be compromised away by the agency when the court directed us to mediate a settlement. The young lady challenged the provision on the basis that she was a journalism major and should not be required to show competency in basic math, since she would never be required to use math in her field of work. (Our failure to teach math might also explain how an elected member of the state board of education at a public meeting multiplied 1,000 by 200 and came up with 201,000. He was the same member who objected to placing computers in classrooms because, as he said in complete earnestness, "There are some teachers who still don't know what to do with floppy dicks." We thought we had misheard until he repeated the phrase as applying to himself as well.) In any event, back to the courtroom. As evidence of her readiness to practice her profession of journalism, she submitted an article she had written and had published on her experiences working in a topless bar. No math or rocket scientist required there either. We stood firm on our standard and the case was resolved in our favor.

I have been putting off discussing ethics and morality in the public service with you but I guess the time has come. I have been giving much thought to this and I will put together a letter for you on that topic next month.

Your nagging

Uncle Ken

re: *Ethics and morality in public service*

If you think you *might* be able to get away with doing it, don't do it.
— Texas Senator Carl Parker

Unanimity . . . is so valued within the organizational context
that it often carries more weight with the individual than his
own conscience.
— Warren Bennis

Unfettered ambition can destroy one's innate awareness of
ethical principles.
— Albert Speer

Mankind are very odd creatures: One half censure what they practice,
the other half practice what they censure; the rest always say and do
as they ought.
— Benjamin Franklin

There is no moral precept that does not have something
inconvenient about it.
— Denis Diderot

FEBRUARY

Dear Kim

Now I come to a special topic I have been putting off talking with you about. It is perhaps the heaviest of the subjects I've written to you about. Very soon you will start thinking about ethical behavior in your career because it will inevitably confront you, as it does every public official. You will not escape it, that I guarantee you. In the hope that perhaps another bureaucrat's experience may get you started thinking on this question,

I will give you some sense of my own personal search for guidance for my behavior in public jobs during my career.

John Steinbeck sums up the dilemma well in one of his novels. His plot is built on a decision made by the French to reinstate their monarchy after the collapse of yet another one of their republics. As I recall, they locate the heir to their throne in Petaluma, California, where he's running a chicken farm. When he comes to rule as Pippin IV, he begins to deal with public issues and immediately he faces questions of good versus bad, having to pick among the best of bad choices, and having to compromise what he wants to do or what he feels is right. In grappling with such moral and ethical questions, he asks a trusted adviser, "What is a person to do?" His adviser replies that one usually does what one is.

That, although a keen observation, is far too simple and simplistic advice to be of much help. So what can I give you from my experience and thinking about this topic that might help you as you have to confront such conundrums? I can only share with you some of my own odyssey in trying to find my way among rocky shoals.

All successful public executives spend a lot of time in apprenticeship as subordinates. It is there you will first be tested. As an ambitious person, you will experience two things that can or should result in disappointment in yourself or even self-disgust. One is to have to carry out orders you feel are wrong or unfair to those affected or improper in how they are being carried out. The other is to compromise your own integrity in order to further your career or not to hurt your advancement. It is from the choices you are forced to make in these kinds of situations that you will learn much about who you really are. How you handle difficult options that come to you in subordinate positions will begin to shape the kind of leader you will become.

I have to confess to you that in my own career I have experienced both forms of self-loathing. I cannot be proud that I carried out orders when I was younger that I would refuse to execute now. Or that I cut corners and did ignominious things because I wanted to get the recognition or approval of my bosses. I have remained silent when I should have disagreed. And I have felt I betrayed myself and what I want to stand for because I longed so much to be on the inside alongside those pressing for action, even if I felt what they were doing was in some ways improper. I did not refuse, on occasion, to carry out an order or disagree on the cusp of action when I had serious reservations. In part, I didn't refuse because I thought to do so could harm my standing with my superiors and retard my future advancement.

Abraham Maslow helps us to rationalize that these feelings are not all bad. He points out that experiencing self-repugnance can have a positive outcome. One of two things can happen to you—one bad, one good. You can become neurotic. Or you can make atonement for your sins against yourself and others.

In my case, these few incidents in my early years made me reassess how I would conduct myself in public office thereafter. I am speaking of the kinds of things that lead you to ask yourself, "If I am willing to do this much or go this far, how much more would I be capable of doing if I am pressed hard enough on it?" Not only do you think about atonement, you start thinking about limits to how far you will permit yourself to be pushed in the future. Or about revisiting your courage and about what you need to do to regain your own self-respect. And until you have confronted hard choices of what is right or wrong in your behavior on the job, you will not think meaningfully about where you draw that line behind you, across which you refuse to be pushed. Until you have discovered the need for such a line, you are unlikely to give it much thought.

I am not going to try to convey to you the guilt and disappointment I felt about betraying myself. And I am certainly not going to describe in writing, even to you, those particular events in which I was involved and allowed myself to be misused and where I played a less than noble role. Suffice it to say that, as Maslow suggests, those experiences caused me along the way to want to make redress for my earlier transgressions. In my career I never had occasion to make one grand recompense like Joseph Conrad's "Lord Jim," but in little ways I have expiated my earlier sins against myself and the public I was responsible to. As I think about the future you face and your driving ambition, I know with certainty what you too will encounter along your way.

Subordinates throughout government willingly carry out bad, unwise, and unfair orders and routinely compromise themselves to please their bosses in order to seek career advancement. And this is not limited to government careers. As I say, having behaved in such ways myself, I can now recognize it more quickly in others. And I understand fully the temptations and rationalizations that lead to ignoble behavior.

As I have implied already, this present letter is certainly not the first time I have thought seriously about this aspect of a public service career. Knowing these self-destructive temptations, I have tried over the years to discover some rationale to guide my own conduct. Perhaps I need to explain why I feel this matter of personal comportment is so critical. It involves far more than just the pain or personal revulsion of individual workers here and there in government as they go about their daily duties. It is the accumulation of individual actions that define the kind of government we have and the way it serves the people. Plato said, "What is honored in a country will be cultivated there." Certainly what is rewarded by an organization will be encouraged there. What leaders sow they will harvest. So, how each of us acts is essential to the outcome of the whole of American government.

Performing effectively in the public service is mostly a matter of carrying out routine and even repetitive activities. In our daily work we spend most of our time fulfilling ministerial functions. Most of what we do is apply the tools of our trade to keep the machinery of government operating efficiently and effectively. But every once in a while we must face a crisis that tests our deepest convictions about our *system* of government. Those are always the most difficult times in a public career, for they often occur in an emergency situation, in a time of pressure, confusion, and uncertainty, at a turning point. And all of these are circumstances that hold the potential for serious error of judgment. These are moments when we might compromise away our own values. These are the times when bosses sometimes decide that for the good of the nation they must violate laws or the Constitution in order to save the republic. As Benito Mussolini put it, "The 'reasons of state' must, on this occasion, take precedence over legality." Even Abraham Lincoln had to rationalize a decision when he said, "I should consider my official oath broken, if I should allow the Government to be overthrown, when I might think the disregarding [of a] single law would tend to preserve it. . . . We have a case of rebellion, and . . . the public safety does require the qualified suspension of the privilege of the writ of habeas corpus, which I authorized to be made." Both were self-justifying reasons for actions that could be questioned legally. When do we know what is justified?

Chances are you will never face times and events as momentous as those faced by Lincoln. But that does not mean that some public figure someday will not rationalize some illegal action "in order to save the nation" or the state or to save the people from themselves. And such bosses have to give orders to subordinates, whom they expect to act on their directions. The mere possibility that every public servant could be given such orders brings us to you and the years just ahead for you.

All the rest of administering government business is relatively easy. It's like the comment about flying an airplane: interminable periods of monotony interrupted by moments of sheer terror. But it is for those moments of testing that we need to be best prepared. Wouldn't it be marvelous to have an immutable formula to turn to that could tell us how to conduct ourselves when embroiled amidst good and evil and near good and near evil, and when we are tempted to take upon ourselves extraordinary authority in order to save the people from themselves and a horrific future?

In a sense I have been in quest of a universal moral and ethical code that I might turn to in seeking out appropriate personal actions and in conducting public business in the most demanding of times. I certainly wouldn't dedicate one of my letters to you on this arcane subject of personal behavior if I had not found during my own career that this quest has been of major importance to me. So here is a brief description of my own quest.

In my search I turned first, of course, to religious upbringings and religious heritage. But here I quickly came to the conclusion that any guidance based solely on religion is founded far less on God's commandments and directions than it is on the wishes of those who interpret God's will. Experience has made me suspicious of interpreters, for what else is an emergency decision to disregard something in the Constitution but an interpretation? And *whose* God and which dogma shall govern us in a bureaucracy made up of public servants from so many different faiths? If there is indeed a God-given truth from the universe, it has all too often been misused through the interpretations rendered by those who declare themselves to be God's priests here on earth. Torquemada was convinced he was doing God's will in burning heretics under the Inquisition. The slaughter of the Huguenots was done in God's name. The Thirty Years War was fought over differing religious interpretations. The massacre of the infidels during the Crusades and the near annihilation of the Native Americans from Mexico south were based on religious fanaticism. A number of countries in the East continue to struggle with whether their governments will be God-directed, that is, guided by clergy interpreting a God-given dogma. A few years ago we saw pictures of beheadings in parking lots and portable gallows at work to enforce such interpretations.

Bloody Mary got her name from the executions carried out under her religious direction. Barbara Tuchman described the decimation of the European population as, among all the other reasons for conflict in the fourteenth century, the Church split over which of two popes was the true deputy of God. Our own burning of witches and our statutes passed in colonial days to persecute the Quakers are examples of the misuse of religious authority by sects acting under the guise of correct religious thought.

The American philosopher Horace Kallen summed up his experience this way, speaking of his childhood in Boston, "The Christians ganged up not only on the Christ-killers; they ganged up on one another, however Christian—as Protestants, as Catholics, as Yankees, as Micks, as Wops, as Polacks, as Dutchies. . ." And today the social standards proposed for all Americans by the so-called Christian Right could be imposed upon me only by what I would see as a totalitarian government. (But I would similarly oppose government imposing upon me ideas from the modern left as to how I am supposed to live my life.)

Therefore, I concluded there are simply too many religious points of view and too many interpretations and too many standards of morality fixed from above for me to turn to them to establish a single and objective guide to personal behavior in public office.

But if my religion, handed down by my own family and community, could not serve as the sole guide I sought, I needed to turn elsewhere. Maybe we should look to the individual's conscience, which comes out of childhood upbringing. The problem here is that all the bad people of the world also had childhoods and upbringings. And the result was they developed consciences that later governed them to their own full satisfaction in all the horrors they perpetrated upon humanity.

I remember your dad told me that he found you inadequate and a disappointment one too many times. He told me you said, "Where did I go wrong, Dad? Was it my heredity or my upbringing?" It had to be upbringing that implanted Daddy Warbucks' conscience. In the musical, "Annie," he states it simply, "It doesn't matter how you treat people on the way up if you're not planning to come down again."

All right, as public servants it seems fitting we might look to the idea of the preeminent importance of the state, our great nation. Can complete devotion to the state perhaps serve as an adequate guide? After all, very early we are all taught loyalty to our nation. "My country, right or wrong" goes back through most of our nation's history. The bumper sticker, "Love it or leave it," of the Vietnam protest era says the same thing. Much of your youth and mine were spent conditioning us to be loyal to our country. We've learned the Pledge of Allegiance and the Scout Oath. Therefore, loyalty to "the state" might seem to be a possible touchstone to govern all we do in performing our personal duties as public officials.

But let's look further at this. Mussolini described the advantages of fascism this way, "The individual exists only insofar as he is subordinated to the interests of the state, and as civilization becomes more complex, so the liberty of the individual must be increasingly restricted." Ignazio Silone in a short novel about fascist Italy, *Bread and Wine,* has one of his protagonists describe what it is like to live in such a state, "[E]very idea is crystallized into formulas. . . . It is entrusted to a body of interpreters so that it may be preserved. . . . And if it becomes the official doctrine of the state no more escape is possible. A carpenter or a laborer can perhaps adapt himself . . . and eat, digest, procreate in peace; but for an intellectual there is no escape. He must either bend the knee and enter the ranks of the dominant clerks, or

resign himself to hunger and defamation and being killed off at the first fa-
vorable opportunity."

By the time Silone wrote this in 1937, the world was watching films
of Nazi Nuremberg. The Sportzplatz was filled with hundreds of thousands
of screaming Germans pledging themselves to the good of the state over all
else, including, of course, over the good of each and every individual.

During our own McCarthy episode at a congressional hearing Arthur
Miller was harassed and pressured. The government was trying to force him
to provide the names of colleagues and friends. The Un-American Activities
Committee began to look as un-American as the communists they sought
to discover. As Adolf Hitler said so boastfully, "The greatest strength of the
totalitarian state is that it will force those who fear it to imitate it." When
Arthur Miller refused to name associates, he was held in contempt of Congress. John Steinbeck said of him, "A man who is disloyal to his friends could
not be expected to be loyal to his country."

In 1970, I was sorely tested as to how much loyalty I thought my country deserved from me. At that time I had the single most chilling experience
in government in all my working career. In Austin, students at the University of Texas (UT) were holding a noisy and angry but peaceful demonstra-
tion on the mall in front of the UT tower and main building to mourn and
protest the killings the day before at Kent State University by the Ohio National Guard. The seven or eight thousand students gathered on the mall
were vociferous and some of their speakers menacing. The students were
being harangued to go down the block and attack the National Guardsmen,
who were lined up on the edge of the campus in assault gear.

My office was at the front of the tower building overlooking the speakers' microphone. A man came into my office, where several regents and we
administrators were standing watching. Without asking anyone for permission he pulled the blinds closed and then cracked open one blind and set
up a movie camera on a tripod and began to film the students and protes-
tors. It was explained to us that he was from an intelligence branch of the
U.S. Army, and our government wanted to identify opponents to the war
and collect evidence for possible future use.

To this day I recall the sense of dread I felt in the pit of my stomach at
that moment. This was *my* government, the one I trusted so completely,
doing this, and using the military, intended to defend us against foreign
threats—and my government was doing it from my own office. There could
be no doubt that my government saw these people out there as our enemy.
Were these films going to be used to put some of them in concentration
camps? I understood the line, "Stop the world; I want off." I was ashamed,

but more than that I was very frightened that my government was resorting to such steps against our own people, our university students. I had seen up close the gap that can suddenly appear in a crisis between the theory of democracy and the actions that some officials feel are appropriate to save a democracy from itself.

The impossibility of choosing blind loyalty to the state above all else as a guide for personal behavior had already been obvious to me from my reading of history. And now I had had my own personal experience with the state acting reprehensibly. Once again I unlearned an earlier childhood instruction.

Thus far we have looked at religion, conscience, and loyalty to the state as a basis for ethical behavior. If these haven't worked for us, we can turn with even less confidence to the idea of loyalty to one's boss and to following orders from above in our search for an adequate or appropriate guideline.

Nam is a book about personal experiences in the war in Vietnam. It contains an account of how an officer and his detachment captured a remote village in Cambodia and reported by radio that they held sixty to seventy women, children, and old men as prisoners, probably "friendlies." The field officer was shocked to receive orders to kill them. This order came from another *American* officer. The officer in the field again described his prisoners and asked for confirmation of the order at a higher level. In a few minutes he was directed to carry out his orders. That meant still *another* American officer was ordering a massacre of civilian prisoners. Unfortunately the officer wrote that he carried out his orders.

Incidentally, there has been abundant evidence accumulated that German soldiers who refused during World War II to carry out orders to execute civilians and Jews were not punished or ill-treated by their superiors. Yet Rudolf Franz Höss, commandant at Auschwitz, pled in his defense, "I had been given an order and I had to carry it out. Whether the mass extermination of the Jews was necessary or not was something on which I could not allow myself to form an opinion, for I lacked the necessary breadth of view." He went on to say, "My pity was so great that I longed to vanish from the scene: yet I might not show the slightest trace of emotion. I had to see everything. I had to watch hour after hour, by day and by night, the removal and burning of the bodies, the extraction of the teeth, the cutting of the hair, the whole grizzly interminable business. I had to stand for hours on end in the ghastly stench, while the mass graves were being opened and the bodies being dragged out and burned. I had to look through the peephole of the gas chamber and watch the process of death itself. . . ."

If relying blindly upon one's country or one's boss clearly provides no reliable guidance for ethical behavior, let's look inside ourselves. After all, have we not been instructed from our earliest years, "To thine own self be true, and it must follow as the night the day, thou canst not then be false to any man." Yet no man in history has been more true to his own self than Adolph Hitler, unless it is Stalin. And Himmler, one of Hitler's most trusted followers, uttered immortal words on being true to oneself and remaining a decent human being. Addressing SS troops responsible for the Nazi program of genocide, he said:

> "The Jewish race is being exterminated," every party member says. "That's quite clear, it's in our programme. Elimination of the Jews, and we're doing it." Not one of all those who talks like this has witnessed it, not one has been through it. Most of you will know what it means when 100 corpses are lying side by side, when 500 are lying there or when 1,000 are lying there. To have stuck this out and at the same time—apart from exceptions due to human weaknesses—to have remained decent fellows, that is what has made us hard. This is a page of glory in our history which has never been written and is never to be written.

There's another possible guide. But I can tell you at the outset I have no confidence in it. Could there be any guideline in what might be called historical imperatives? Some historians say there are historical cycles that repeat themselves. Even if it's true how can this help us? Such a view is too macro to satisfy our micro needs of knowing what to do day by day on the job. We need to know more specifically what is one to do that is right right now. While I advised you earlier to read biographies, they are too micro for general guidance. They are too specific to provide a universal guide even if they do give you important insights into ethical choices and how decisions get made in the heat of crises and turmoil.

This seems to leave us only one last place to turn: reason. Did I find our touchstone there, in philosophy? Here we can track Bentham as he plays with ledgers to record relative pleasures and pains in all policy choices, as though we could accurately quantify such values for different people and groups and make public policy by bookkeeping. We can look at Nietzsche and how his "will to power" has been misused, despite much of the good sense he makes otherwise. And Hegel has simply created a separate and special universe where his reasoning may work, but where it fails most reality checks on planet earth. Kant set out to prove God existed and ended up reasoning that He did not, but then Kant couldn't admit it. Kierkegaard goes along very convincingly until he has to rely on a leap of faith to get back from where his reasoning took him to where he had hoped to be when he started out.

And the existentialists seem such a doleful and teary lot, dwelling on our brief period of consciousness amidst the cold and uncaring dust of the universe. Yet I did find I could at least relate to the existential sentiments contained in an epitaph on a tombstone in the Spoon River cemetery. This is the one at the grave of the man who was killed pursuing his hobby of flying machines:

> . . . It is fitting that the workman
> Who tried to chisel a dove for me
> Made it look more like a chicken.
> For what is it all but being hatched,
> And running about the yard,
> To the day of the block?
> Save that a man has an angel's brain,
> And sees the ax from the first.

When we compare the thoughts of philosophers with the actions of public servants and how little most career bureaucrats know about formal philosophy, we can see how indeed small need be our fear that our government will ever be seized from us by "philosopher kings." For our world of politics and public policymaking is precisely as John Dewey described it, "While saints are engaged in introspection, burly sinners run the world."

We can look to hosts of other philosophers and we still come full circle and my question remains: How can we reduce the sins of the burly activists in government? I suspect my recounting of my search has become downright discouraging to you. It certainly has been for me. I have found only modest solace in the rationalization that negative findings have their uses. But simply because I have found many of my lifelong teachings and tenets to be wanting in my search for some universal code for moral behavior does not totally discourage me.

Let me tell you what keeps driving me on in my search. Arthur Miller created a scene in *After the Fall* that keeps me looking for my guidelines. One character describes his thoughts upon looking at the remains of a guard tower at a Nazi death camp. He says, "Yes, believers built this, maybe that's the fright—and I, without belief, stand here disarmed."

I refuse to be discouraged because I refuse to stand disarmed. We can never permit ourselves to be half-hearted for what is good as we oppose those who are wholehearted for what is evil.

You must be tired of my discarding card after card. You must be ready to call my hand. If I am not disarmed even after so long a search, you have a right to insist I lay down my cards and show you such arms as I have.

First, I believe there does exist what Maslow calls an "intrinsic conscience, a court of ultimate appeal for the determination of good and bad, of right and wrong." This is not the traditional conscience, the small voice that originates in childhood upbringings and helps you sense what is right or wrong. This "inner nature" is inborn in most of us to tell us when we are being stultified, misused, or compromised in our inner natures. Most people can feel when their needs for fulfillment are being denied, when they must represent mendacity or falseness as truth, when they are required to do something unprincipled or against their own self-concept or self-defined sense of what is proper. Maslow says "every falling away from species-virtue, every crime against one's own nature, every evil act, *every one without exception records itself* in our unconscious and makes us despise ourselves" (Maslow's emphasis). He is quick, however, to acknowledge that when a person feels uncomfortable with a situation, we cannot tell automatically whether that is good or bad. But at least it is an alarm, a starting place.

If your very being, your sense of personal destiny and capacity, and your psychological center are touched in certain circumstances in some way that causes you to feel violated or at least uncomfortable, whether by external forces or by your own decisions, pay attention. Here is a chance for you to ask why you feel that way. Here is a chance for you to raise that inner feeling to the surface for more complete examination.

Isaiah Berlin felt the same. "We are moral beings: we would not qualify as human if moral considerations, however false or inadequate, were absent from our deliberations. And from . . . our shared language of moral discourse we know the inhuman when we encounter it."

That was what I was saying at the very beginning of this letter. Working inside organizations, you will feel pressures to carry out orders you feel uneasy about, and, to get ahead, there will be temptations to compromise yourself and your principles or instincts. If you have a weak "intrinsic conscience," you may never in the least be pricked or prodded by it. Therefore, reliance on the inner nature of each of us can be only marginally useful in searching for a touchstone for moral behavior in public office. Yet I do believe that most people possess that intrinsic conscience that can help to guide them to avoid improper behavior—if they will just pay attention to it.

Second, for all my apparent cynical rejection of religion, upbringing, loyalty, being true to oneself, and history and philosophy as guides to conduct, I do readily accept the judgment of humankind over time: All of these reference points I have examined make their contributions to rational and ethical comportment. From these sources come attitudes, frames of reference, a part of the "intrinsic conscience," and elements of social lubrication that will assist you in tough choices on public issues. Not one of them alone is adequate to serve as a universal basis for public decision making and action. But they do, together, deliver valuable aids that promote humane responses and empathy and understanding. Consequently, they will be helpful as part of your guide to proper conduct. So don't give up on them.

For myself, from philosophy I have gleaned further useful guidance and reinforcement for my instinctual feelings about my duty as a public servant. Since philosophy can get pretty heavy for an informal letter like this, let me quote instead from a play to state the rationale for social action that I discovered in John Dewey's pragmatism. In one of his plays George Bernard Shaw has one of his most provocative characters speak about administrative organization and the "greatest of our evils and the worst of our crimes," poverty. The protagonist Undershaft says, "You see, my dear boy, when you are organizing civilization you have to make up your mind whether trouble and anxiety are good things or not. If you decide that they are [good], then, I take it, you simply don't organize civilization. And there you are, with trouble and anxiety enough to make us all angels! But if you decide the other way, you may as well go through with it."

What Shaw is saying is that if we are to be civilized we have no choice but to use our knowledge and skills to overcome the troubles and ills and anxieties and poverty of the world we find all around us. This means we have to apply what we know and what we can discover in order to act responsibly to improve the lot of humanity. Or more simply, we must choose either to let the events shape us or we undertake to shape the events. To fail to do this is to relegate the improvement of ourselves to some kind of "natural law" by which some "hidden hand" will mete out blessings and burdens among those from the most privileged at the top to the lowest underclasses. And we know from long experience that that "hidden hand" will not do this equally or reasonably or fairly. Because favoritism and partiality and bias exercised by the privileged classes will always influence the natural law and its so-called "hidden hand." "Property will purchase power, or power will take over property," as one of our founding fathers put it. But as Shaw (along with the pragmatists) says, leaving the "natural law" to deal with mankind's problems is neither organized *nor* civilization. It is abdication. Rather than be master of our destiny, we would be content to drift rudderless into our future. That is not why you and I chose the public service as a career.

And if we pursue a rational civilization, it can be organized only through legislative, judicial, and administrative actions. In the modern world no government can sit on the sidelines and permit some mindless social mechanism to define how we all relate to one another. Government must be the major organized intelligence in a society for pursuing the interests and progress of all the people. No other institution can do it. No hidden hand will do it equitably. So I reject any "natural law" and I take my public service totem from pragmatism: We can maintain continual progress and improve the condition of humankind through the application of intelligence to our problems and conditions. We will always have adequate injustice and problems to work with.

Now, lastly, I finally come to what I can give you as one universal guide. I will label it simply the Democratic and Constitutional Imperative. Let us start by accepting this premise: "Presume not God to scan; the proper study of mankind is man." The subject I believe we must examine is the truly democratic person.

People live together most productively and harmoniously if four conditions are met. First, if they have the opportunity and freedom to participate and be heard in setting the goals and purposes of their society. Second, if they have the opportunity to share in the country's productive capacity and to participate in the actions and work of their society. Third, if they may share reasonably equitably in the benefits of their society. And fourth, if they are free from oppression and unnecessary constraints on their mobility, thoughts, and other liberties.

I don't think I need to develop these points any further for you. Obviously what I am describing is our functioning democracy. The cohesion and satisfaction of a people will be stronger if the processes of the state minimize the intervention of government into individual decisions and choices and facilitate sharing in goal setting, actions, production, and benefits. These are, of course, the fundamental elements of our government which were established or, at minimum, hinted at in the writing of our Constitution. Over most of our history, we have bit by bit improved upon the democratic ideals given to us that summer in Philadelphia over two centuries ago. The founding fathers gave us a Constitution that prescribed the structure and processes of a government and a Bill of Rights to define the individual's protections under that government.

A more perfect democracy has evolved by extending and increasing these primary elements in our system of government: broader participation in goal setting, wider participation in production and actions, and more equitable sharing of society's benefits while constraining unnecessary government encroachment upon individual freedoms. And remarkably this more perfect democracy has been achieved despite the desires of some in the dominant classes in our society to control government for their own benefits.

Now from that reasoning I will hand it to you on a platter. Here is the only sure touchstone I can find to guide behavior and moral choices of public servants: the Democratic and Constitutional Imperative. In your particular agency you must, through your own policies and management practices, protect and enhance those constitutional values I just described. Specifically, you must actively work to see that your agency remains open, that information is shared, that secrets do not stifle informed participation by the general public so that conflicting values and views can be played out and negotiated to acceptable resolution. You must encourage community involvement and ensure that all affected groups have access to participate and to perform roles in the decisions and work of your agency and public activities sponsored by your agency. You must see that the benefits or sanctions administered by your agency are applied equitably and fairly. And you must strive to constrain and minimize unnecessary government intrusions and restrictions upon the people affected by your agency while at the same time not granting or endorsing unfair privileges to some over the rest.

Now, beyond your own agency responsibilities, as you are able to influence government more generally, there are related principles you should take every opportunity to promote. First is the essentiality of sharing and spreading knowledge. Participation and sharing require government assurance of access to education. This is necessary to enable the people to make informed decisions and to protect themselves against exploitation. Moreover, education prepares the people to organize and assume positions of advocacy on their own behalf, the sine qua non of self-help. Second, increasing public participation and sharing also require government actions against discrimination; actions to fairly distribute income and essential needs and services; actions to facilitate social mobility; and actions to control privileges, power, or wealth that are misused.

Third, participation means that the forum for public debate must be forever kept open—both to influence decisions and to learn from the debate that must go on. Democracy really works only when it is one large cybernetic system, making decisions related to all its parts, carrying out actions, trying to benefit all, and getting public feedback for more decisions and fine tuning.

So we come back to that question we began with, Pippin IV's query, "What is a person to do?" For your moral decisions in your personal life consult your religious beliefs and upbringings, your conscience, your loyalty to our nation and your boss, your idea of being true to yourself, history, and biography, and philosophy. For your decisions in your public role consider the same sources. But in your public role pay special attention to your "intrinsic conscience" and devote yourself to promoting the Democratic and

Constitutional Imperative. Short of attracting attention to yourself or appearing stuffy, you should not be reluctant to see yourself as a model of
ethical behavior, someone whose conduct could ideally serve as a guide to
all members of society. This will at least make you more responsible for your
own behavior even if you never become a model worthy of a pedestal. We
might make this goal a subpart of the Democratic and Constitutional Imperative and call it the Bureaucratic Code of Comportment: Conduct yourself so that your behavior may serve as the pattern for the behavior of every
bureaucrat.

   If this sounds "old hat" and tautological, this means that your sense of
the public philosophy that guides our nation is still intact and you are in
accord with the founding fathers. If this is the case, I am preaching to the
choir. But if you do hold this view it means you are standing between the
two extremes of alternative public philosophies being preached as more appropriate to rule our country. On the one extreme are those who believe that
America has a special place in God's plan denied to all others on the planet
and that we will prevail over the rest of the world if we pursue materialistic
success and militant hatred of rivals and those of competing beliefs. Senator
Albert Beveridge's announcement near the beginning of the twentieth century still holds with many today, "God has marked the American people as
His chosen nation to finally lead in the regeneration of the world. This is
[our] divine mission."

   On the other extreme lie the postmodernists. They claim to have discovered a new way to see what is real in our contemporary society. They are
"post" because they have moved their observations and description of society beyond the "modernists." The label "modernism" has been used in art,
music, literature, and elsewhere. Modernity was also a label applied by social scientists to their discovery of how we see ourselves. The social science
modernists found that we had come to have faith in specific truths, in science, in certainty, and in a belief that these were verifiable and could be used
by us to make progress in improving the human condition.

   The postmodernists have found fault with these "modernist" as-
sumptions and observations about how present society actually works. To
them our world is not certain, there are many truths, and truth changes with
experience, and the consequent reality is that we are controlled by myths.
Those myths include the belief that entrusting government to people of reason (that's *you* and *me* they're talking about) is a subterfuge for distancing
government from the citizens and having government run and controlled
by an elite (you and me and other people of reason in the public service).
Postmodernist reasoning finds that representational government and de-

mocracy are perpetrating illegitimate governance upon the public. And as to the career you have embarked upon, they hold that "public administration is an inherently anti-democratic approach to governance." Underlying all this is the revelation that the Constitution itself is not legitimate. It serves, along with the reasoning of our founding fathers, as a dangerous basis for public administration. According to the postmodernists, guiding our behavior by these "myths" makes it impossible for us in the public service to determine what is in the public interest.

Commonplace or not, dated or not, I still take my reassurance from a public philosophy that is based on our essential freedoms, that provides for a system of social justice, and that assumes certain rights and responsibilities of the individual. Within that system I believe that the conflicting and multiple values of the peoples, classes, and communities of our nation can coexist and play out against each other and permit us to make progress together. Tolerance and pluralism are workable and working concepts. A general acceptance of a public philosophy is what holds a country together. You will need to make your stand on this and to know that it matters because it is we public servants who must facilitate and lubricate these processes of citizen self-governance.

So now we return to the one question I left hanging. Is it enough to declare, "My country, right or wrong?" No. We need to remember the rest of Carl Schurz's quotation engraved on the wall in the old Philadelphia Customhouse: "Our country, right or wrong. When right, to be kept right; when wrong, to be set right." So if all else fails, remember in performing your public duties that disobedience and insubordination in a democratic government do, on occasion, have their place.

What you have here is an intimate and true tracing of my own prolonged trek through the public service in search of a code or discipline for personal behavior in acting for public good. We all have to undertake our own search and find our own answers.

You will now begin your own tests and your own quest. You'll do fine. As a friend said to his colleague about to start work in the White House, "It's going to be very hard. Try to do right."

Your absolving

Uncle Ken

re: *A few thoughts on leadership*

The administrator who is willing to be an administrator and not merely an officeholder will find that the strain is chiefly upon his character, rather than his mind. — *Robert Maynard Hutchins*

If you are getting kicked in the rear it means you are in front.
— *Chinese fortune cookie*

If you compromise vital issues you will always lose friends and never appease your enemies. — *Arthur Schlesinger, Jr.*

Leadership is getting people to do what they don't want to do, and to like it. — *Harry S. Truman*

M A R C H

Dear Kim

So you've been sharing my letters with your friends. Now you say they want me to tell you more about leadership specifically. Who said I was going to take requests? You realize, I'm sure, that leadership is largely what I have been talking to you about all along. But at risk of repeating here and there what I've already said about it, I will say a little more on the topic.

There are no prescriptions I can give you for leading. Leadership is an art, not a science nor a set of axioms or formulas, despite all the revealed secrets and recorded tapes and miracle manuals available on the market. I'm certain no one is born with it; you learn it. There are skills and techniques you can observe and study and practice, but as I watch leadership in practice I have become convinced instinct and intuition play a big part in how leaders exercise their unusual talents. But then, of course, instinct and intuition come out of experience with all of life. Being a leader is a continuing challenge because regardless how good you get at it, there is always something new to learn or perfect or try out or to achieve through the use of it.

My key advisers taught me something about my own leadership style one day at a staff meeting. As I came in they were all laughing, and they said before we got down to business they wanted to talk about what they had been discussing. Someone had brought in the findings of a study described in the *Harvard Business Review* on how many of the most effective executives make decisions. You've been through ad infinitum the usual guidelines on how to make decisions: get the facts, analyze the facts, consider alternative actions and their consequences, and then decide on action. The research showed, on the contrary, that the more effective leaders decide very early in the process of dealing with a crisis or problem about how they will resolve the issue. This is in contrast to the less effective managers who want to gather and study all the facts before deciding what to do and before taking action.

Another surprise finding was that top leaders often decide what to do and *then* consider the consequences. And a third characteristic of top executives revealed by the study was that they often go with their instincts: they will make a decision based on very rudimentary information and do not wait for careful analysis.

All of this obviously runs exactly contrary to the prescribed formulas on how decisions should be made.

My staff found this interesting because they said it described so closely how I had been making decisions for years. That's what they had been laughing about. Although I protested at the time that surely I was a more reasoning person than this implied, I must confess on later reflection they had me pegged pretty well.

What convinced me was their further description of my process—I should say, *our* process together. When faced with a crisis or dilemma they said I nearly always set a course early and very quickly for what we would do. And then I would say, "Now let's see what kind of case we can put together to support or justify that—or defend that—or make that work"—or whatever. This gave everyone a direction in which to move together. They said the staff understood my initial position to mean, in addition to trying to beef up the quick decision, that they had complete license to point out what could go wrong with it, why it wouldn't work, why another approach might work better. In other words, there was still a lot of room for movement after our general direction had been set. The result was that my initial position would often stand firm and would turn out to be a workable response to the circumstances we faced. But my initial position also often ended up being modified, based on our facing realities we weren't aware of at the outset or on turning up new facts or because of perceivable bad outcomes. And they said I would have to admit that on occasion my initial position had proved to be totally indefensible and was abandoned entirely for another approach.

My staff said that my particular approach to decisions and their willingness to accept it only worked because I always remain open to contrary arguments and can accept bad news and criticism. As they sometimes said about me, "Maybe wrong, but never in doubt." But if we were wrong it could be—and would be—set right.

They said they thought the value of this approach was that the staff never leaves a meeting with a crisis left hanging with no sense of where we are all going and what we are going to try to do about the problem. The assurance of having some kind of direction, even if a hasty and tentative one, gives them a sense of security in not having some extremity still pending with no plan of any kind to respond to it. And, I must say, this seems to provide a calming effect among the uncertain and excitable few.

In addition, there is less risk that staff members will be riding off in different directions to deal with the problem. There is a sense that this new, terrible crisis, too, can be managed and that in the meantime we are not in disarray or in limbo.

But I know too that if my approach is initially reassuring or comforting to some of the staff, there is a subsequent benefit as well. As we labor together to make my initial proposition work (or to modify it or find another that will work better) we come together as a team. Everyone is encouraged to make his input and there is buy-in from working together. That is, the decision does not become exclusively *mine;* it becomes everybody's.

Yet I suspect that as top executives react to crises in this way, bypassing the usual approaches to decision making, it is in part due to the time they have spent in the trenches and their experience with similar situations they have witnessed or been through before. Often the leader has the institutional memory and the historical context to see more clearly than others which options are available and which path of action stands the best chance of success. In his mind he is assessing the responses of those to be affected by the decision and weighing positive and negative reactions. He is making connections and measuring gains and losses, acceptance and criticisms, sizing up the consequences of action and inaction.

But I also think that the leader remains more unflappable and cool in crises than do the specialists who direct the divisions of her organization. Partly this is due to having survived far worse than the one at hand. And partly it is probably because by the nature of her being at the top, this present crisis is just one of several she is dealing with at the moment, whereas with her subordinates and division heads, this situation seems to be one of much more dire consequences. She also knows if she doesn't set some direction for this particular problem right now, she will have to find time to think the whole thing through again later and decide then what to do. When is she going to find time for that with all else she is dealing with?

Maybe if we spent more time studying the followers and not the leaders we would find out why people will get behind some leaders and not others who want so desperately to be leaders. The Japanese say when someone points at the moon only a fool looks at the finger. In primarily studying leaders we may be looking at the wrong thing.

Scholars who have looked at followers rather than at leaders have found that most people do not have feelings of certainty or assuredness, especially in dealing with emergencies and crises or confrontations. And such people tend to want to follow others who show they do have a sense of assuredness and confidence. A person who "may be wrong, but never in doubt" can attract followers. You will often be followed if you convey the sense that you clearly believe you know what you are doing and you know where you are going.

That sense of assuredness and confidence usually comes from special knowledge the leader has that the followers do not. While I was in the U.S. Navy I encountered a metaphor that stands for what I learned much later as an executive. A weathered, old guitar-playing sailor on our ship told us one day about his playing in hillbilly bands in Tennessee when he was a youth. He said there were lots of guitar and banjo players in the mountains but most of them had the same serious problem. They could play the C chord just fine, and the G chord and the F chord. Their problem was they didn't know when to change chords in the different pieces they played. But our old friend said he knew when all the changes had to be made. So as he patted his foot, he pointed it straight ahead for the C chord, to the left for the F chord, and to the right for the G chord. The band immediately sounded miraculously better, even if everybody but him and the fiddle player were staring at the floor.

I suspect they became dependent on him and nobody else learned when the chord changes had to be made. Another metaphor lurking here somewhere?

I have discovered there are a couple of paradoxes of leadership you have to learn to balance. As I said, you need to appear to have assuredness and certainty about where you are going, but there is a fine line between certainty and autocracy. A sense of rightness can evolve into righteousness and arrogance. Having the courage to act on your assuredness can easily devolve into dictatorial behavior and overconfidence in your own judgment. And hubris has probably brought down more leaders than even corruption and inaction.

The other paradox of leadership is this: You must decide and you must direct, but you must also listen and take advice. You must not be deciding and directing when you ought to be listening and taking advice. And more importantly, you should not be listening and taking advice when you need to be deciding and directing.

Simple enough? I told you there are no formulas, but I have just given you two. Go forth and make of them a leader.

Even if it means looking at the finger rather than the moon, let's go back and consider a few characteristics of leaders. I've already discussed in earlier letters a host of qualities of leaders such as integrity, courage, accessibility, loyalty, sensitivity, vision setting, and sitting with your opposition. And I know you are reading entire books on leadership that label the different types for you, transactional, managerial, transforming, innovative, agitating, inspirational, visionary, charismatic, and all the rest. So what can I add? Well, here are some characteristics that are often associated with leaders and not with followers or nonleaders.

First, leaders care about their people. Being able to get the right people in the right positions and looking after them will do more to make a leader successful than probably any other single thing he does. I've already referred to the risk of hiring second- and third-class people, but there are a couple of elements I haven't touched on yet. One is the ability of leaders to figure out the needs and wants of their followers, and this means their own staff as well. Leaders work to satisfy and fulfill those needs and wants. These might be the need for recognition, a chance for advancement, the wish to correct a wrong or make a difference, or the desire to be associated with a successful effort to ameliorate a social ill. Or their wants may be more mundane: a nonthreatening work environment, flextime, child care, a pleasant and social setting, or a locker room to shower in after noontime jogging.

In looking after their people, leaders are most solicitous of their closest advisers and colleagues. They push them and often overload them, they give them new challenges, they inspire them, and they stretch them to become better than they realize they can be.

Second, leaders protect their people and look after their welfare. Leaders take the blame and spread the credit. No leader will last long who lets his subordinates take the fall for his errors or the organization's mistakes. Even when a subordinate is to blame for some mistake within the organization, the executive should take the hit in public; she can settle accounts with the employee in private. At a board meeting when something goes wrong or there is a clear error or oversight, if I take the blame and promise to take care of it, I am always amazed how that puts an end to the matter with the board. They are quick to move on to a new item as though they do not want to embarrass me about the matter any further. And most of the time they know full well the mistake was not mine personally.

It is only at the very top that someone can say, as President John Kennedy did kiddingly to his advisors in the State Department, "I sure hopes this works because if it does I plan to take credit for it. If it doesn't you will have to take the blame." But after the Bay of Pigs fiasco, he knew full well, as Harry Truman had said, "The buck stops here."

It is probably this human side of effective leaders that makes them empathetic even to those whose hopes and aspirations they must dash. Most good leaders have a way of saying "no" that often, almost surprisingly, permits them to retain the respect and admiration of those whose plans have been denied. Somehow they convey the sense, without stating it, that they are thinking, "If you were in my position we both know you'd be doing about the same thing I am, and I know that too. And if I were in yours I'd probably be in your situation. Nothing personal here. We each have to do what's expected of us." There's another leadership paradox here (another formula for you). You need to convey that your decision is not personal, yet you have to find a way to be personable in your demeanor as you exercise your authority.

For example, effective leaders usually have a way of lubricating difficult situations with humor or inquiry about something he and his adversary have a common interest in or a mutual acquaintance. They know not to deprive their opposite of dignity and face. Above all, they are not mechanical and heartless. They imply that while the two of you could not be in agreement in this particular situation, you very well may be on another occasion.

There are heads of agencies and government offices who remain convinced that the way to get people to give their most is to instill fear in them, to intimidate them. These are usually the same managers who use up people and toss them aside with little or no appreciation for service and have no compunctions about abusing their employees. It is a shame anyone has to suffer such a boss, but unfortunately they do exist—in far too great a number.

Another characteristic of leaders is they have a lot of energy and they expend it in specific ways. Their energy manifests itself in commitment and drive as well as in never giving up. And they spend a lot of their energy in making professional contacts and friends. I can usually spot a leader in the making. They are continually building new relationships, creating networks, getting to know more people, joining another association or professional organization. They push new ideas and they don't quit easily. They have dogged determination to change things and they keep after what they want to accomplish. They are often persistent to the point of being annoying or even obnoxious, and their commitment to an idea is often revealed in their propensity for opportunism. They rarely miss a chance to advance their ideas, and they use their wide net of contacts to get help and mobilize support.

One skill you will need to learn along the way to becoming a leader is to assume the role appropriate to the occasion. Some circumstances require minor roles, some ceremonial and symbolic roles, some supporting roles and some call for starring roles. You have to learn to take the right voice, the correct part. By the time you stand before the employees of one of your departments whose jobs are threatened by pending legislation to provide them reassurances, you will know this is not ceremonial, nor is this an occasion to take a minor or supporting role. When you come to share the podium with a governor, you will have learned to avoid anything touching on the title role. When you stand before all your employees at an agencywide staff meeting, you won't step back, waiting for someone else to take the principal part. As smooth and practiced as people may appear in such different roles, these are learned lines and parts. Leadership is part theatre as well as content, image as well as substance, persona and charisma as well as purpose and meaning. As I advised you in one of my first letters, rehearse these roles as your boss or bosses play them out. "Chance favors only the prepared mind," as Pasteur advised us.

I have sort of moved away from describing characteristics of leaders and gone to giving advice again. But you can get all the characteristics and qualities stuff about leadership elsewhere. So it's back to preaching and telling you about leadership based on my own experience.

Although it is no longer a politically correct aphorism, there is a saying, "Don't shoot at sparrows and eagles will come to you." A leader should not get bogged down in details and doing the small jobs just because he has learned over the years how to do them well or because he enjoys them or because he is willing to spend the extra hours in the office necessary to get them all done. Each time you move up in job responsibilities you have to learn to stop doing some of the things you used to do. There are new duties and a new perspective you need to take on. Just because you *can* do something does not mean you *should* continue to do it. Especially when you get to the top you will find that if the leader leaves the big issues unaddressed, they will likely remain unaddressed. Others cannot easily step into the leader's role of planner and forward looker. As a policymaking leader you should be concerned in the policy process with public and social problems and with developing solutions to them and getting those enacted and funded, and with coordinating the tactical and strategic work of your staff to do these things, not with the details of implementation or housekeeping functions at your agency.

I assure you that focusing on the small tasks and details will keep you from your principal responsibilities. You need to be thinking and gaining perspective on the issues your agency faces and what will be coming your way. You, of all the people in the agency, need to be looking ahead. You need to be making outside contacts. You need to be reading. You need to be recharging your batteries. Henry Kissinger said somewhere that the difficulty with top-level jobs is that you cannibalize the knowledge and information you have in your head when you take the job. You use up your intellectual capital because you never have the time to replace it. When you get to the top your attitude toward what is your unique job in the total enterprise needs to change. In short, don't waste your time by becoming a micromanager.

And while I'm on the subject of small tasks and details, there is another aspect of smallness that separates the mediocre from most leaders. The "wannabe" leader often falls back on the smallness of the martinet. He gives disproportionate importance to procedures, rules, and regulations or spit and polish at the sacrifice of what is truly significant in the situation at hand. Not being able to see or know what really needs to be done, wannabe leaders will immerse themselves and those they supervise or command in routine motions, procedures, and doing things by the letter. In the military enlisted men and women are the first to spot a small person trying to fill a big job. Paul Fussell summed it up neatly when he said, "Chickenshit refers to behavior that makes military life worse than it need be: petty harassment of the weak by the strong; open scrimmage for power and authority and prestige; sadism thinly disguised as necessary discipline; a constant 'paying off of old scores'; and insistence on the letter rather than the spirit of ordinances. Chickenshit is so called—instead of horse- or bull- or elephant-shit—because it is small-minded and ignoble and takes the trivial seriously." And then he hits at the heart of it: "Chickenshit can be recognized instantly because it never has anything to do with winning the war." You see any message here on leadership?

Personally I have found that one of the most difficult adjustments I have had to make in coordinating matters with my staff and staying posted on what they are doing is this: As we meet on a problem or project, I will just get involved deeply in the issue brought to me by a division or a study group or committee, and it will be time to meet with another group on another topic. I have to wash that old topic out of my mind and get my brain around a new subject or problem. That can be very difficult for me, as the issues just raised and their ramifications are still bouncing around in my head. But I have to force it to happen; I get into the new subject. Then in ten or fifteen minutes I have to do it all over again.

This shifting of gears all day long is one of the most vexing aspects of my work. Added to that are the interruptions by telephone calls that I have to take from board members, legislators, or staff aides to the governor or other agency heads or university presidents. Very typically a day is a long series of ten- and fifteen-minute sequences and problems, leaving me with stripped gears in my head. And as the day comes to an end, and I finally sign the last papers on my desk, there at last I uncover what I laid out to work on or read when I first came to work that morning.

If you do not find ways to capture some time for your own thinking and vision, every day can become programmed to pass in this way. That's the life you are headed toward. Don't let it inundate you. And don't let yourself be nibbled to death by mice, the minutiae of management.

An additional word of advice: No problem or issue is ever resolved with finality. They remain and they come back because, as issues affecting a changing society and culture, they can hardly ever be totally resolved; they are only attenuated temporarily and they arise anew in fresh variations. They are like the flu virus; they are cyclical, they mutate, and they can come back even more virulent.

As you come to suffer the slings and arrows of outrageous allegations and confrontations associated with leadership remember Victor Frankl's philosophy. You cannot control the things that happen to you, but you can control your *attitude* toward what happens to you. Frankl calls it our "last freedom," to "choose one's own way."

Man's "unique opportunity lies in the way in which he bears his burden." Be positive. Keep perspective. There is no such thing as fairness about life; know that the universe owes us nothing. If economics is the dismal science, politics, which is really the business of leadership, has to be the cheerful science. A leader, a politician, a public administrator truly believes he or she can make a difference, things can be made better, a brighter future can be achieved through organization, hard work, and the relentless application of professional skills.

There are so many things I have left unsaid about leadership, but I have to go.

Alas, I must meet with the council of university presidents. They will wish to give me instructions on how I should do my job and inform me further on where my many deficiencies lie.

Your arrant relation,

Uncle Ken

re: *A summing up*

If men were angels, no government would be necessary. If angels were to govern men, neither external nor internal controls on government would be necessary. In framing a government which is to be administered by men over men, the great difficulty lies in this: You must first enable the government to control the governed; and in the next place oblige it to control itself.   — *James Madison*

We must learn to trust our democracy, giant-like and threatening as it may appear in its uncouth strength and untried applications.
                                                                          — *Jane Addams*

The business of politics is not with theory and ideology but with accommodation.   — *Alexander Bickel*

A   P   R   I   L

Dear Kim

With your final papers approaching and graduation just ahead, it is time I bring these epistles to an end. This will be the last installment of my gratuitous and unsolicited advice. And I am enclosing a list of some of my favorite reading over the years that I promised you some months ago.

I must conjecture that if you shared my renditions of some of my stories with others who were present, they might say I have not always overburdened myself with objectivity. But I stand with Alice and her wonderland adventures: this is *my* story. My intent has been to increase a little your understanding of the world you are about to enter, and along the way perhaps enhance your sensitivity to the nuances and subtleties of relationships you will encounter.

Sensitivity is a key element of your future success. You will have to learn to be insensitive enough to be able to go home and sleep at night, insensitive enough not to let every disappointment and denial you inflict on others eat at your gut or make you indecisive. Being excessively sensitive or worrying will waste your energy. Yet you will need to be sensitive enough to know when you need to trim your sails, when you do need to temper your appetite and settle for less than the whole hog, when your opponents from both sides are about to summon a convention to call for your head. And to maintain that necessary sensitivity, just short of oversensitivity, you will need to circulate constantly among the communities you affect by your decisions.

Some scholar of the mind described the unconscious as the substance inside an egg with a porous shell. The shell is the persona of how you want to be seen by the outside world. A strong persona or ego makes for a less porous shell, and less of the unconscious "you" is revealed to the outside world. I would extend this metaphor to say that the effective public servant needs a porous shell to let the outside world in as well. Too tough a shell will keep you from sensing the outside world's response and reactions to you and your decisions. But, on the other hand, too porous a shell will leave you as just a wet spot on the pavement as events speed by.

I know that in drawing on my own personal experiences to illustrate my little lessons for you in public policymaking and management, the range and breadth of cases have been limited. Yet I hope there has been here and there something of use. But I hope most of all that what I have shared with you reveals that there is excitement at all levels of government and quasi-government work. The so-called devolution of federal activities to state and local governments and nonprofit organizations does not mean that the demands and experience and quality of life are any less at these other levels. Also I hope you will recognize that there is much commonality of behavior and experiences irrespective of the level of public service, or whether you work for a board or commission or an independent agency or a lobbying organization or special interest group. In being a profession of the highest calling, the public service is an honorable field of work that will demand your absolute best at all times as you pursue the public good, regardless of where you are working in the system. There is a substantial universality of experience in government that transcends geography or agencies or levels of government.

When I was a child and there was some disaster like a house on fire or my grandmother cut herself badly or a hay truck ran off the road and turned over, I always wanted to jump up and run around. I was tremendously exhilarated. Is that why I've found a happy spot in the public service? I don't know, but when things come apart or there's a clear need to do something, I want to be in the middle of it somehow. The main thing I have learned in the meantime is not to jump up and run around. I hope you find that same excitement in your career.

I'm not going to assume you have gotten the subtle message I have been sending throughout my notes to you. (Be thankful for small things; subtlety is the mitigating condition to offset creeping curmudgeonism.) Therefore I will be direct to be certain you get the point. I am but one among tens upon tens of thousands who have experienced what I have tried in small part to describe to you in these epistles. The little vignettes from my own career may serve to show that even an insignificant public servant who "struts and frets his hour upon the stage" among those of far greater accomplishments can, nonetheless, live an exciting life and, amidst the sound and the fury, make an occasional contribution and signify something.

If, in recounting some of my experiences and retelling "war stories," I have made it sound as though these jobs may not sometimes be mean, cruel, punishing, and exhausting, it is only because the human mind works to protect us by helping us to forget the truly worst aspects of living through unpleasant circumstances. There will be some days that are more gut wrenching than others. Part of this will be because you are learning and the only way to gain some of what you need to know to serve in the public arena is to live through it. Part of it will be because you can't understand what is happening to you and why—or know what you should do about it. Part of it will be because you have made a mistake and there is no way to undo your actions and get back to where you were when you made the mistake in order to try a better approach or apply what you've learned in the meantime.

And part of it is because it is just the nature of these jobs that you will stand in the vortex among intense and bitter differences among people who uncompromisingly want and demand certain preferences and benefits from government for themselves or those they represent. And some of those you deal with are heartless; they have probably never smiled at anything in life except someone else's misery, and they are totally unremitting in pursuing their own selfish wants. Just stand firm in the knowledge that you have as much right to hold your view as they do theirs and that despite the reigning silence there *are* friends out there for your position.

I have always found it helpful to imagine the worst that could happen to me in some terrible situation I have gotten myself into, and I have been amazed at how often I have concluded, "I can live with that."

While in the letters I have sent you I have often made light of the confrontations and situations I have experienced, I would do you a disservice if I did not say forthrightly that there is a large measure of unpleasantness and disappointment that goes along with top-level government positions. Just don't let it get the upper hand with you. One tactic of your opponents is to make you feel discouraged and to wear you down; that leaves the field to them. Keep playing the game. As Secretary of State George Schulz so wisely remarked, "It's never over." Live to fight another day. And if nothing else will keep you going forward, you might reflect on Wisconsin Governor Lee Dreyfus's "seriousness scale." He said on a scale of one to ten, his fighting on Okinawa was a ten, and nothing since then has ever scored a two.

Disappointments and defeats bring growth and understanding. Someone wisely said that no one should be permitted to work in the White House who is not over forty and hasn't suffered at least one major disappointment in life. A large part of your preparation for a position of leadership will come through the toughening and conditioning experiences of your earlier years. Many of us were tempted frequently along the way to find some other line of work where we hurt less, felt humiliated less often, sensed our inadequacies less acutely. And some do drop out. But remember that other people are less concerned than you may think with your foibles and mistakes. And the pain *will* recede. And out of it you learn and grow. In time you will become ready. You are permitted to be frustrated, but you must never let yourself become thoroughly discouraged or disenchanted.

Let me assure you that some of your defeats will come about because of dumb or even downright stupid things you do or say. You can't remain silent and do your job. And having to take positions on issues will force you to express opinions that offend others or embarrass you. You can't learn unless you get into the fray. You are not permitted in this business to sit on the bench or outside the game until you have mastered it. You can't master it without playing it. So don't be too hard on yourself about your stupidities. Learn from your self-afflictions, but also learn to be forgiving of yourself and get up and get on with the game.

In one of my earliest letters I chided you about entering the public service to fulfill your desire to play a hero role, to want to make a difference, to want to become a meaningful figure during your lifetime. "The urge to heroism is natural, and to admit it is honest." But the particular model you create for "the hero" you wish to become is crucial to the role you will seek to fulfill. This is why it is important for you to read history and biographies in order to have hero role models beyond the present moment. Our founding fathers knew they were playing hero roles because they were students of

history, the classics, governments, and figures from previous times. I can't
expect you to go back to the classics, but there are hosts of men and women
worthy of your knowing about and their accomplishments and their values,
heroes worthy of your emulating them. And the very best of them are those
who conform to a standard articulated by many over the centuries: A society
is judged not by the benefits it bestows on its privileged but by how it cares
for its needy and dispossessed.

Luckily, due to our time and place in history, we are able to talk with
confidence about your personal career and to consider procedures and practices of government in the context of a civilized society. My experiences and
your plans for a career are so unique in the longer history of mankind that
we hardly realize how unusual are our present times. We so readily and
quickly take them for granted. Catastrophe and war put only a few of us
where, as Michael Herr put it, "[S]afety is provisional, [where] early death,
blindness, loss of legs, arms or balls, major and lasting disfigurement—the
whole rotten deal—could come in on the freakyfluky as easily as in the so-
called expected ways . . . to die in firefights and mortar-rocket attacks." For
example, to be among those demobilized Russian soldiers at the end of
World War II who were on one of three trains left on a siding near Odessa
and neglected somehow in the bureaucracy until they all froze to death. Or
to die by the throw of the dice that placed you among the two million Ar-
menians marched into the desert to disappear during World War I, not because you were a belligerent, but because of your race and ethnicity. Or to
suffer similarly in any of the hundreds of other decivilizing events of the recently closed century.

In our present civilized world we have grown to expect that the universe owes us so much. But the universe out there owes us nothing. Every
piece of civilization, without exception, is a creation of humankind. It is all
so very tenuous. We are blessed and privileged with the choices we are free
to make about sane things to do with our lives as a result of the works of
all those before us. I will risk sounding preachy to say that this is due almost
entirely to the many institutions of society that promote our security and material well-being and the seeming continuous advancement of humankind.

But of all those institutions the most important is our own democratic
form of government. Every other social, religious, economic, scientific, and
political institution is enhanced and shared in by the people because of our
democracy. If you will recall, this is where I started, something I said to you
last year in my very first letter. Science and technology play a tremendous
part in our progress and well-being, but equally important are the institu-

tions that bind our society together, that give all its members a sense of sharing in its goals and plans, and that provide some equity about the distribution of the opportunities and products of that society. You will now find your role in all that.

During your lifetime there will be episodes of terror and public irrationality and unforeseen social crises and political turmoil or worse. In such situations the simple experiences I have shared with you to help to get you started in your career will be of little value. But if you can learn in the meantime to manage institutions of government and never forget that it is always the people whom you serve, you may be prepared to be of help in those times of special trouble. And remember this one terrifying thought: You will hold a unique position, along with a small handful of other leaders out of all the population, to make a difference in how events play out.

The profession of public service you have entered has only recently emerged. Government service was, until practically the twentieth century, largely service to the rulers or to the "nation," not service to the public, the people. That is where your profession is relatively new and different from what the so-called public service was in the past. Consequently you will bear a special obligation. Too many public servants are merely functionaries. But if you are worth your salt you will strive to be part of the elite of the public service. You will be inside government or working with associations or in other public positions that promote good government. Part of your duty to your profession will be to serve as a crusader and activist inside government to protect constitutionalism and open democratic governance. In your own area of special concern as a public servant it will be your responsibility to see that the processes of a functioning democracy are not compromised or misused. This will be your principal duty as a servant of the public: to nurture the legal structure in which you work in order to protect the people you serve.

As I reflect back on what I have gleaned from my experience in government and what I have shared with you in these letters, they strike me as quite inadequate to launch you or anyone on a public career. It is a somewhat fearful and uncharted course you have set for yourself. But a touch of danger is needed to make for excitement. And being uncharted, it may take you anywhere, and you may choose any star for your guide.

But if, by chance and by diligence and by talent, you achieve some exalted position, from time to time you might remember to reflect on Washington Irving's observations upon passing a few hours in Westminster Abbey: "It almost provokes a smile at the vanity of human ambition, to see how [the gravestones] are crowded together and jostled in the dust; what parsimony is observed in doling out a scanty nook, a gloomy corner, a little portion of earth, to those, whom, when alive, kingdoms could not satisfy. . . ."

I know you will do well. All my very best wishes.

Your proud colleague,

Uncle Ken

Afterword

While they are, of course, absolved from any responsibility for what I have written here, I do want to acknowledge several people who have been particularly helpful and influential in my development and career as a public servant and who directly and indirectly contributed to what I have had to say in these pages. These include Louis Brownlow, with whom I was fortunate to share office space in two of my beginning years in the public service. "Brownie," through his anecdotes, made me recognize early that the actualities of human events and our own stories about them come before the theories we may later build around them. We experience before we generalize and we fashion stories from our lives to help us understand—and to convey our understandings to others. And we recount our versions of events as we create our own sense of truth and puzzle over what it all means.

"Brownie" was born in the nineteenth century and would, at the turn of this new century, have been 121 years old. A founder of the American Society for Public Administration (ASPA) and other "1313" professional organizations in Chicago and Washington, he died at 82, making a speech on the public service. As I tell stories of my own experiences to a new generation of public servants and refer back to Louis Brownlow, I recall Margaret Mead's definition of living history in her biography, *Blackberry Winter*: "The human unit of time, the space between a grandfather's memory of his own childhood and a grandson's knowledge of those memories as he heard about them." We have our own shared human unit of time among the author, Louis Brownlow, and my intended young readers, a unit of time that covers most of the history of public administration as a profession.

And to Emmette Redford, my teacher and a mentor and confidant, I owe much. He listened to my experiences and advised me on occasion on issues and problems (again, he is excused of any responsibility for my later actions). And then he pushed me to write about them.

Now a few acknowledgments are fitting to friends who encouraged me to write this "oddball" approach to a textbook. They include Don

Wilson, while he was executive director of the Bush Presidential Library Foundation at Texas A&M University; Pat Shields, who read almost all my early drafting and spurred me on; and Steve and Kitty Klaidman, a journalist and an artist, respectively, who read a very early draft and were among the first to see something in this unusual approach to imparting lessons from the practice of my profession. Suggestions, comments, and support flowed from others as well: Dean Ed Dorn of the Lyndon B. Johnson School of Public Affairs at the University of Texas, and Arnold Vedlitz at the George Bush School of Government and Public Service at Texas A&M University. Paul Van Riper's great enthusiasm for the book helped give me the final push to complete it. And although he has recently moved to the Cato Institute from the Georgetown University Press, John Samples, while directing the press, expressed the interest in publication that made it possible for others than my own students to see these pages. Gail Grella, as the interim director, and Deborah Weiner, the editorial manager, took the book on and moved it quickly ahead to publication.

A number of librarians helped with one task or another along the way, and I am grateful to them all. But Jenifer Putalavage, a library science graduate student at the University of Texas, was especially helpful in running down references that seemed such a nuisance to a person who has spent far more of his time speaking and quoting others than writing and having to make formal attribution with specific citations.

Then there are two groups that I especially wish to thank: my students for their enthusiasm for their chosen field of work and their response to my teaching methods, and to Texas A&M University I am especially indebted for providing facilities and support while I wrote the book.

Penultimately, I wish to express my pleasure that my work on this book put me in close touch again with Harlan Cleveland, who, in my youth, offered me a scholarship and additional support when I applied for admission to the Maxwell School of Citizenship and Public Affairs at Syracuse University. Harlan Cleveland has always been "Dean" to me, even when he ascended to far more august titles. He insisted as we discussed my work on this book that I should now address him as Harlan. He said he did not want to have to start calling me Commissioner or Professor.

And finally my appreciation to Emily, who, along with all else we share, has been an indispensable sounding board, enthusiast, critic, and partisan throughout this effort. In living with a self-styled raconteur, her dubious recompense has been to hear a number of these tales more than once.

Notes

OCTOBER

Re: Working with politicians

p. [1]. Arthur Miller quotation from interview by Terry Gross, National Public Radio, *Fresh Air,* 25 November 1987.

p. [21]. James Q. Wilson quotation in *Bureaucracy: What Government Agencies Do and Why They Do It* (New York: Basic Books, 1989), 299–300.

p. [21]. George C. Marshall quotation in Ed Cray, *General of the Army George C. Marshall, Soldier and Statesman* (New York: W.W. Norton, 1990), 661.

p. [22]. McPherson quotation in Harry McPherson, *A Political Education* (Boston: Little, Brown & Company, 1972), 5.

NOVEMBER

Re: Working with the press

p. [23]. Justice Jackson quotation in *U.S. v. Ballard,* 322 US 78 (1944).

p. [23]. Alexander Bickel, *The Morality of Consent* (New Haven: Yale University Press, 1975), 83.

p. [23]. Harrison E. Salisbury, *A Time of Change* (New York: Harper and Row, 1988), xi.

p. [29]. Nancy Stancill's reports appeared in a series published in the *Houston Chronicle* in 1987 and 1988.

DECEMBER

Re: Learning from your boss

p. [34]. Holmes quotation in "Life as Joy, Duty, End," in Max Lerner, *The Mind and Faith of Justice Holmes* (New York: Random House, 1943), 42.

p. [34]. Sir Edgar Williams quotation on Montgomery in Carlo D'Este, *Decision in Normandy* (New York: Harper Collins, 1983), 204.

p. [34]. Tacitus quotation (regarding the Emperor Galba) in *The Histories, Book 1,* chapter 49 (regarding the Emperor Galba).

p. [36]. F. Scott Fitzgerald quotation in Edmund Wilson, ed., *The Crack-Up* (New York: James Laughlin, 1945), 69.

p. [38]. In my discussion of the new attacks on the federal government, I have drawn heavily on Alan Brinkley, Nelson W. Polsby, and Kathleen M. Sullivan, *New Federalist Papers* (New York: W.W. Norton, 1997), especially chapters 2, 3, and 17.

p. [39]. The citation of "to care for him who shall have borne the battle . . ." derives from President Abraham Lincoln's second inaugural address.

p. [39]. Edith Hamilton quotation is a translation in *The Greek Way* (New York: W.W. Norton, 1930), 20.

p. [40]. Harlan Cleveland quotation from his lectures at Syracuse University in 1959, transcribed by the author.

p. [40]. Citation from *New York Times* in Peter Gradenwitz, *Leonard Bernstein: The Infinite Variety of a Musician* (Leamington Spa, Warwickshire, England, and New York: Berg Press, 1987), 35, 37.

p. [41]. John Dean quotation in John W. Dean, *Blind Ambition: The White House Years* (New York: Simon & Schuster, 1976), 20.

p. [43]. John Stuart Mill quotation in Mill, *On Liberty* (Indianapolis: Bobbs-Merrill Company, 1956), 45.

JANUARY

Re: Dealing with unpleasant and difficult people

p. [45]. Presciliano Rangel quotation is from his daughter, Irma Rangel, longtime state legislative representative from Kingsville, Texas, to the author.

p. [45]. Dan Vittorio Segre quotation in Segre, *Memoirs of a Fortunate Jew: An Italian Story* (Bethesda, Md.: Adler & Adler, 1987), 117.

p. [45]. "Life is fired at us point blank" citation from José Ortega y Gasset, *Mission of the University* (Princeton: Princeton University Press, 1944), 73.

p. [48]. T.V. Smith in Smith, *A Non-Existent Man* (Austin: University of Texas Press, 1962), 251.

p. [49]. Story about Ross in Dale Kramer, *Harold Ross at the New Yorker* (Garden City: Doubleday & Company, 1951), 106.

p. [51]. In this passage I have relied on the "lexicon of intentionally ambiguous recommendations" in Robert J. Thornton, "I Can't Recommend the Candidate Too Highly," *Chronicle of Higher Education,* 25 February 1987, 42.

FEBRUARY

Re: More on unpleasant people

p. [54]. Garry Wills quotation in Wills, "Hurrah for Politicians," *Harpers,* September 1975, 45–54.

p. [57]. California Congressman John McGroarty reference is from John F. Kennedy, *Profiles in Courage* (New York: Harper & Brothers, 1955), 10.

p. [57]. Sam Rayburn story told to the author by Joe Kilgore in 1969.

p. [57]. "Tinkerbell" citation from Tom Loftus, *The Art of Legislative Politics* (Washington, D.C.: Congressional Quarterly, Inc., 1994), 94.

MARCH

Re: Subordinate leadership, getting help from above

p. [63]. Lyndon B. Johnson quotation in Robert Dallek, *Lone Star Rising: Lyndon Johnson and His Times, 1908–1960* (Oxford: Oxford University Press, 1991), 528.

p. [63]. Benjamin Disraeli quotation from Disraeli, speech at Edinburgh, 29 October 1867.

p. [63]. Benjamin Franklin quotation in "Sayings of Poor Richard," *Almanack*, January 1733.

pp. [70–71]. Passage on Franklin D. Roosevelt regarding Learned Hand and Supreme Court appointment of Rutledge in William O. Douglas, *Go East, Young Man: The Early Years* (New York: Random House, 1974), 332.

APRIL

Re: Taking the initiative, or risk taking inside government

p. [73]. William O. Douglas quotation in Douglas, *Go East, Young Man: The Early Years* (New York: Random House, 1974), 271.

p. [73]. David Lloyd George quotation in Joseph E. Persico, *Casey: From the OSS to the CIA* (New York: Viking Penguin, 1990), 492.

p. [73]. William Wordsworth quotation in "Lines left upon a seat in a yew tree," from *Lyrical Ballads*.

MAY

Re: The kinds of pressures and influence used on you

p. [82]. Sir Edward Coke quotation in Catherine Drinker Bowen, *The Lion and the Throne* (Boston: Little, Brown & Company, 1956), 287.

p. [83]. President Woodrow Wilson quotation in Henry Beach Needham, "Woodrow Wilson's Views," *Outlook*, 26 August 1911, 940.

p. [87]. Eleanor Roosevelt quotation in Doris Kearns Goodwin, *No Ordinary Time* (New York: Simon & Schuster, 1994), 311.

p. [87]. Robert Wagner quotation in Robert Caro, *The Power Broker, Robert Moses and the Fall of New York* (New York: Random House, 1975), 728.

SEPTEMBER

Re: Relations with a governing board

p. [89]. Milton Mayer quotation in Mayer, *They Thought They Were Free: The Germans 1933–45* (Chicago: The University of Chicago Press, 1955); 162.

p. [89]. Horace Mann quotation from Mann, commencement address, Antioch College, 1859.

OCTOBER

Re: More on governing boards

p. [102]. Admiral Arleigh Burke quotation in Ken Jones and Hubert Kelly, Jr., *Admiral Arleigh (31-Knot) Burke* (Philadelphia: Chilton Books, 1962), 180.

p. [102]. Robert Lewis Stevenson quotation in Stevenson, *Father Damien: An Open Letter to the Reverend Dr. Hyde of Honolulu* (New York: Scribner's Sons, 1916), 17.

NOVEMBER

Re: Bona fide bureaucratic behavior

p. [121]. C.S. Lewis quotation in Lewis, *The Screwtape Letters* (New York: MacMillan, 1960), x.

p. [121]. Colleen McCullough quotation from McCullough, *The First Man in Rome* (New York: Avon Books, 1990), 163.

p. [125]. Henry Wriston quotation from Clark Kerr and Marian Gade, *The Many Lives of Academic Presidents* (Washington, D.C.: Association of Governing Boards of Universities and Colleges, 1986), 193.

p. [127]. General Joe Stilwell quotation from Barbara Tuchman, *Stilwell and the American Experience in China 1911–1945* (New York: MacMillan, 1971), 232–33.

p. [123]. Unitarian minister quotation from "Loving thy neighbor through acts of Congress" by Reverend A. Powell Davies in Unitarian Church in Washington, D.C. [n.d.].

DECEMBER

Re: "Walking with kings"

p. [134]. George Bernard Shaw quotation from Shaw, "Mrs. Warren's Profession," Act II, in *Complete Plays with Prefaces* (New York: Dodd, Mead and Co., 1963), 65.

p. [134]. Robert Shaw quotation from National Public Radio programming the day after his death, 26 January 1999.

p. [139]. José Ortega y Gasset, *Mission of the University* (Princeton: Princeton University Press, 1944), 42.

p. [140]. "Do you long for the conversation . . ." quotation from John Ruskin, *Sesame and Lilies* (Boston: Houghton Mifflin, 1900), 12.

p. [141]. Pericles quotation from Thucydides, *The Peloponnesian Wars* (New York: Random House, 1951), 116.

p. [141]. Harry Golden quotation from Golden, "How to Live With a Chair You Hate," *Saturday Review*, 17 June 1967, 14–17.

p. [142]. Mark Twain quotation from Twain, "Fenimore Cooper's Literary Offenses," in *How to Tell a Story, and Other Essays* (New York: Harper, 1902).

pp. [143–144]. Duke of Gloucester (William Henry) quotation from Henry Digby Best, *Personal and Literary Memorials* (London: H. Colburn, 1829), 68.

JANUARY

Re: Delegating, or working for your subordinates

p. [145]. George Marshall quotation from Ed Cray, *General of the Army George C. Marshall, Soldier and Statesman* (New York: W.W. Norton, 1990), 591.

p. [145]. Edith Hamilton quotation from Doris Fielding Reid, *Edith Hamilton* (New York: W.W. Norton, 1967), 45.

p. [145]. General George Patton quotation from Carlo D'Este, *Patton: A Genius for War* (New York: Harper Collins Books, 1995), 223.

p. [145]. Julius and Augustus Hare quotation from *Guesses at Truth, 1827*, Series 1, p. 137, in *Oxford Dictionary of Quotations* (Oxford: Oxford University Press, 1992), 326.

p. [149]. Lord Salisbury quotation from Robert K. Massie, *Dreadnought* (New York: Random House, 1991), 202–203.

FEBRUARY

Re: Ethics and morality in public service

p. [152]. Senator Carl Parker quotation from Parker speech at the 1998 Annual Conference of the Southern Regional Education Board, Chapel Hill, North Carolina.

p. [152]. Warren Bennis quotation from Bennis, *The Leaning Ivory Tower* (San Francisco: Jossey-Bass Publishers, 1973), 100–101.

p. [152]. Albert Speer quotation from Gitta Sereni, *Albert Speer: His Battle with Truth* (New York: Knopf, 1995), 636.

p. [152]. Benjamin Franklin quotation from "Sayings of Poor Richard," *Almanack,* June 1752.

p. [152]. Denis Diderot quotation from Robert and Mary Collison, eds., *Dictionary of Foreign Quotations* (New York: Facts on File, 1980), 235.

p. [153]. The story of Pippin IV from John Steinbeck, *The Short Reign of Pippin IV: A Fabrication* (New York: Viking Press, 1957).

pp. [153–154]. Abraham H. Maslow references from Maslow, *Toward a Psychology of Being*, 2nd ed. (New York: D. Van Nostrand, 1968), especially pages 4–8.

p. [155]. Benito Mussolini quotations from Denis Mack Smith, *Mussolini* (New York: Random House, 1983), 303.

p. [155]. President Abraham Lincoln quotation in Carl Sandburg, *Abraham Lincoln: The War Years,* vol. 1 (New York: Harcourt Brace, 1939), 281.

p. [156]. Barbara Tuchman quotation in Tuchman, *A Distant Mirror: The Calamitous 14th Century* (New York: Knopf, 1978).

p. [156]. Horace M. Kallen quotation in Kallen, "How I Bet My Life," *Saturday Review,* 1 October 1966, 27–30.

pp. [157–158]. Ignazio Silone quotation in Silone, *Bread and Wine* (New York: Harper, 1937), 176.

p. [158]. Adolph Hitler quotation from Joseph E. Persico, *Casey: From the OSS to the CIA* (New York: Viking Penguin, 1990), 538.

p. [158]. John Steinbeck quotation in Steinbeck, "The Trial of Arthur Miller," *Esquire,* June 1957, 47.

p. [159]. Passage on Vietnam from Mark Baker, *Nam: The Vietnam War in the Words of the Men and Women Who Fought There* (New York: Morrow, 1981), 196.

p. [159]. Rudolf Franz Höss quotations in Höss, *Commandant of Auschwitz,* translated by Constantine FitzGibbon (London: Weidenfeld and Nicolson, 1959), 124, 144.

p. [160]. "To thine own self . . ." citation from Shakespeare, "Hamlet," Act I.

p. [160]. Heinrich Himmler quotation in *Nazi Conspiracy and Aggression,* 12 vols. (Washington, D.C.: Government Printing Office, 1946–47): IV, document 1919-PS, 563.

p. [161]. Tombstone epitaph citation from tombstone for Franklin Jones in Edgar Lee Masters, *Spoon River Anthology* (New York: Macmillan, 1962), 104.

p. [161]. John Dewey quotation in Dewey, *Reconstruction of Philosophy* (New York: Holt and Co., 1920), 196.

p. [161]. Reference to Arthur Miller's play from Miller, *After the Fall* (Toronto: Penguin Books, 1980), 15.

p. [162]. Isaiah Berlin's views are cited in Michael Ignatieff, *A Life: Isaiah Berlin* (New York: Henry Holt and Company, 1998), 249.

p. [162]. Abraham H. Maslow references from Maslow, *Toward a Psychology of Being,* 2nd ed. (New York: D. Van Nostrand, 1968).

p. [163]. The play referred to is George Bernard Shaw, *Major Barbara* (New York: Modern Library, 1956); the lines are spoken near the end by Undershaft to his son, Stephen.

p. [163]. "Property will purchase power . . ." quotation by Virginian Benjamin Watkins Leigh, cited in Arthur M. Schlesinger, Jr., *The Age of Jackson* (Boston: Little, Brown & Company, 1945), 13.

p. [164]. "Presume not God to scan . . ." quotation in Alexander Pope, *Essays on Man*, Epistle II, 1.1 (1733).

p. [164]. "People live together most productively and harmoniously . . ." statement based in part on Bronislaw Malinowski, *Freedom and Civilization* (Bloomington: Indiana University Press, 1944).

p. [166]. Senator Albert Beveridge quotation in Henry Allen, "The American Century," *The Washington Post* (national weekly edition), 4 October 1999, 6.

pp. [166–167]. "Public administration is an inherently anti-democratic approach to governance . . ." quotation from O.C. McSwite, *Legitimacy in Public Administration* (Thousand Oaks, Calif.: Sage Publications, 1997), 28.

p. [167]. Carl Schurz quotation from Schurz speech in the U.S. Senate, 1872.

p. [167]. "It's going to be very hard . . ." quotation by Francis Pickens Miller in Harry McPherson, *A Political Education* (Boston: Little, Brown & Company, 1972), 236.

MARCH

Re: A few thoughts on leadership

p. [168]. Robert Maynard Hutchins quotation in Clark Kerr and Marian Gade, *The Many Lives of Academic Presidents* (Washington, D.C.: Association of Governing Boards of Universities and Colleges, 1986), 190.

p. [168]. Arthur Schlesinger, Jr., quotation is a paraphrase of President Andrew Jackson's style of dealing with opponents, in Schlesinger, *The Age of Jackson* (Boston: Little and Brown, 1945), 40.

p. [168]. Harry Truman quotation in Robert Debs Hienl, Jr., ed., *Dictionary of Military and Naval Quotations* (Annapolis, Md.: U.S. Naval Institute, 1966), 173.

p. [169]. The *Harvard Business Review* article discussed here is Daniel J. Isenberg, "The Tactics of Strategic Opportunism," *Harvard Business Review*, March/April 1987, 92–97.

p. [173]. President John F. Kennedy quotation from Harlan Cleveland as told to author.

pp. [175–176]. Paul Fussell quotation in Fussell, *Wartime* (New York: Oxford University Press, 1989), 80.

p. [176]. Victor Frankl quotation in Frankl, *Man's Search for Meaning* (New York: Simon & Schuster, 1963).

APRIL

Re: A summing up

p. [178]. James Madison quotation in Madison, *The Federalist*, no. 51 (New York: Random House, Modern Library, 1937), 337.

p. [178]. Jane Addams quotation from Residents of the Hull House, *Hull-House Maps and Papers* (New York: Thomas Y. Crowell, 1895), 198.

p. [178]. Alexander Bickel quotation in Bickel, *The Morality of Consent* (New Haven: Yale University Press, 1975), 19.

p. [181]. George Schulz quotation from James Q. Wilson, *Bureaucracy: What Government Agencies Do and Why They Do It* (New York: Harper Collins, 1989), 300.

p. [181]. Lee Dreyfus's remark was made at a conference on the role of governors in higher education held at Racine, Wisconsin, March 1985.

p. [181]. "The urge to heroism . . ." quotation is by Ernest Becker in Becker, *The Denial of Death* (New York: Macmillan, 1973), 4.

p. [182]. Michael Herr quotation in Herr, *Dispatches* (New York: Random House, 1977), 14.

p. [183]. Washington Irving quotation in İrving, *Sketchbook* (Boston: Allyn and Bacon, 1942), 197.

A Hundred Really Good Books

BIOGRAPHIES AND AUTOBIOGRAPHIES

Morris Abram (civil rights activist in U.S. South)
Abram, Morris. *The Day Is Short*. New York: Hartcourt, Brace, Jovanovich, 1982.

John Adams
Bowen, Catherine Drinker. *John Adams and the American Revolution*. Boston: Little,
 Brown & Co., 1950.

Isaiah Berlin (English political theorist)
Ignatieff, Michael. *A Life: Isaiah Berlin*. New York: Holt, 1998.

Prince Otto Eduard Leopold von Bismarck
Cruikshank, Edward. *Bismarck*. New York, Penguin, 1983.

Martin Bormann
Lang, Jochen von. *The Secretary, Martin Bormann: The Man Who Manipulated Hitler*.
 New York: Random House, 1979.

U.S. Admiral Arleigh Burke
Potter, E.B. *Admiral Arleigh Burke*. New York: Random House, 1990.

Lord Burghley (Sir William Cecil, advisor to Queen Elizabeth)
Hume, Martin. *The Great Lord Burghley*. New York: McClure Phillips & Co., 1906.

Clark Clifford
Clifford, Clark with Richard Holbrooke. *Counsel to the President*. New York: Random House, 1991.

Sir Robert Coke (English legal giant)
Bowen, Catherine Drinker. *The Lion and the Throne*. Boston: Little, Brown & Co., 1956.

Crazy Horse and General George Armstrong Custer
Ambrose, Stephen. *Crazy Horse and Custer*. New York: Meridian, New American
 Library, 1975.

John Dean (general counsel to President Richard Nixon)
Dean, John. *Blind Ambition*. New York: Simon & Schuster, 1976. (Focused on
 Watergate scandal.)

Justice William O. Douglas
Douglas, William O. *Go East, Young Man: The Early Years*. New York: Random House, 1974.

Dwight D. Eisenhower
Ambrose, Stephen E. *Eisenhower: Soldier and President*. New York: Simon & Schuster, 1990.

Eleanor of Aquitaine
Meade, Marion. *Eleanor of Aquitaine*. New York: Hawthorne/Dutton, 1977.

Queen Elizabeth
Jenkins, Elizabeth. *Elizabeth the Great*. New York: Coward-McCann, 1959.

Benjamin Franklin
Van Doren, Carl. *Benjamin Franklin*. New York: Penguin, 1991.

Galileo Galilei
Sobel, Dava. *Galileo's Daughter: A Historical Memoir of Science, Faith, and Love*. New York: Walker & Co., 1999.

Ulysses S. Grant
Grant, Ulysses S. *Personal Memoirs of U.S. Grant*. New York: C.L. Webster & Co., 1885–86.

King Henry VIII
Baldwin Smith, Lacey. *Henry VIII: The Mask of Royalty*. Chicago: Academy Chicago Publishers, 1987.

Adolph Hitler
Bullock, Alan. *Hitler: A Study in Tyranny*. New York: Harper & Row, 1971.

Oliver Wendell Holmes
Lerner, Max. *The Mind and Faith of Oliver Wendell Holmes*. New York: Random House, 1943.

Sam Houston
James, Marquis. *The Raven: Biography of Sam Houston*. Indianapolis: Bobbs-Merrill, 1929.

Andrew Jackson
Schlesinger, Arthur, Jr. *The Age of Jackson*. Boston: Little, Brown & Co., 1945.

Lyndon Johnson
Caro, Robert. *The Path to Power: The Years of Lyndon Johnson*. New York: Random House, 1975.
Dallek, Robert. *Lone Star Rising: Lyndon Johnson and His Times, 1908–1960*. Oxford: Oxford University Press, 1991.
———. *Flawed Giant: Lyndon Johnson and His Times, 1961–1973*. Oxford: Oxford University Press, 1998.

Meriwether Lewis (Lewis and Clark expedition)
Ambrose, Stephen. *Undaunted Courage*. New York: Simon & Schuster, 1996.

Huey Long
Williams, T. Harry. *Huey Long*. New York: Bantam Books, 1970.

Henry Luce
Swanberg, W.A. *Luce and His Empire*. New York: Scribner's Sons, 1972.

Douglas McArthur
Manchester, William. *American Caesar: Douglas McArthur*. Boston: Little, Brown & Co., 1978.

Harry McPherson (aide to President Lyndon Johnson)
McPherson, Harry. *A Political Education*. Boston: Little, Brown & Co., 1972.

Jeb Stuart Magruder (aide to President Richard Nixon)
Jeb Stuart Magruder. *An American Life: One Man's Road to Watergate*. New York: Atheneum, 1974.

Andre Malraux (twentieth-century French literary and political figure)
Malraux, Andre. *Anti-Memoirs*. New York: Holt, Rinehart and Winston, 1968.

George C. Marshall
Cray, Ed. *General of the Army George C. Marshall, Soldier and Statesman*. New York: W.W. Norton, 1990.

John Marshall
Beveridge, Albert. *The Life of John Marshall*. Atlanta, Ga.: Cherokee Publishing Company, 1990.

Margaret Mead
Mead, Margaret. *Blackberry Winter*. New York: Touchstone, Simon & Schuster, 1972.

Edward R. Murrow
Persico, Joseph E. *Edward R. Murrow: An American Original*. New York: Bantam Doubleday Dell Publishing Group, 1988.

Benito Mussolini
Smith, Denis Mack. *Mussolini*. New York: Random House, 1983.

Napoleon
Ludwig, Emil. *Napoleon*. New York: Boni & Liveright, 1926.

Tip O'Neill
O'Neill, Tip, with William Novak. *Man of the House: The Life and Political Memoirs of Speaker Tip O'Neill*. New York: Random House, 1987.

General George Patton
D'Este, Carlo. *Patton: A Genius for War*. New York: Harper Collins, 1995.

Peter the Great
Massie, Robert K. *Peter the Great*. New York: Alfred Knopf, 1980.

Sam Rayburn
Hardeman, D.B., and Donald C. Bacon. *Rayburn: A Biography*. Austin: Texas Monthly Press, 1987.

Franklin D. Roosevelt
McGregor Burns, James. *Roosevelt: The Lion and the Fox*. New York: Hartcourt, Brace & World, 1956.

Theodore Roosevelt
Morris, Edmund. *The Rise of Theodore Roosevelt*. New York: Ballantine Books, 1979.

Albert Speer
Speer, Albert. *Inside the Third Reich*. New York: Avon, 1971.
Sereny, Gitta. *Albert Speer: His Battle with Truth*. New York: Alfred Knopf, 1995.

Josef Stalin
Ulam, Adam B. *Stalin*. New York: Viking, 1973.

General Joe Stilwell
Tuchman, Barbara. *Stilwell and the American Experience in China*. New York: Macmillan, 1971.

Henry Lewis Stimson
Stimson, Henry Lewis, with McGeorge Bundy. *On Active Service in Peace and War*. New York: Harper, 1948.

Harry Truman
McCollough, David. *Truman*. New York: Simon & Schuster, 1992.

George Washington
Flexner, James T. *Washington: The Indispensible Man*. New York: Mentor, New American Library, 1974.

Theodore H. White (American journalist and writer)
White, Theodore H. *In Search of History: A Personal Adventure*. New York: Harper & Row, 1978.

Edward Bennett Williams (Washington lawyer, adviser, lobbyist)
Thomas, Evan. *The Man to See: Edward Bennett Williams*. New York: Simon & Schuster, 1991.

Cardinal Thomas Wolsey (adviser and cardinal under Henry VIII)
Ferguson, Charles W. *Naked to Mine Enemies: The Life of Cardinal Wolsey*. New York: Time Life Books, 1965.

ARTISTS AND WRITERS

Henry Adams
Adams, Henry. *The Education of Henry Adams*. New York: Modern Library, Random House, 1931.

Maria Callas
Stassinopoulos, Arianna. *Maria Callas: The Woman Behind the Legend*. New York: Ballantine, 1981.

Edith Hamilton
Reid, Doris Fielding. *Edith Hamilton*. New York: W.W. Norton, 1967.

Moss Hart
Hart, Moss. *Act One: An Autobiography*. New York: Random House, 1959.

Samuel Johnson
Bate, W. Jackson. *Samuel Johnson*. New York: Hartcourt, Brace, Jovanovich, 1975.

Arthur Miller
Miller, Arthur. *Timebends: A Life*. New York: Grove Press, 1987.

Sergei Prokofiev
Seroff, Victor. *Sergei Prokofiev*. New York: Taplinger, 1979.

Mary Renault
Sweetman, David. *Mary Renault*. London: Pimlico, 1994.

Pierre-Auguste Renoir
Renoir, Jean. *Renoir, My Father*. San Francisco: Mercury House, 1988.

Artur Rubinstein
Rubinstein, Artur. *My Young Years*. New York: Alfred Knopf, 1973.

Thornton Wilder
Harrison, Gilbert A. *The Enthusiast: A Life of Thornton Wilder*. New York: Fromm International Publishing Corporation, 1986.

COMING-OF-AGE BIOGRAPHIES

Baker, Russell. *Growing Up*. New York: Signet, New American Library, 1984.
Campbell, Will. *Brother to a Dragonfly*. New York: Seabury Press, 1977.
Catton, Bruce. *Waiting for the Morning Train*. Garden City: Doubleday, 1972.
Karr, Mary. *Liar's Club*. New York: Penguin, 1995.
Morris, Willis. *North Toward Home*. Oxford, Mississippi: Yoknapatawpha Press, 1996.
Styron, William. *A Tidewater Morning: Three Tales from Youth*. New York: Random House, 1993.
Wright, Richard N. *Black Boy: A Record of Childhood and Youth*. New York: Harper, 1945.

HISTORY

Bergamini, David. *Japan's Imperial Conspiracy*. New York: Simon & Schuster, 1972. (Origins of Japan's involvement in World War II.)
Boorstin, Daniel J. *The Discoverers*. New York: Random House, 1985.
Bowen, Catherine Drinker. *Miracle at Philadelphia: The Story of the Constitutional Convention, May to September, 1787*. Boston: Little, Brown & Co., 1966.

Ceram, C.S. *Gods, Graves, and Scholars*. New York: Bantam Books, 1976.

D'Este, Carlo. *Decision in Normandy*. New York: Harper Collins, 1983. (D-Day landing in Europe, World War II.)

Goodwin, Doris Kearns. *No Ordinary Time*. New York: Simon & Schuster, 1994. (Franklin and Eleanor Roosevelt in the White House.)

Hamilton, Edith. *The Greek Way*. New York: W.W. Norton, 1930.

Herr, Michael. *Dispatches*. New York: Random House, 1977. (Considered by many to be the best book on the war in Vietnam.)

Hibbert, Christopher. *The House of Medici: Its Rise and Fall*. New York: Morrow Quill, 1980.

Jaworski, Leon. *The Right and the Power: The Prosecution of Watergate*. New York: Reader's Digest Press, 1976.

Keegan, John. *The First World War*. New York: Alfred Knopf, 1999.

Massie, Robert K. *Dreadnought*. New York: Random House, 1991. (History of the battleship and the origins of World War I.)

Manchester, William. *The Glory and the Dream*. Boston: Little, Brown & Co., 1973. (A narrative history of the United States, 1932–1972.)

——. *A World Lit Only by Fire: The Medieval Mind and the Renaissance—Portrait of an Age*. Boston: Little, Brown & Co., 1992.

Moore, Lt. General Harold, and Joseph Galloway. *We Were Soldiers Once . . . and Young*. New York: Harper Collins, 1993. (On the Vietnam War.)

Morgan, Ted. *An Uncertain Hour: The French, the Germans, the Jews, the Barbie Trial, and the City of Lyon, 1940–1945*. New York: Arbor House/William Morrow, 1990.

Shaara, Jeff. *The Last Full Measure*. New York: Ballantine, 1998. (The last two years of the U.S. Civil War.)

Shaara, Michael. *The Killer Angels*. New York: Ballantine, 1974. (Battle of Gettysburg, U.S. Civil War.)

Sheehan, Neil. *A Bright Shining Lie: John Paul Vann and America in Vietnam*. New York: Random House, 1988.

Shirer, William. *The Rise and Fall of the Third Reich*. New York: Simon & Schuster, 1959.

Smith, Page. *A New Age Now Begins: A People's History of the American Revolution*. New York: McGraw Hill, 1976.

Stone, Irving. *Men to Match My Mountains: The Opening of the Far West, 1840–1900*. Garden City: Doubleday, 1956.

Williams, Harry T. *Lincoln and His Generals*. New York: Vintage, Random House, 1952.

GENERAL INTEREST

Becker, Ernest. *The Birth and Death of Meaning*. New York: Free Press, Macmillan, 1971.

——. *Denial of Death*. New York: Free Press, Macmillan, 1973.

Berlin, Isaiah. *Four Essays on Liberty*. Oxford: Oxford University Press, 1969.

Bickel, Alexander. *The Morality of Consent*. New Haven: Yale University Press, 1975.

Index